Narrating the Slave Trade, Theorizing Community

Cross/Cultures

READINGS IN POST/COLONIAL
LITERATURES AND CULTURES IN ENGLISH

Edited by

Gordon Collier
Geoffrey Davis
Bénédicte Ledent

Co-founding editor

†Hena Maes-Jelinek

Advisory Board

VOLUME 207

The titles published in this series are listed at *brill.com/cc*

Narrating the Slave Trade, Theorizing Community

By

Raphaël Lambert

BRILL
RODOPI

LEIDEN | BOSTON

Cover illustration: Wiktor Górka, poster for the film *Tamango*, 1958 (detail). Courtesy of Henryk Górka.

The Library of Congress Cataloging-in-Publication Data is available online at http://catalog.loc.gov
LC record available at http://lccn.loc.gov/2018057844

Typeface for the Latin, Greek, and Cyrillic scripts: "Brill". See and download: brill.com/brill-typeface.

ISSN 0924-1426
ISBN 978-90-04-37758-5 (hardback)
ISBN 978-90-04-38922-9 (e-book)

Printed by Printforce, the Netherlands

Contents

Acknowledgements

I wish to thank my editor, Gordon Collier, for his guidance, comments, bon mots, and professionalism. I owe a special debt of gratitude to Patrice Petro for her support throughout the years and her suggestions on my initial proposal. I am also very grateful to Chris Bongie for his appraisal of an earlier version of Chapter 4, and to Taras Sak for his observations on a later version of the same chapter. My appreciation further extends to Peter O'Connor for his reading of a fledgling version of Chapter 3, and Etsuko Taketani for her advice and reliability in the preliminary stages of this project. Special thanks also go to Ania Pochmara for securing the rights to the Wiktor Górka illustration that graces the cover of this book. Finally, I am obliged to Takayuki Tatsumi, Yoshiko Uzawa, and the Tokyo Chapter of the American Literature Society of Japan for inviting me to introduce my research on the slave trade and theories of community (2011). Subsequently, I was given the opportunity to present some of the arguments developed in *Narrating the Slave Trade* at the Kansai Chapter of American Literature Society of Japan (2012), the Society for Cinema and Media Studies conference in Montreal (2015), the Collegium for African American Research conferences in Liverpool (2015) and Málaga (2017), and on the occasion of a talk at the University of Seville (2018). *Narrating the Slave Trade* also includes expanded and revised versions of various publications: Chapter One is based on two essays, "The Conservative Dispositions of *Roots*," *Transition* 122 (January 2017): 96–112, and "The Strange Career of *Tamango*: From Prosper Mérimée's 1829 Novella to Its 1958 Film Adaptation," *Film International* (February 2011): online. Chapter Two draws on two essays, "Political Principles and Ideologies in Charles Johnson's *Middle Passage*," *Transatlantica: American Studies Journal* 1 (2015): online, and "Patriotism in Charles Johnson's *Middle Passage*," *Critique: Studies in Contemporary Fiction* 58.3 (2017): 175–192. And Chapter Three is an extended version of "Barry Unsworth's *Sacred Hunger*: Birth and Demise of a Community," *Journal of Modern Literature* 41.1 (2017): 118–136. Finally, I am beholden to my wife, Kyoko Yoshida, for her critical reading of each and every chapter, and not least importantly, her patience, encouragement, and endearment.

Introduction: All in the Same Boat

It may seem incongruous, perhaps even inappropriate, to bring together the story of the transatlantic slave trade, which evokes uprootedness, agony, and dehumanization, with the notion of community, which evokes stability, comfort, and altruism. But a community means more than a reassuring feeling of togetherness and a sense of belonging. A community implies commitment, responsibility, and obligation to others. It may be unified or fragmented, close-knit or welcoming, coercive or permissive, or imposed by circumstances the subject cannot control. It may be ideological, cultural, religious, or political. And it may be a mere abstraction, an idealization, or a projection. There is no satisfactory definition of community, but community is an ontological issue, and this is how the idiom "in the same boat" should be understood: in no way does it imply that those on board a slave ship, above and below deck, share the same fate. Rather, it means that the slave trade implicates all parties involved, generates all kinds of interaction, and influences the nature of existence in many different ways across time and space.[1] Hence, the fundamental issue of community, from its most concrete to most metaphysical dimension, imbues

---

1 In *The Black Atlantic: Modernity and Double Consciousness* (1993), Paul Gilroy conjures up "the image of the ship" (4)—especially the slave ship—in order to "rethink modernity via the history of the black Atlantic and the African diaspora into the western hemisphere" (17). In a similar fashion, *Narrating the Slave Trade, Theorizing Community* looks at the slave ship as a chronotope in order to delve into the "micro-politics of the slave trade and its relationship to both industrialisation and modernisation" (17). However, it does so through the prism of community, which eventually leads to considerations beyond the circumscribed notion of the black Atlantic and its historical backdrop. It should also be noted that Charles Johnson's *Middle Passage* (1990) and Barry Unsworth's *Sacred Hunger* (1992)—respectively the objects of the second and third chapters herein—were published prior to *Black Atlantic* and raise issues that strikingly overlap Gilroy's argument about the "instability and mutability of identities" (xi) and "cultural insiderism" (3). Finally, Édouard Glissant's seminal work on the notion of creolization, which is at the heart of the fourth and last chapter of the present study, is never really acknowledged as a major source by Gilroy even though Glissant's "The Open Boat," the prefatory piece of creative non-fiction to *Poetics of Relation* (1990), features the slave ship as a chronotope linking the birth of the Creole people in the New World and the creolized world of today. As for Glissant's *Le discours antillais* (1981), which theorized key concepts of cultural syncretism and hybridity more than a decade ahead of Gilroy's *Black Atlantic*, it is only mentioned in passing in the first chapter (in re Michael Dash's partial and controversial translation, *The Caribbean Discourse*), and again in the form of a brief endnote to the third chapter to acknowledge that the concept of diaspora is "suggestively explored by Glissant in *Carribbean Discourse*" (236n16).

© KONINKLIJKE BRILL NV, LEIDEN, 2019 | DOI:10.1163/9789004389229_002

fiction of the slave trade. The notion of community proves to be an effective tool for understanding the workings of the slave trade, and slave-trade fiction proves to be a propitious terrain for bringing latent but crucial issues of community to light.

It may also seem superfluous to study the slave trade through fiction when the outpouring of historical literature over the past two decades seems to have exhausted the topic. In fact, *Narrating the Slave Trade, Theorizing Community* does rely on this rich historical background, but it also aims to broaden slave-trade studies beyond historical knowledge. Even when historians turn their attention to the human drama of the Middle Passage, as Marcus Rediker does in *The Slave-Ship: A Human History* (2008), or when they vow, like Stephanie E. Smallwood in *Saltwater Slavery: A Middle Passage from Africa to American Diaspora* (2007), to excavate from all available documents "something of the slaves' own experience of the traffic in human beings and of life aboard the slave-ship,"[2] they can only do so within the limits of their discipline, which steers clear of subjectivity and pathos. This is where fiction becomes relevant as it uncovers territories that have remained either untapped by or inaccessible to historians.

One of these uncharted territories is community, which pervades fiction of the slave trade. By exploring the latter through the prism of community, *Narrating the Slave Trade* reverses Paul Veyne's claim that "history is true fiction"[3] and posits fiction as a reliable source of knowledge—historical and otherwise.[4] References to a plethora of historical documents related to the slave trade, from logbooks to medical records, newspaper clippings, letters, testimonies and legal proceedings, pervade slave-trade fiction, but the purpose of such fiction is not so much to present and analyze as to mold and transform such primary material into a work of imagination designed by convention to entertain, and bound by its nature to afford the reader greater insight into the

---

2 Stephanie E. Smallwood, *Saltwater Slavery: A Middle Passage from Africa to American Diaspora* (Cambridge MA: Harvard UP, 2007): 5.

3 Paul Veyne, *Comment on écrit l'histoire: essai d'épistémologie* (Paris: Seuil, 1971): 10.

4 When Paul Veyne argues, in *Comment on écrit l'histoire*, that "history is true fiction" (10), he means that writing history is akin to writing fiction insofar as it requires sorting out, simplifying, and organizing information in order for the narration to take shape and become coherent. Of course, history is not meant to entertain but to inform. It is based on documents and aims at objectivity. However, Veyne argues, after Gérard Genette, that "history is *diegesis*; not *mimesis*" (15), thus exposing, on the one hand, the porosity existing between historical and fictional narration, and, on the other, implying that fiction may also entail historical relevance.

transatlantic slave trade.[5] In this study, fiction is not to be understood as the obverse of fact. And while the works under scrutiny do not purport to lay claim to any special form of truth, they can hardly be apprehended, by virtue of their loaded content, apart from their cognitive import.

However, it is not these works' respective contributions to slave-trade history that will be the object of analysis but the notion of community as it invariably arises, in its various dimensions, in all these works. Recent years have seen an explosion of interest in both community studies and slave-trade studies in academia and the wider cultural world. While *Narrating the Slave Trade* is not intended to uncover the deeper reasons lying behind this concomitance, it may be relevant to note that such prominent contemporary thinkers as Jean-Luc Nancy, Roberto Esposito, Giorgio Agamben, and Alphonso Lingis have examined in considerable detail the notion of community, answering an urge to dispel misconceptions and clichéd generalizations at a time of profound social, cultural, and political upheavals in the world: the collapse of Communism both as a political system and as an ideology; the mass migrations from poor and war-torn regions of the world toward the more affluent and peaceful European and North American continents; and the rise of economic liberalism and ensuing disintegration of the social fabric across postmodern societies. Indeed, the simultaneous impetus to rethink the notion of community and revisit the slave trade comes at a time when the same triumphant free-market ideology, which arguably fueled and justified the slave trade, is back and ascendant.[6]

---

5 This pedagogical orientation in no way diminishes the artistic quality of slave-trade literature, and it has been a characteristic of the genre since its inception. Quite logically, it is particularly tangible in abolitionist poetry (e.g., William Cowper in England, and John Greenleaf Whittier in America), and first-person narratives such as Ottobah Cugoano's *Thoughts and Sentiments* (1787) and Olaudah Equiano's *Interesting Narrative* (1789), not only because these authors doubled as anti-slavery activists but also because readers were largely ignorant of the realities of the so-called triangular trade. Not all early narratives constituted an indictment of the slave trade, though. Famously, Ukawsaw Gronniosaw's *Most Remarkable Particulars* (1772) seemingly condones slavery, while the eponymous royal slave in Aphra Behn's *Oroonoko* (1688), despite being deceived and molested by some of his white captors, seems to have no qualms when it comes to his own war prisoners in Africa, whom he sold to British slave traders for his own profit.

6 Ian Baucom makes the link between the mercantile logic underlying the slave trade and today's global market economy explicit when, borrowing Giovanni Arrighi's concept of "the long twentieth century," he describes what he calls the "the eighteenth- to late-twentieth-century Atlantic cycle of capital accumulation"; Baucom, *Specters of the Atlantic: Finance Capital, Slavery and the Philosophy of History* (Durham NC: Duke UP, 2005): 161. Expectedly, champions of the free-market economy do not acknowledge this continuum between the slave trade and globalization. Instead, they argue that the transnational movement of goods, technologies, services, and capital benefits all and is the only way for the underdeveloped

Recent news items featuring forced migrations, sweatshop labor, and human-rights violations ad nauseam find an eerie echo in the exploitation of human capital (from slavery in the New World to working-class misery in Europe) typifying the modern era, and more especially the transatlantic slave trade. This trans-historical parallel may explain why the slave trade—a paradigmatic phenomenon of modernity—has been rescued from collective amnesia and acknowledged for its profound and lasting impact on the societies involved in it. In the United States, mainstream culture reflected this trend with Steven Spielberg's film *Amistad* (1997), although *Amistad*, which re-acquainted the wider public with the story of the slave trade twenty years after the very successful TV miniseries *Roots* (1977), proved to be a soothing courtroom drama rather than an unsettling human tragedy.[7] Academia also went through a more than two-decade hiatus from Philip Curtin's *The Atlantic Slave Trade: A Census* (1969) to a new wave of slave-trade research in the 1990s, which culminated in the release of David Eltis and Stephen D. Behrendt's *Trans-Atlantic Slave Trade: A Database on CD-ROM* (1999). Poetry experienced a similar gap: Robert Hayden's seminal "Middle Passage" (1962) was not emulated until David Dabydeen's "Turner" (1994)—a scathing reinterpretation of J.M.W. Turner's celebrated painting, "Slavers Throwing Overboard the Dead and Dying" (1840). Other important works followed, including James A. Emanuel's "Middle Passage Blues" (1999), Elizabeth Alexander's "Amistad" (2005), M. NourbeSe Philip's *Zong!* (2008), and Kevin Young's *Ardency: A Chronicle of the Amistad Rebels* (2011). Fiction was no exception to the rule, but novelists on either side of the Atlantic were the first to respond to the paradigm shift of the late twentieth century: Charles Johnson with *Middle Passage* (1990), Barry Unsworth with *Sacred Hunger* (1992), Caryl Phillips with *Crossing the River* (1993), Graeme Rigby with *The Black Cook's Historian* (1993), and Fred D'Aguiar with *Feeding the Ghosts* (1997)—to mention but some of the

---

world to overcome the scourge of poverty. For instance, the IMF website promotes economic globalization thus: "There is substantial evidence, from countries of different sizes and different regions, that as countries 'globalize' their citizens benefit, in the form of access to a wider variety of goods and services, lower prices, more and better-paying jobs, improved health, and higher overall living standards"; Julian Di Giovanni et al., "Globalization: A Brief Overview," *International Monetary Fund: Issues Brief* (May 2008): online (accessed 28 December 2016).

7   Haile Gerima's *Sankofa* (1993) should be mentioned as the first narrative film of the 1990s to engage with the transatlantic slave trade, but, for all its qualities, it failed to reach a mass audience. It could also have made its way into this study, as it addresses issues of community when Mona, an African-American fashion model, travels back in time to a plantation in the Caribbean and ends up joining a maroon community and its fight for freedom.

most remarkable achievements of that decade—all offered original, thought-provoking perspectives on the slave trade, its history, significance, and legacy.

While all works of fiction on the slave trade could probably be analyzed from the unique perspective of community, *Narrating the Slave Trade* does not aim to be exhaustive. Instead, it focusses on a very limited number of works whose selection was determined in relation to their potential to reveal the most various and enlightening aspects of community. This book is made up of four chapters, with each chapter concentrating on a specific dimension of community as it permeates one, sometimes two, works of fiction. The first chapter devotes its attention to the captives in the hold of slave ships. It revolves around issues of racial consciousness while also exploring the socio-political context and ideologies informing the works under scrutiny. The second chapter discusses political ideologies and the gestation of social organizations aboard a slave ship during the Middle Passage. The third chapter explores the creation of an ideal society—a classless, gender-equal, and multiracial isonomic community born out of a premeditated shipwreck and dramatic beginnings on the wild shores of the New World. And the fourth and last chapter shows how the story of the slave trade, especially the trauma of the Middle Passage, can help reassess the notion of community and take it in new directions.

The first chapter considers the most mundane aspect of the encounter between slave-trade studies and community theory: the racial community. Slave-ship captives, dazed and exhausted, chained in the hold, often came from very different geographical, cultural, and linguistic horizons. It was difficult for them to communicate, let alone organize a rebellion. Yet, driven by a basic need for survival, and perhaps interpreting their common dehumanization as a rallying sign, captives did engage in mutual support and plotted together whenever possible. In the popular imagination, the rebellion is the moment when the ethnic diversity characterizing most shiploads of captive slaves dissolves into a unifying racial consciousness. The reality, of course, was different: no more than their European captors did African captives define themselves in terms of race. Yet, once in the New World, this white–black divide on which the power structure was based took hold and came to characterize the entire social edifice. In the United States, for instance, *de facto* and *de jure* racial segregation became the norm, and it remained so long after slavery was abolished.

Racial pride and solidarity became tools of resistance and helped establish the type of racial consciousness displayed in slave-trade lore even though the human cargo in the hold did not think and act as a race. Yet anachronistic depiction of racial solidarity in slave-trade fiction is not mere historical ignorance. It serves an ideological purpose, implying a continuum between the

subjugation, deportation, and exploitation of Africans in the slave-trade era
and the lot of their descendants in post-slavery times, as if racial consciousness
were intrinsic to the black community rather than circumstantial and socially
constructed. This re-writing of history is particularly striking in Prosper Mérimée's novella *Tamango* (1829), which the blacklisted Hollywood director John
Berry adapted in 1958, and in Alex Haley's *Roots: The Saga of an American
Family* (1976) and its 1977 televised version. Both *Tamango* and *Roots* feature a
mutiny aboard a slave ship, and both address issues of racial consciousness and
allegiance in the African-American community. Mérimée's *Tamango*, allegedly
an abolitionist piece, makes purported racial differences the linchpin of its
argument and ends up bringing the socio-political climate of Mérimée's age
into the light of day. Berry retained the idea of the slave rebellion in Mérimée's
novella but revamped the rest of the story to fit his own agenda and reflect his
slant on historical reality. Accordingly, Berry put the beautiful mulatto Aiché,
both slave and mistress of the slave-ship captain John Reinker, in a terrible
dilemma: remaining faithful to the captain who promised to free her, or sacri-
ficing herself for the cause of the rebels on the grounds of racial identity and
freedom—an early and appropriate metaphor for the issues of racial solidarity
and militancy that will take centre stage in the ideological debates of the up-
coming civil rights movement.

    Roots and its televised version came out in the aftermath of the civil rights
movement, almost two decades after the film *Tamango,* and, just like *Tamango*,
Roots gives prominence to race consciousness in its Middle Passage segment.
In *Roots*, the hold is the place where a sense of pan-African solidarity emerges,
first out of a unanimous hatred of the toubob (the white man), and second out
of a need for group identification and self-preservation. *Roots* suggests that the
afrocentric sensibility of the cargo is inborn, that it lay dormant until it was
revived by white violence and negrophobia. Thus, *Roots* may be interpreted
as an indictment of the discourse of racial superiority that once underpinned
the slave trade and portended the systematization of racial discrimination
in the twentieth century. Yet, the slave uprising in both Haley's *Roots* and its
adaptation is a failure. Resistance is quelled and order is restored: a narrative
choice that ought to be interpreted in terms of its historical context and political
ideology. While some reviewers and critics deemed Haley's novel a provocative
work of fiction, others praised the miniseries as a groundbreaking event in the
history of prime-time television. The first chapter, however, overcomes this
alleged opposition arguing that *Roots*, whether on paper or on screen, conveys
conservative values. After the botched uprising, the protagonist Kunta Kinte
is sold into slavery, but the story neutralizes the disturbing and often shocking
nature of slavery by emphasizing family values and making black characters
as non-threatening and conventional as possible. These are the mid-1970s: the

general anxiety triggered by the success of black radicalism has receded, and the white majority is much less overtly prejudiced than it once was. In fact, the white majority ostensibly welcomes the end of segregation in the South and the overall achievements of the civil rights movement. Yet it is eager for a status quo ante in which racial hierarchies are quietly reinstated. The return of a conservative agenda as early as 1968 with the election of Richard Nixon reflects this sentiment as more subtle, but nevertheless effective, policies of racial discrimination are implemented.[8] *Roots* inadvertently reflects this new national mood and sheds an unexpected light on a form of race consciousness rarely seen as such: white ethnocentrism.

The evolution of European monarchies toward democracy in the eighteenth and nineteenth centuries occurred while the transatlantic slave trade was in full swing, and the nations most involved in the trade are also the nations that made the creed of the Enlightenment, especially the notions of individual freedom and the right to "the pursuit of happiness," the core principle of their constitutions. Although these lofty principles were presented as universal, they were often circumscribed to benefit the citizens of the nation that laid them down. Thus, Americans made it clear that all the ambitious goals set in their Constitution are for "ourselves and our Posterity." The role of a constitution is to cement national unity; a nation is created out of a set of characteristics in which citizens recognize themselves and common rules by which they agree to abide. Benedict Anderson, at the beginning of *Imagined Communities* (1991), defines a nation as "an imagined political community—and imagined as both inherently limited and sovereign."[9] A nation, Anderson further writes, is a community in which all citizens feel a communal bond: "regardless of the actual inequality and exploitation that may prevail in it, the nation is always conceived as a deep, horizontal comradeship" (7). The relationship between citizens and their national community, however, is never so smooth and harmonious. Some

---

8 Michelle Alexander shows how the conservatives capitalized on the frustrations of the most vulnerable sections of the white community in the presidential campaign of 1968: "Competing images of the poor as 'deserving' and 'undeserving' became central components of the debate. Ultimately, the racialized nature of this imagery became a crucial resource for conservatives, who succeeded in using law and order rhetoric in their effort to mobilize the resentment of white working-class voters, many of whom felt threatened by the sudden progress of African Americans"; Alexander, *The New Jim Crow: Mass Incarceration In The Age of Colorblindness* (New York: The New Press, 2010): 46. By 1968, Alexander goes on to argue, "81 percent of those responding to the Gallup Poll agreed with the statement that 'law and order had broken down in this country' and the majority blamed 'Negroes who start riots' and 'Communists'" (46).

9 Benedict Anderson, *Imagined Communities: Reflections on the Origin and Spread of Nationalism* (1991; London: Verso, 2006): 6.

self-styled patriots may violate, knowingly or not, the values their nation holds most dear, while other, ostensibly more authentic patriots may simply feel forsaken by their national institutions. The Constitution itself can never be completely neutral, and it may be divisive; it may also have established standards the nation cannot or will not meet. More generally, national communities are unsteady because they are unable to unite behind a reassuring consensus, and they find themselves overshadowed by political ideologies that often clash with one another and hamper national unity. All these issues of patriotism and political allegiance are at the heart of the second chapter, which focusses on Charles Johnson's *Middle Passage* (1990).

Middle Passage is all about the slave trade, yet it never uses the tropes of slave-trade narrative even when it evokes the horrors undergone by the human cargo. A bildungsroman, a farce, a picaresque novel, a historical fiction, and a philosophical meditation all at once, *Middle Passage* tells the story of Rutherford Calhoun, a former slave and unscrupulous rascal of twenty-two years of age who, after a brief experience of living by his wits in New Orleans, stows away on the Africa-bound slaver the *Republic* in order to escape both the mob and an enamoured schoolmarm. Aboard the *Republic*, Calhoun is exposed to three antagonist entities embodying radically different political models against which he is going to forge his own opinion and mold his destiny. The first of these models is that of Ebenezer Falcon, the tyrannical captain of the *Republic*. Falcon is described as a genuine American hero, a man of Manifest Destiny who pillages faraway lands for the benefit of both his nation and private employers. But while Falcon incarnates the conquering spirit and ruthless materialistic culture of his nation, he remains above all a soldier of fortune whose patriotism is purely self-interested. Through Falcon, the early section of this chapter not only probes the foundations of the nation that has seen itself, since its inception, as the most democratic in the world, but also the various levels of civic commitment to the Constitution. The second of these models is embodied by the crew, a group of disparate lowlifes whose sole purpose is to kill the captain and sell the cargo for profit. The crew is neither ideologically nor politically driven, since lucre is their primary stimulus. Yet, their motive for mutiny is inspired by a need for regime change aboard the *Republic*. The third model is that of the Allmuseri, a mythical African tribe of whom forty members are shackled in the hold of the *Republic*. The Allmuseri are initially associated with virtues of non-violence, tolerance, and unity, but their successful insurrection and subsequent takeover of the *Republic* will split them into rival factions and unleash forms of behavior no better than those of their former oppressors. The suggestion, advanced by the story itself, that the contact with the Western world of Falcon has vitiated the pacifist nature of the

Allmuseri is not only tenuous but also misleading. Focussing on the Diamelo character, a ne'er-do-well tribesman turned top dog after the insurrection, the chapter demonstrates that Allmuseri culture, behind its façade of perfection, is as flawed as any other culture.

Although each of these three groups is ready to take Calhoun in, Calhoun feels that he fits into none of them and decides to turn his allegiance to his own nation, its institutions, and the values it purportedly promotes. Considering the way black individuals (whether free or not) were treated at the time, and bearing in mind Calhoun's visceral attachment to individual freedom, the latter's claim, toward the end of the story, that he is a patriot is enough to take the reader aback. As the final section of this chapter argues, however, Calhoun's newfound ideals can be understood in relation to the decision of the nameless protagonist in Ralph Ellison's *Invisible Man* to come out of the underground lair where he has been holed up and play his role as an American citizen. Both protagonists know that the odds are against them, but both believe that the nation's institutions have the potential to build a truly democratic society for all Americans. It is this unwavering faith in the values of equality and tolerance on which the nation was built that makes Calhoun and the Invisible Man genuine constitutional patriots.

Victims of the slave trade, when they did not die in coffles on the way to the coast of West Africa or during the Middle Passage, rarely escaped their fate: they became slaves on the plantations of the New World, beasts of burden whose life-expectancy, especially in the early days, could be as short as six or seven years. A few slaves managed to run away, however, and some of them formed communities often hidden high in the mountains, deep in the swamps, or in the secluded recesses of pathless woods. Such communities survived either by relying on the munificence of nature or by pillaging nearby plantations. They were autonomous and created their own political rules, social norms, and cultural values. With the notable exceptions of Harriet Beecher Stowe's *Dred: A Tale of the Great Dismal Swamp* (1856), Édouard Glissant's *The Fourth Century* (1964), and, to a lesser extent, Harold Courlander's *The African* (1967) and Michelle Cliff's *Abeng* (1984), very few fiction writers have treated the topic of maroon communities in depth. Scholarship on the topic, from Richard Price's seminal anthology *Maroon Societies* (1973) to such recent works as Sylviane Diouf's *Slavery's Exiles* (2014) and Neil Roberts's *Freedom as Marronage* (2015), attests to the overwhelmingly African pedigree of such communities. However, Eric Williams's remark, in *Capitalism and Slavery* (1944), that "unfree labor in the New World was brown, white, black, and yellow"[10] is a reminder that some

---

10   Eric Williams, *Capitalism and Slavery* (1944; Chapel Hill: U of North Carolina P, 1994): 7.

of these communities were racially mixed and even included individuals of European extraction.

A black and white community is featured in the final part of Barry Unsworth's *Sacred Hunger* (1992), a historical novel that begins in Liverpool in 1752, the year the African Company of Merchants takes control of the British slave trade, and ends in the wilderness of Florida's Atlantic coast in 1764, a year after Spain has ceded Florida to the Kingdom of Great Britain in the aftermath of the Seven Years' War. The white crew and the black cargo of a slave ship, after joining forces and slaying their brutal, lunatic captain, beach and de-mast the vessel before settling in the unmapped jungle beyond the shoreline. Under the guidance of Delblanc, a young idealist of good birth, the small group of survivors becomes a leaderless, egalitarian community, which has abolished property, adopted a quid pro quo exchange system, and obliterated parental exclusivity. But Delblanc's idyllic society never becomes the El Dorado Voltaire's Candide chances upon in South America.[11] Soon the community crumbles due to both its internal contradictions and the refusal of some members to abide by the established common rules. Thus, *Sacred Hunger* does not so much depict daily, down-to-earth existence in a utopian community as the founding, growth, and undoing of such a utopian community. To a certain extent, this third chapter furthers the previous chapter's analysis of the factors that help form political opinions, but it is also an autopsy of a failed experiment in community living. The creation of the settlement is the opportunity to imagine what a concrete application of the theories of such early contractualists as Thomas Hobbes, John Locke, and Jean-Jacques Rousseau might have led to. Rousseau's aversion to private property as well as his idea of making the people both sovereign and the subjects of their own sovereignty by giving them full political power and entrusting them with the destiny of their society are closest to Delblanc's own conception of a truly democratic society. However, Delblanc's promotion of individual commitment to the well-being of the entire community is a disembodied ideal; Delblanc's own distrust of any form of ruling authority,

---

11   It is very likely that Barry Unsworth created Delblanc's community from a variety of examples, both fictional and real. The El Dorado in *Candide* (1759) is an interesting candidate for comparison not only because, like Delblanc's ideal society, it is secluded and in the New World, but also because it is a harmonious, peaceful society which has developed an excellent educational system, eradicated poverty, and done away with government and religion. Staying within the timeframe of the story, Étienne-Gabriel Morelly, the purported author of *The Code of Nature* (1755), also comes across as a good match for the Delblanc character in *Sacred Hunger*. Indeed, in Morelly's *Code*, such essential features of modern societies as politics, trade, and law are abolished on the ground that they thwart individual freedom. As for private property, it is the source of all evil—a stance Delblanc would gladly adopt.

combined with a form of absolute but eventually coercive equality, comes to undermine the sense of unity he had managed to forge among the survivors in the aftermath of the mutiny. Delblanc's failure to foster enduring group identification leads to the resurgence of clannish behavior and strategies of self-advancement on the part of the more entrepreneurial individuals in the settlement.

The rise of these businessmen and the normalization of selfish, greedy, and unethical practices epitomizing their success constitute an eerie parallel with the neoliberal mentality that resurged in force in the 1980s as a consequence of Thatcherism in the United Kingdom and Reaganism in the United States. Thus, what happens in the settlement leads to two diverging interpretations. On the one hand, it suggests that the development of business, the accumulation of wealth, and the inequality resulting therefrom constitute an inexorable process in the history of mankind. On the other, it implies that the economic model that free-market advocates managed to impose on the rest of the world at the end of the twentieth century is a regression to a type of primitive capitalism—a capitalism without social safeguards, and one that has made the slave trade and other forms of exploitation possible. It is the second interpretation that Unsworth intended to impart, and the ravages of unbridled laissez-faire capitalism form an enlightening subtext of trans-historical significance in *Sacred Hunger*. But the communal adventure upon which Delblanc and his fellow survivors have embarked is also an opportunity to explore the notion of community beyond the contingencies of politics.

The story of the settlement in *Sacred Hunger*, by giving the reader access to the mindset of those who have decided to disown the community to which they owe their life, enables a detailed exploration of the notion of community, what makes it possible and what undermines it, what its benefits and demands are, and, ultimately, what it means to live together. Relying both on Jean-Luc Nancy's argument that "being-in-common" with others is intrinsic to the human experience and on Roberto Esposito's emphasis on duty and responsibility to others—characteristics embedded in the etymological core of the word "community"—this chapter dwells on why some individuals choose to abstract themselves from a community that has provided them with a degree of serenity and a quality of life they could never have hoped for after being trapped, either as cargo or crew, in the machinery of the global slave trade. By going to the roots of Delblanc's failure, this chapter endeavors to uncover the complex system of human interactions that regulate a community.

In *The Atlantic Sound* (2001), Caryl Phillips devotes a few paragraphs to Sullivan's Island, the place where many slave ships would unload their cargo for the auction block of nearby Charleston, South Carolina. With measured irony,

Phillips calls Sullivan's Island the Black Ellis Island and describes the Middle Passage experience in an unusual way:

> An arrival in America. Having crossed the Atlantic in the belly of a ship. An arrival. Here in America. Step ashore, out of sight of Charleston. To be fed, watered, scrubbed, prepared. To be sold. Back home, a similar climate. Different vegetation. Different birds. Family. An arrival. Low, low land. Water. The mainland lying low in the hazy distance. Charleston. Farewell Africa. Welcome America.[12]

Phillips's lines echo verses in Robert Hayden's poem "Middle Passage" (1962) a few decades earlier: "Middle Passage: / Voyage through death / to life upon these shores." In "Middle Passage," Hayden does not spare the reader the agony undergone by the cargo chained in the hold during the crossing of the Atlantic, but he begins and ends the poem with these verses, as if to enclose the horrifying experience of the Middle Passage in a hopeful vision of life in the New World. This same idea of the Americas as the place of a new start appears in *Sacred Hunger* as well when Matthew Paris reflects on Delblanc's clear-sightedness: "In the landfall itself, where others saw merely a refuge, Delblanc must have seen a violent birth."[13] Finally, Édouard Glissant picks up this idea of birth in "The Open Boat," the short piece that opens his seminal *Poetics of Relation* (1990). At once poetic prose fiction, historical account, and philosophical essay, "The Open Boat" works both to remember and to transcend the trauma of the Middle Passage. Under Glissant's pen, the life-affirming statement of Hayden's poem has become an axiom—a universal principle that not only informs the *Poetics of Relation* but his ensuing philosophical reflection as well.

The hold, in Glissant's poetics, is the unknown—a place where human beings are uprooted, dissocialized, and depersonalized. The unknown is also the marine abyss in which so many captives, dead or alive, were casually dumped, and it is the loss of reality in the New World where the everyday has become unreal, and the familiar of the ancestral land a fading memory. While describing the first dread of the hold as "a fall in the belly of the boat,"[14] Glissant re-interprets the hold as a womb whence a new people emerged. Thus, in spite of all those who have been sacrificed, Glissant sees the experience of the hold as a beginning, the advent of a new humanity, a nothingness that has finally become knowledge. This knowledge is neither the pre-established knowledge

---

12   Caryl Phillips, *The Atlantic Sound* (London: Vintage Random House, 2001): 257.
13   Barry Unsworth, *Sacred Hunger* (New York: W.W. Norton, 1993): 537.
14   Édouard Glissant, *Poetics of Relation*, tr. Betsy Wing (*Poétique de la Relation*, 1990; Ann Arbor: U of Michigan P, 1997); 6. Further page references are in the main text.

of hegemonic cultures nor knowledge limited to Glissant's own Creole culture. Rather, it is an all-embracing knowledge leading to the Glissantian notion of Relation. Relation, Glissant argues, "is not made up of things that are foreign but of shared knowledge" (8). Relation, which started in the "nonworld"—that is, in the darkness and anonymous promiscuity of the hold—has developed into the "total world" (*tout-monde*). The purpose of the total world is to foster diversity as a bulwark against uniformity and inertia. Glissant criticizes what he calls "continental thinking," as it thwarts cultural exchange and tends toward the homogenization of society and culture. To the negative concept of "root-identity" Glissant opposes a rhizomatic view of humankind whereby the specter of the Middle Passage, of its violence and oppression, can be transcended. Relation is revealed through creolization, which is both a theory and a praxis meant to resist any form of totalitarianism and nurture cultural fragmentation. Creolization, Glissant argues, "carries along into [...] the incredible explosion of cultures" (34). But this explosion, he continues, "does not mean [these cultures] are scattered or mutually diluted. It is the violent sign of their consensual, not imposed, sharing" (34).

Echoing Giorgio Agamben in *The Coming Community* (1990), Glissant questions the fact that the individual only exists in his/her relation to the community, which curtails his/her freedom. The conditions of freedom are such, Glissant argues, that the individual ought not to be governed by a universalizing history or limited by a territory. Through the concept of Relation, Glissant militates not for the end of borders but for greater cultural communication. Glissant's targets are essentialism and what he calls filiation (the constitution of identity through the creation of founding myths), which generate self-legitimization and violence. To experience Relation is to experience chaos, because the contacts among cultures are not fixed by ideologies but are constantly changing and moving. Glissant prefigures Alphonso Lingis's notion of "the community of those who have nothing in common" when he describes the "Relation-identity" as something that "does not think of a land as a territory from which to project toward other territories but as a place where one gives-on-and-with rather than grasps" (144). Glissant also anticipates the work of Esposito on the suffix *munus* in the Latin root of the word "community," which implies "an obligation or a debt"[15] to the community. Glissant writes:

> Thought of the Other is sterile without the other of Thought. Thought of the Other is the moral generosity disposing me to accept the principle of alterity, to conceive of the world as not simple and straightforward,

---

15   Roberto Esposito, *Communitas: The Origin and Destiny of Community*, tr. Timothy Campbell (*Communitas: origine e destino della comunità*, 1998; Stanford CA: Stanford UP, 2009): 6.

> with only one truth—mine. But thought of the Other can dwell within
> me without making me alter course, without "prizing me open," without
> changing me within myself [...]. The other of Thought is precisely this
> altering. Then I have to act. That is the moment I change my thought,
> without renouncing its contribution. I change, and I exchange.
>
> *Poetics of Relation* 154

In other words, belonging to the community is not, to paraphrase Esposito, an
addition but a subtraction; it is an onus. Lingis posits the *"other community"*[16]
as an alternative to the rational community of the "individual of modern culture" who "sets out to produce his individuality as that of a nature closed upon
itself" (9). The other community, Lingis continues,

> forms when one recognizes, in the face of the other, an imperative. An
> imperative that not only contests the common discourse and community
> from which he or she is excluded, but everything one has or sets out to
> build in common with him or her.
>
> *The Community of Those Who Have Nothing in Common* 10–11

Agamben presents a similar idea with his notion of "whatever singularity,"
contending that the community of tomorrow is not defined by the affirma-
tion of identity or "representable condition of belonging" (86), but by the
"co-belonging" of singularities itself. A community is not something already
constituted—or, worse, artificially constituted. It is not a passive idea. It is dy-
namic, always in development, and, like the boat of Glissant, open and ready
to sail for all.[17]

Agamben's notion of "co-belonging" is an explicit reference to Jean-Luc Nancy's concept of coexistence. To coexist means that we do not exist without being
related to others, or, to use Nancy's terminology, without being-in-common. As
Nancy puts it in *Being Singular Plural*, the "question of Being and the meaning of
Being has become the question of being-with and of being-together."[18] In *The Inoperative Community*, Nancy postulates an "originary or ontological 'sociality'"[19]

---

16   Alphonso Lingis, *The Community of Those Who Have Nothing in Common* (Bloomington:
      Indiana UP, 1994): 10.

17   The exact sentence, which concludes "The Open Boat," reads: "Our boats are open, and we
      sail them for everyone" (9) ("Nos barques sont ouvertes, pour tous nous les naviguons").

18   Jean-Luc Nancy, *Being Singular Plural*, tr. Robert D. Richardson & Anne E. O'Byrne (*Être
      sigulier pluriel*, 1996; Stanford CA: Stanford UP, 2000): 35.

19   Jean-Luc Nancy, *The Inoperative Community*, ed. Peter Connor, tr. Peter Connor et al.,
      foreword by Christopher Fynsk (*La Communauté désoeuvrée*, 1983, rev. 1986; Minneapolis:
      U of Minnesota P, 1991): 28.

that exists before any form of socialization. Glissant's metaphor of the womb in "The Open Boat" postulates that the minds of the captives are, like the minds of newborns, a tabula rasa. Hence, the encounter with the unknown other in the hold of the slave ship is a striking illustration of Nancy's theory: "Although you are alone in this suffering," Glissant tells those in the hold, "you share in the unknown with others whom you have yet to know" (6). Focussing on the analogies between Glissant's and Nancy's theories (especially the remarkable similarities of their respective key concepts of Relation and being-with), this last chapter aims to rethink the notion of community in an entirely new light.

Both Glissant and Nancy have reached rather ominous conclusions as to the state of the present world, which is plagued with social and economic disparities, the disempowerment of political institutions as a consequence of the economic liberalization of world markets, the ensuing standardization of life, and the proliferation of various forms of cultural isolationism as a response to an overwhelming sense of alienation. But while Glissant and Nancy identify the problems, they fail to come up with viable solutions. Even if the entire world, as Glissant would have it, is being creolized, the forces of free-market capitalism, rather than the impetuous, fruitful exchanges of ideas among cultures, decide our destinies. Even if the utter fragmentation of our world, as Nancy argues, has fostered the conditions for a better world to be created *ex nihilo*, such a creation remains a concept rather than a practical project. Nicolas Bourriaud's notion of the "radicant" appears to constitute a way out of this theoretical impasse. While acknowledging the rhizome as a valid metaphor for Glissant's creolized globality, Bourriaud, through the radicant, re-inscribes the importance of enrooting, not in the form of a unique, homogenizing root but as a process whereby momentary roots form news roots in the random and infinite network of relationships developed by individuals caught in the perpetual flow of populations and cultural values typifying the twenty-first century. The radicant works as a remarkable revealer of the zeitgeist of our age, but Bourriaud's focus on the art world reduces the scope of the phenomenon, romanticizes its turbulence, and overlooks its deleterious effects on at-risk populations. The radicant is all but a panacea to the ills of the world. By contrast, Glissant and Nancy urge us to reconsider community in order to shape a better future, but in doing so, they dismiss the very notion of community as obsolete and even prejudicial. Instead of thinking beyond community, it is perhaps advisable to accept community as an ontological phenomenon and tackle its negative tendencies lest our world hearkens back to a darker past, a past when such practices as slave trading were business as usual.

CHAPTER 1

The Slave Trade and Racial Community: *Tamango* and *Roots*

The moans of the Foulah shivered through the black hold. Then, after a while, a clear voice called out in Mandinka, "Share his pain! We must be in this place as one village!" The voice belonged to an elder. He was right.[1]

: .

Both *Tamango* and *Roots* feature a slave-ship insurrection, and both present the insurgents as a racial monolith. While some of the captives may stand out and claim their difference from their peers, they are still perceived as oppressed blacks pitted against their white oppressors. The circumstances of the Middle Passage seem to dispel such a simple categorization, since the composition of passengers below and above deck was, historically, anything but homogeneous. Yet, this radical separation of crew and cargo along racial lines aboard slavers serves as the premise to Marcus Rediker's *The Slave-Ship*:

> In producing workers for the plantation, the ship-factory also produced "race." At the beginning of the voyage, captains hired a motley crew of sailors, who would, on the coast of Africa, become "white men." At the beginning of the Middle Passage, captains loaded on board the vessel a multi-ethnic collection of Africans, who would, in the American port, become "black people" or a "negro race." The voyage thus transformed those who made it.[2]

But this process leading from ethnic diversity to racial polarization is not what *Tamango*, *Roots*, and most other fictional accounts of the Middle Passage are interested in. Rather, such stories posit the white–black dialectic as originary and immutable because it bolsters an ideological agenda, which may vary

---

1 Alex Haley, *Roots: The Saga of an American Family* (1976; New York: Vanguard, 30th Anniversary Edition 2007): 175.
2 Marcus Rediker, *The Slave-Ship: A Human History* (New York: Viking, 2007): 10.

across time, from one author to the next, and from one original text to later versions.[3]

Prosper Mérimée's *Tamango* (1829) and its 1958 movie adaptation by John Berry, as well as Alex Haley's *Roots* (1976) and its televised version the following year, must be understood with these parameters in mind. In all cases, the hold of the slave ship is the place where African captives from all origins are molded into blacks: i.e. defined primarily in terms of race, with all the connotations and consequences such a term entails. Both versions of *Tamango* and both versions of *Roots* rely on this racial criterion, and all of them are meant to be an indictment of the slave trade. Yet, all these *Tamango* and *Roots* versions fail to send a truly progressive message. In fact, the more these stories make racial community the core element of their argument, the more the argument back-fires. The question of whether racial difference should be emphasized, because it is either natural, beneficial, or necessary, is recurrent throughout this and the following chapters.

Both Mérimée's *Tamango*[4] and its film adaptation by Berry must be under-stood in their historical context. Set in the 1820s, Mérimée's *Tamango* is full of ambiguities—it denounces both the slave trade and the French government's disingenuous support of it, while also depicting Africans in an unflattering and objectionable light. Berry's *Tamango* is less oblique than Mérimée's but no less complex, and equally influenced by its political environment. The Cold War, decolonization, and the American civil rights movement constitute a diffuse but significant backdrop to the film. While remembered as an audacious, even provocative film, Berry's *Tamango* promotes values that are quite different from Mérimée's but not necessarily more broad-minded.

---

3   This white–black paradigm of race is at the core of Daniel Black's *The Coming: A Novel* (2015). *The Coming* portrays the destiny of the black community from life in Africa prior to any con-tact with whites, to the Middle Passage (the main focus of the novel) and slavery in the New World. Black emphasizes the tribal diversity of the Africans shackled in the hold, and while he names all his protagonists, he also chooses to treat them as a unified whole, a community that resolves to survive, thrive, and tell the tale. The collective "we" of the Africans and their descendants is used throughout the story. Contrastively, the voice of the whites is eclipsed, only laying bare the atrocities they perpetrated. Thus, Black embraces the racial dichotomy that was manufactured on the slave ship in order to appropriate it and celebrate black iden-tity. *The Coming* may be read as a reparative novel making up for Haley's lies about the his-torical veracity of *Roots* (a point later discussed in section 1 of this chapter).

4   Mérimée's *Tamango* is a simple case of the biter bit: Tamango, an African slave dealer, is captured along with the people he has just sold to a French captain. Once in the hold of the slave-ship with his former victims and now fellow captives, Tamango organizes a successful revolt in which all the whites on board are massacred. Unable to steer the ship back to Africa, the insurgents succumb to thirst and starvation except for Tamango, who is rescued and goes on to live the forlorn life of an alcoholic cymbalist in the British colony of Jamaica.

   Alex Haley's *Roots* (1976) and the miniseries it inspired prompted a great
deal of contradictory and impassioned criticism. Arnold Rampersad praised
the novel for "yielding startling insights into the psychological process of American slavery" (24). Conversely, Russell Adams deemed most characters in the
novel "boringly akin to stock-figures."[5] As for the miniseries, it was commend-
ed for being an eye-opener about the harsh realities of slavery and an enhancer
of race relations in the United States. Vernon Jordan, the former Urban League
president, called the miniseries "the single most spectacular educational experience in race relations in America."[6] Negative reviews abounded, too, with
many critics and academics arguing that the *Roots* miniseries was a bowdler-
ized and conservative version of Haley's original work. According to Lauren
Tucker and Hemant Shaw, the miniseries distorted Haley's story, marginalizing
"the black cultural experience" while elevating "the white perspective on the
black American experience."[7] Leaving polemics aside, this chapter does not
find fundamental differences between Haley's bestseller and its immensely
popular adaptation: both owe their success not so much to their novelty and
boldness (captivating the mainstream with a story about slavery) as to their
conservative overtones (perpetuating the reassuring, traditional values of the
dominant culture).
   This chapter first places Mérimée's *Tamango*, Berry's adaptation thereof,
and both versions of *Roots* in their respective social, cultural, and political
context so as to understand how each work evinces the zeitgeist of its era.
Thus, Mérimée sets *Tamango* in the 1820s, a time when France, pressured by
England, has officially signed off on banning the slave trade. While Mérimée
presents himself as an abolitionist, his take on the slave trade, and especially
his portrayal of the protagonist Tamango, suggests strong racial biases while
also foreshadowing his nation's colonial ambitions on the African continent.
Coincidentally, Berry's own version of Mérimée's *Tamango* came out when
the French colonial empire was beginning to crumble, while, in the United
States, the African-American community was coming together to defy direct
and institutional violence, and to fight for equality and justice. Through his
adaptation of *Tamango*, Berry endeavors to show, with varying degrees of success, his unwavering support for the black cause on both the national and

---

5   Russell L. Adams, "An Analysis of the 'Roots' Phenomenon in the Context of American Racial
    Conservatism," *Présence Africaine* 116.4 (1980): 131.
6   Quoted in Frank A. Salamone, "*Roots* (Haley, 1976), in *Encyclopedia of Slave Resistance and
    Rebellion*, ed. Junius P. Rodriguez (Santa Barbara CA: Greenwood, 2006), vol. 2: 427.
7   Lauren Tucker & Hemant Shaw, "Race and the Transformation of Culture: The Making of the
    Television Miniseries *Roots*," *Critical Studies in Mass Communication* 9.4 (December 1992):
    328.

the international stage. The context for Haley's *Roots* and its adaptation is the post-civil rights era. By then, much had been achieved in terms of reducing racial inequality in the United States, but rather than offering a profound reflection on issues of race, *Roots* makes family the central theme of the plot—a strategy that proved to be an ideal vehicle for roping in a nation eager for normalcy and the soothing vision of a color-blind society held together by a set of universal values.

The hold of the slave ship is often interpreted as the place where Africans from many different tribes coalesce into a race. In Mérimée's *Tamango*, however, the captives are not given a voice and cannot convey a sense of racial solidarity (if any). The narrator, whose view of the slave trade remains ambiguous throughout the text, is the one who assigns a racial identity to the Africans, and in order to do so, he resorts to a litany of stereotypes that were already rampant in the early nineteenth century. In Berry's *Tamango,* the hold has become a crucible of black militancy. Tamango and his fellow tribesmen have failed to take control of the ship as they do in Mérimée's original. They are trapped in the hold and condemned to certain death. But their self-sacrifice is a moral victory, a symbol of resistance, and a demonstration of race allegiance. In *Roots*, the cargo is less homogeneous than in Berry's *Tamango*. Differences are acknowledged, especially in the novel, and disagreements among captives with various backgrounds precipitate a failed insurrection. But those subtleties tend to disappear behind collective hatred of the white oppressor. Racial consciousness resurfaces, but, as a comparison of the Middle Passage segment in both the novel and the miniseries shows, it is carefully constructed so as to avoid any parallel with negative perceptions of black radicalism at the time.

The plots of *Tamango* and *Roots* hinge on the notion of race. The perception of race in Mérimée's *Tamango* seems to be that of his age. The story is filled with crass stereotypes about Africans, and while Mérimée's credentials as an abolitionist seem impeccable, his rhetorical way of dealing with issues of race may leave some readers perplexed about his intended message. Berry's plot is more down-to-earth and aims at showing what a sense of community, mediated by racial solidarity, can accomplish. The use of racial identity by both Haley and the miniseries in *Roots* is more circumspect than Berry's. Still, it remains central to the plot inasmuch as Haley once presented *Roots* as a story that his (African-American) people could make theirs. A thorough analysis of the Middle Passage segment suggests, however, that *Roots*, for ideological motives, downplays the significance of the African-American community in the history of the nation. Symptomatically, these stories' dramatization of the racial community as a way of denouncing the slave trade backfires and ends up promoting the kind of values they purportedly meant to criticize.

1   *Tamango* and *Roots* in Context

Mérimée published *Tamango* in the midst of a fierce national debate about the slave trade. On the occasion of the Treaty of Paris (1815), the restored Bourbon monarch Louis XVIII had been compelled to sign a treaty with England whereby France forswore slave-trading activities. But many in France believed that England's efforts to enforce its 1807 ban on the slave trade was in fact a deliberate attempt to stifle an already ailing French economy. In this perspective, violating the ban became not only a necessity but also a patriotic stance. This accounts, early in Mérimée's story, for the attitude of the French officials who, upon inspecting Captain Ledoux's brig, turn a blind eye to "the obvious objective of the ship's travels, tacitly support[ing] Ledoux's illegal money making scheme."[8] While this is a clear indictment of the French government's connivance in the slave trade, Mérimée still panders to his readership's proverbial anglophobia: at the end of the story, when Tamango is rescued by English sailors and brought to Jamaica, the local British governor reasons that since the men Tamango murdered "were only Frenchmen," Tamango will be set free—that is, the narrator hastens to explain, "made to work for the government."[9] This ending to the story is disconcerting because it tends to dampen the difference between the pathetic life of a destitute musician in a colonial regiment and that of a plantation slave in the Americas. This way of blowing hot and cold typifies Mérimée's way of presenting the slave trade throughout the text.

From the outset, Captain Ledoux seems to live up to his name. He comes across as a gentle, bonhomous veteran, a true patriot who lost a hand at Trafalgar and regrets that the war is over. Ledoux is an entrepreneur at heart, and slave trading naturally suggests itself to him as a lucrative venture. The good-natured Ledoux imparts his joie de vivre by naming his brig *L'Espérance* (Hope). But there will be very little hope for his human cargo. Ledoux is a tight-packer who leaves only three feet four inches in height for his human cargo and questions the need for the slaves to stand up in the hold, since, "when they arrive in the colonies [...] they'll spend more than enough time on their feet" (73). Cynicism peaks when, after he has decided against filling the narrow space between rows of slaves with even more slaves, a contentious Ledoux declares: "You have to be humane and allow a black man at least five feet by two in which to flex his limbs during a voyage lasting six weeks or more" (73).

---

8   Corry Cropper, "Prosper Mérimée and the Subversive 'Historical' Short Story," *Nineteenth Century French Studies* 33.1–2 (Fall 2004–Winter 2005): 66.

9   Prosper Mérimée, "Tamango" (1829), in Mérimée, *Carmen and Other Stories*, tr. Nicholas Jotcham (New York: Oxford UP, 2008): 92. Further page references are in the main text.

The measurements, incidentally, are a bit less than the room left for a human corpse in a coffin,[10] while the choice, in the original, of the infinitive *s'ébattre* ("to flex his limbs") connotes the purported puerility of Africans. Further on, this supposed puerile nature of Africans merges with the myth of the "happy darky" when the captives are made to dance above deck, for health purposes, to the tune of the fiddler:

> On these occasions it was remarkable to see them all turn their black faces towards the musician, gradually lose their expression of abject despair, laugh loudly, and even applaud when not prevented from doing so by their chains.
>
> "Tamango" 80

The stereotype of African childlikeness is one of many, but it is recurrent and essential to refining our understanding of Mérimée's ideological position when he wrote *Tamango*.

The title character Tamango also embodies the ostensible callowness of Africans. Tamango first welcomes Ledoux, a potential slave-buyer, with two wives and a small retinue under a makeshift straw shelter. Tamango dresses up for the occasion, and his mismatched, ill-fitting attire, "an old blue military tunic which still had a corporal's stripes" (74) complemented by "a large cavalry sabre [hanging] from a cord at his side" (74), makes him look ludicrous and fickle. From a narrative point of view, it is difficult to decide whether this demeaning description of Tamango is meant to meet the expectations of Mérimée's contemporaries, or if it is meant to offend them and thus arouse their antislavery sentiments. Mérimée's narrator's jeering remark at the end of the paragraph does not help, as it hammers home the notion of Tamango's racial inferiority: "In this rigout, the African warrior adjudged himself more elegant than the most consummate dandy to be found in Paris or London" (74). The narratorial voice in *Tamango* is disturbing, as it seems to shift from one viewpoint to another throughout the story. Depending on the situation, the narrator is sometimes detached, sometimes not; sometimes omniscient and sometimes

---

10   This comparison between coffins and individual space in the hold is established in the endnote to the 1967 Garnier edition of *Tamango*. The preceding endnote in that same edition also suggests that Mérimée was probably familiar with the report by Auguste de Staël, of the Société de la morale chrétienne (Society for Christian Morality), about torture in the slave trade. The death metaphor that envelops the slave trade is nothing original at the time of Mérimée. Stephanie E. Smallwood reports: "Slave-ships were called *tumbeiros* in the eighteenth-century Angolan trade [...] a term historians have translated as 'floating tombs' or 'undertakers'" (*Saltwater Slavery*, 137).

limited; more importantly, it occasionally gets entangled with the voice of the unsavory Ledoux character. Yet, Mérimée's sincerity about ending the slave trade can hardly be questioned, as he chose to publish *Tamango* in the *Revue de Paris*, a new literary magazine that published such noted abolitionists as Benjamin Constant and Victor Schoelcher. Mérimée's narrative strategy may be patterned after Montesquieu's famous condemnation of slavery in *The Spirit of the Laws* (1748).[11] In the essay "Of the Slavery of the Negroes" (Book XV, Ch. 5), Montesquieu mocks the attitudes of the supporters of slavery by putting himself in their shoes: "Were I to vindicate our right to make slaves of the negroes, these should be my arguments [...]." A series of statements, each more outrageous than the last, ensues, and Montesquieu concludes: "It is impossible for us to suppose these creatures to be men, because, allowing them to be men, a suspicion would follow that we ourselves are not Christians" (250). In the same fashion, Mérimée endeavors to infuriate his reader by a series of egregious comments and scenes so as to expose the ignominy of the slave trade and those who profit from it.

John Berry's *Tamango* bears little resemblance to its nineteenth-century literary source. Aiché, the favorite Tamango had given to the captain in the original, has become the captain's long-standing mulatto girlfriend. As for the obnoxious, vain, heartless slave trader Tamango, he has been replaced by a principled, fearless lion-hunter who refuses to obey his cruel oppressors and convinces his fellow captives that it is better to lose one's life in righteous combat than to be sold by the white man into slavery. This complete rewriting of plot and characters reflects the historical and political context of the film. On the level of world politics, the 1955 Asian–African Bandung conference in Indonesia not only opposed both European colonialism and neocolonialism by the USA and the USSR, but also aimed at promoting the "Recognition of the equality of all races and of the equality of all nations large and small."[12] As for France, the Algerian war of independence had started in 1956, and respected intellectuals from the colonies such as Frantz Fanon, Aimé Césaire, and Léopold Sédar Senghor had been debunking negrophobic stereotypes and celebrating Africanness. In the United States, African-American civil-rights activists had been fighting for social, political, and racial equality, bringing to the attention of the world the contemptible spectacle of lynching and institutional racism. In this

---

11   The connection between Mérimée's prose and Montesquieu's provocative statement in "Of the Slavery of the Negroes" is suggested by Gonzague Truc in his notes for the Garnier edition of *L'esprit des lois* (1748).

12   This is the third of the ten principles of the Asian–African conference held in Bandung on 18–24 April 1955.

context, in which white injustice is brought to the fore all over the world, it is hard to imagine how John Berry could have created a faithful version of Méri-mée's African protagonist who sells his own people and seems to confirm all too well pervasive notions of inherent black inferiority and savagery.

The release of *Tamango* in France did not go without its share of trouble. *Tamango* was censored in French colonies and overseas territories. American columnists naturally offered an American interpretation of the ban. *Tamango* was banned in the French colonies, a *New York Times* columnist explained, "as being too inflammatory, since it has romantic scenes between a Negro woman and a white man."[13] It is highly unlikely that miscegenophobia was the reason for censorship in the colonies.[14] More likely, the story of fearless, rebellious slaves silenced to death by a brutal white master came across as an undesir-able candidate for screenings in African theatres. In 1956, France was facing growing resentment in its African empire and decided to grant the inhabitants of its African colonies full status as citizens in the hope that such measures would stave off nationalist movements and calm a climate of violence. 1956 is also the beginning of France's anti-colonialist troubles in the North African littoral.[15] Berry, an American director exiled in Paris, must have been conscious of French susceptibilities as Ledoux, the French captain, has become Reinker, a Dutch captain.[16]

Roots came out in the 1970s, a time that marked the apogee of the progres-sive politics of the 1960s in the United States. Richard Nixon had resigned as

---

13   A.H. Weiler, "By Way of Report," *New York Times* (13 September 1959): X9.

14   About a decade prior to *Tamango*, the African-American jazzman Miles Davis had almost married the French singer Juliette Greco, and although interracial relationships weren't the norm, Greco and Davis weren't treated as pariahs, either. And a couple of years after *Tamango*, in 1960, the film director Claude Bernard-Aubert made *My Baby Is Black!* (*Les lâches vivent d'espoir*). This is a rather daring interracial romance between a white French woman and an African student. It focusses on people's hostility toward their relationship, which, in consequence, starts to falter. Such candidness was unthinkable in 1958 America. Incidentally, 1958 is the year Richard and Mildred Loving, a Virginia mixed-race couple with three children, were charged by a court in Virginia with the crime of marrying each other. They were sentenced to one year in prison—a sentence that could be suspended provided that they left Virginia at once and did not return together or at the same time for twenty-five years. The Lovings took their case to the Supreme Court of America and finally won in 1967. See United States Supreme Court, "*Loving v. Commonwealth of Vir-ginia*, 1967," in *Interracialism: Black–White Intermarriage in American History, Literature, and Law*, ed. Werner Sollors (Oxford & New York: Oxford UP, 2000): 28.

15   On the radio show *Le Masque et la Plume* in 1958, the critic Jacques Doniol-Valcroze, although dismissive of *Tamango*'s scenario as flat, acknowledged that the film is coura-geous and meaningful in such a historical context and that, as a matter of fact, "the cen-sorship made no mistake about it" ["la censure ne s'y est pas trompée"].

16   Raymond Borde, "*Tamango*," *Les Temps Modernes* 146 (April 1958): 1904.

President in 1974, the Vietnam War had just ended, and the nation was undergoing economic recession. On 23 August 1976, the novelist Tom Wolfe tried to capture the social and cultural climate of the 1970s in "The 'Me' Decade and the Third Great Awakening," a cover story for *New York* magazine in which Wolfe argued that individuals were turning in upon themselves after a decade of deep, personal commitment to political and social change. Communitarianism was out. Individualism was in. Haley's *Roots* came out on 17 August 1976, just a week prior to Wolfe's essay. Like Wolfe, Haley must have felt that Americans were tired of politics and pulling back from both national and international issues in order to focus on themselves. But while Wolfe postulated an atomized, almost asocial withdrawal of the self, Haley did not envisage wholesale rejection of community. Rather, in these times of doubts, Americans sought solace in traditional values, and family, especially family life, was a major integrating factor in this quest for serenity. Haley's *Roots* skillfully tapped into that reservoir of hope by developing such themes as heredity and national identity.

Roots tells the story of Kunta Kinte and his descendants' dogged resilience in keeping their lineage alive. It is nearly impossible for African Americans to trace their family tree back to a community in Africa, as the slave-owning class did its utmost to prevent slaves, either through sexual abuse or property sale, from starting a family and maintaining it over generations. But Kunta's lineage remains strong and indelible because, as Leslie Fishbein argues, "Haley's ancestors exhibited remarkable sexual restraint, with Kunta and Kizzy experiencing prolonged periods of volitional celibacy."[17] Thus, *Roots* harbors conservative values in which American mainstream culture of the 1970s took refuge after the social upheavals of the 1960s. However, the chastity of Kunta and his progeny constitutes more than a response to the sexual liberation of the 1960s: it tends to downplay the sexual violence typifying slavery despite the miniseries' candid depiction of such violence. As a result, *Roots* makes the hardships of slaves as ordinary as the hardships of any other downtrodden minority in America.

The full title of Haley's bestseller, *Roots: The Saga of An American Family*, indicates that, in the story, family must be understood as both phylogenetic (race) and genealogical (kinship). The "roots" in Haley's title refer to Africa and suggest that, despite the uprootedness of the Middle Passage and forced acculturation in the New World, the originary African culture could not be eradicated. From that perspective, the story fosters racial pride and identification. But the second section of the title, *The Saga of an American Family,*

---

17   Leslie Fishbein, "*Roots*: Docudrama and the Interpretation of History," in *American History, American Television: Interpreting the Video Past*, ed. John E. O'Connor (New York: Frederick Ungar, 1983): 287–288.

offsets the emphasis on Africa. While the term "saga," which encompasses at once notions of adventure, legend, fiction, and non-fiction, may be too polysemous and generic for close, objective analysis, the term "American family," which is much more concrete and unequivocal, may be construed—considering the stakes of the civil rights movement (the struggle for equality and civic recognition)—as a statement about the full-fledged American identity of the slaves and their descendants. Although published under the auspices of the US Bicentennial—an ideal context in which to engage the whole nation in a dialogue about issues of citizenship, identity, and race—such a statement must have been rather outdated by the time the novel came out in 1976. But the success of *Roots* across the racial, social, and political spectrums is a reminder of its timeliness and, if recent occurrences of racial strife in the United States are any indication, timelessness. Haley, by celebrating his African heritage (the roots), while also underscoring the Americanness of the black community, had written a novel that accommodated very different sensibilities and satisfied a divided nation's longing for consensus.

From a historical perspective, Haley's preoccupation with family was opportune, reflecting as it did the preoccupation of the era. When *Roots* came out, Assistant Secretary of Labor Daniel Patrick Moynihan's famous report, *The Negro Family: The Case For National Action* (1965), was a decade old and still fiercely debated. Meant to justify the Lyndon B. Johnson administration's push for more welfare programs, the Moynihan Report blamed the foretold disintegration of the African-American community on poverty and the absence of the nuclear family. One of Moynihan's central arguments was that the harrowing experiences of slavery and Jim Crow had "worked against the emergence of a strong father figure."[18] Despite recent civil rights advances, de facto racism lingered on, and without decent jobs and equal treatment, the report implied, African-American men would remain psychologically crippled and unable to assume their marital and paternal responsibilities. The Moynihan Report, however well intentioned it may have been, was accused of stereotyping the black family and, more specifically, black men. Yet, the urban riots of 1967 and 1968 seemed to lend credence to the report, and Moynihan, now Richard Nixon's Counsellor for Urban Affairs, channeled his concern for black joblessness and concomitant welfare dependency into Nixon's Family Assistance Plan (FAP), an ambitious welfare reform project that aimed at replacing ineffective programs with a guaranteed annual income for people in need, provided that they worked or took job training. The FAP, which would eventually be defeated

---

18   Quoted in Glenn David Mackin, *The Politics of Social Welfare in America* (New York: Cambridge UP, 2013): 136.

by the Senate in 1972, avoided direct reference to race, but its primary, un-avowed purpose was to reinstate black men as heads of households, thereby strengthening the black family and restoring social order. This focus on black male leadership at home also implied reducing the need for black women to be both the sustainer of domestic life and the traditional breadwinners in the public workforce, and to enable them to go back home to raise their children more effectively.

Roots does bear witness to the devastating effects of slavery on the black family. For instance, Bell's two daughters from a previous marriage were sold before Bell meets Kunta. But *Roots*, while attaching great importance to the notion of family, does not embrace the Moynihan Report and the FAP's patri-archal vision of the family. Kizzy, who writes a pass for her runaway lover Noah and later becomes the matriarch of the slave quarters on the Moore planta-tion, is the opposite of a passive, subservient woman. As for the virtuous father figures Kunta Kinte and Chicken George, they may be seen as a refutation of the black male stereotypes (idle, irresponsible, and prone to violence) that the Moynihan Report and the FAP contributed to perpetuating.

In no small measure, *Roots* owed its initial success to Haley's claim that his protagonist Kunta Kinte, a slave brought from Africa in 1767, was his direct ancestor. Soon, however, Haley's historical findings were being questioned. As early as 1977, Mark Ottaway, an investigative reporter from England, estab-lished that the fictional Juffure of Kunta's youth, where no white had ever set foot before Kunta's kidnapping, was actually an important slave-trading vil-lage along the Gambia River.[19] Ottaway also discovered that Kebba Fofana, the providential griot who had corroborated Haley's version of Kunta's origins in Africa, was an imposter. As for Kunta turned Toby (John Waller's slave), Gary and Elizabeth Shown Mills, two genealogists of the University of Alabama, concluded that "those same plantation records, wills, and censuses cited by

---

19   Mark Ottaway, "Tangled Roots," *Sunday Times* (10 April 1977): 17, 21. Ottaway's claims were
      soon confirmed by the historian Donald R. Wright, who wrote that Juffure was actually
      one of "two Gambia-River villages where people were most involved in dealings with Eu-
      ropeans during the slave-trading era"; Wright, "The Effect of Alex Haley's *Roots* on How
      Gambians Remember the Atlantic Slave Trade," *History in Africa* 38 (2011): 295. And Wil-
      liam Dillon Piersen is even more explicit about Juffure's involvement in the slave trade:
      "Considering that the historic Juffure, home of Kunta Kinte, was a major trading factory
      along a section of the Gambia heavily involved in slaving for over a century before the
      time of Kunta's capture, Haley's emphasis on kidnapping is probably historically mislead-
      ing, but as a novelist he would doubtless point out it was morally true"; Piersen, *Black
      Legacy: America's Hidden Heritage* (Amherst: U of Massachusetts P, 1993): 49.

Mr. Haley not only *fail to document* his story, but they *contradict* each and every pre-Civil War statement of Afro-American lineage in *Roots!*"[20]

Famously, Haley tried to counter these allegations by claiming that his work was akin to "faction," a portmanteau word defined by *The Popular Press New Dictionary of Black History* as "A literary social-document based upon exhaustive research and characterized by the presentation of historical fact through the medium of fictionalized dialog."[21] Ironically, this definition dismisses *Roots* as "faction," since Haley did not fictionalize, but fabricated, historical facts.[22] Haley also argued that his purpose was not to tell the true story of his family but, rather, to "give his people a myth to live by."[23] More precisely, Haley explained,

> I began to realize then that the biggest challenge I had was to try and write a book which, although [sic] was the story of my family would symbolically be in fact the saga of Black people in this country.[24]

Haley's argument would have been much more convincing had it come before journalists and scholars started to question his genealogical claims. But Haley did not only take liberties with historical facts. He was accused of plagiarizing Margaret Walker Alexander's *Jubilee* (1966) and Harold Courlander's *The African* (1967).[25] The Walker case was dismissed, but Haley was compelled to pay hefty damages to Courlander in an out-of-court settlement.[26]

---

20   Gary B. Mills & Elizabeth Shown Mills, "*Roots* and the New 'Faction': A Legitimate Tool for Clio?" *Virginia Magazine of History and Biography* 89.1 (January 1981): 6.

21   Quoted in Mills & Shown Mills, "Roots and the New 'Faction,'" 3.

22   By contrast with Mills and Shown Mills, David Gerber defines "faction" in such a way as to redeem Haley. According to Gerber, "faction" is "an amalgam of fact and fiction in which the reader is generally kept in the dark about where the former leaves off and the latter begins"; David A. Gerber, "Haley's *Roots* and Our Own: An Inquiry into the Nature of a Popular Phenomenon," *Journal of Ethnic Studies* 5.3 (Fall 1977): 88.

23   Quoted by Philip Nobile, "Was *Roots* One of the Great Literary Hoaxes?" *Toronto Star* (8 March 1993): A13.

24   Quoted in Fishbein, "*Roots*: Docudrama and the Interpretation of History," 290.

25   See, for example, Tyler D. Parry, "The Politics of Plagiarism: *Roots*, Margaret Walker, and Alex Haley," in *Reconsidering "Roots": Race, Politics, and Memory*, foreword by Henry Louis Gates, Jr. (Athens: U of Georgia P, 2017): 47–62; Robert D. McFadden, "Alex Haley Denies Allegations That Parts of 'Roots' Were Copied From Novel Written By Mississippi Teacher," *New York Times* (24 April 1977): 4; Philip Nobile, "Alex Haley's Hoax: How the Celebrated Author Faked the Pulitzer Prize-Winning 'Roots,'" *Village Voice* (February 1993): 1; Stanley Crouch, "The 'Roots' of Huckster Haley's Great Fraud," *Jewish World Review* (18 January 2002): 57–62.

26   In 1978, Harold Courlander went to the U.S. District Court of the Southern District of New York to charge Haley with plagiarizing eighty-one passages from his novel *The African*.

Courlander's *The African* deserves more than being remembered as the novel that Haley pilfered to write his bestseller. *The African* must also be seen as a literary achievement in its own right. It tells the story of Hwesuhunu, an African teenager who undergoes the Middle Passage, becomes a maroon on the Caribbean island of Saint Lucia, then a slave in the state of Georgia, and finally a runaway whose fate, by the end of the novel, remains uncertain. *The African* is a story of black resistance, whose protagonist displays all the virtues of the mythic American hero: dignity, resilience, resourcefulness, charisma, and magnanimity. Race, however, complicates matters: Hwesuhunu, as his new westernized name Wes Hunu indicates, is someone else's property, and his efforts to achieve freedom are constantly thwarted. Wes Hunu is ready to die for what he believes is right, but in antebellum America it is not enough to possess all the qualities of a hero. One must also be of the right color—a circumstance that should have inflamed the entire African-American community. The year is 1967, the Black Power movement is gaining momentum, and race riots venting the anger and frustration of African Americans have erupted across the nation. The lukewarm reception of *The African* is all the more surprising as Wes Hunu is much more heroic and true to his African identity than Kunta Kinte. Kunta is also a proud African who initially refuses acculturation, but after three unsuccessful escapes, he compromises: his freedom has died, but his African heritage will survive as he passes it on to his offspring. And when, generations later, Kunta's descendants achieve freedom, they have managed to keep the bloodline flowing all the way down to Haley and his family.

Haley's *Roots* is credited with triggering a national interest in genealogy that has gone unabated ever since. Americans' obsession with their origins is not surprising if one considers that their ancestors, when they were not brought in chains, often came to America because of dire circumstances at home where they were the victims of either persecution or abject poverty. Genealogy could be described as a tool to "re-member": i.e. a tool with which to put the members of a scattered or shattered family back together again. But genealogy, whose Greek etymology, *genos*, refers to race, also contains less honorable preoccupations with pedigree and purity. In that particular sense, genealogy may be perceived as a rather reactionary hobby, as it encourages individuals to define themselves and, by extension, others in terms of filial, geographical, cultural,

---

"Haley's principal defense," Walter Rucker explains, "was that he had never read Courlander's book, but this was proven false [...]. In the end, Haley settled out of court for $650,000 and issued a public acknowledgment of his wrongdoing"; Walter C. Rucker, "Haley, Alex," in *Encyclopedia of African American History*, ed. Leslie M. Alexander & Walter C. Rucker (Santa Barbara CA: ABC–CLIO, 2010): 792.

and racial origin rather than in terms of character and personal achievements. As James Hijiya, in a 1978 article about Americans' newfound interest in genealogical research, notes: "According to Alex Haley, who you are is not determined by what you do but by where you come from."[27] This concern with the *genus* (the group) may also account for the relative flop of Courlander's *The African* a decade earlier, as the 1970s marked a diminution of interest in self-fashioning individuals like Wes Hunu, and a growing interest in individuals as the product of their lineage like Kunta Kinte. Such a shift may be interpreted as a consequence of the radicalization of the civil rights movement in the late-1960s, which fostered a relative withdrawal within the fold of the racial community—not only the black but also the white community.

2   The Hold and the Idea of Racial Community

The insurrection that takes place aboard *L'Espérance* in Mérimée's *Tamango* is the opportunity to develop yet another black stereotype: cruelty. The text makes it clear that the blacks do not have a monopoly on cruelty. Ledoux and his men are more than a match, and most readers would concur with George Hainsworth that "the sum of the tale, clearly, sets in parallel savagery and civilization, to the greatest glory of neither."[28] Yet the cruelty of the whites comes across as less ruthless than that of the blacks: first, because the narrator's constant sardonic tone takes away some of its ignominy, and, second, because it is circumstantial, the inevitable result of commercial imperatives. By contrast, the cruelty of the blacks is innate: they cannot help it. It is in their nature, and it is blended with other negative attributes in the text. Thus, during negotiations with Ledoux, a little alcohol makes Tamango emotional and irrational (he gives his favorite wife Ayché to the Captain in a fit of rage); he is easy to manipulate and bargains his slaves away. Tamango's hubris and impercipience, however, only match his barbarity: when Ledoux refuses to buy the mother of the children he has just acquired for a glass of brandy, Tamango shoots the mother dead in front of her children. This inhumanity will resurface in the form of utter savagery later on when Tamango kills the captain during the insurrection.[29]

27   James A. Hijiya, "*Roots*: Family and Ethnicity in the 1970s," *American Quarterly* 30.4 (Fall 1978): 550.

28   George Hainsworth, "West African Local Colour in *Tamango*," *French Studies* 21.1 (January 1967): 22.

29   The ferocity of Africans ought to be put in context as well: in 1829, when the story comes out, the French still have in mind what Doris Kadish calls the "black terror" of the Haitian

Before the insurrection, Tamango is temporarily presented in a positive light. Although still a selfish individual who does not hesitate to lie to his fellow captives so as to gain their confidence or aggrandize himself, Tamango is also the one who exhorts them to take action to recover their freedom. Displaying acumen and leadership, Tamango masterminds a perfect uprising, on the occasion of which the animality and savagery of the blacks are underscored. Tamango, who is "as agile as the panthers of his homeland," bites Ledoux in the throat, killing him, while all the other whites are "pitilessly slaughtered" and their corpses "dismembered, chopped up, and thrown into the sea" (86). Even in victory, Africans are represented as merciless, bloodthirsty brutes—a rather stupefying and one-sided view of Middle Passage violence.

The insurrection aboard *L'Espérance* in John's Berry's adaptation is quite different from that of Mérimée, entrenched as it is in the African-American politics of the postwar period. Eager to champion the black cause, Berry has transformed Tamango the victimizer into Tamango the heroic victim. A man of principle, Tamango prefers physical punishment to eating swill served by his white oppressors. "They will never make me a slave!" he warns his fellow captives in the hold; and when they turn against him for getting one of them hanged, he reminds them that everything he does is designed to free them from their chains. A charismatic leader, Tamango teaches his followers resilience and solidarity: "Brothers in life. Brothers in death" becomes their motto when they exchange blood before the uprising. Later, after a half-successful fight and retreat into the hold with Aiché as a hostage and bargaining chip, a magnanimous Tamango pushes the men's new-found sense of community to its limits: "We can stay and fight and even if we die, we'll win, because you can sell living men but you can't sell dead ones. Me, they won't sell me." None of the men—freedom fighters *avant la lettre*—will fail their leader, and they choose to sacrifice themselves for their ideals. The communal feeling of the black captives in the hold is all the more important as it is contrasted with the

revolution, and even if Mérimée, according to Kadish, refuses to "acknowledge Saint Domingue as a historical subtext"—"The Black Terror: Women's Responses to Slave Revolts in Haiti," *French Review* 68.4 (March 1995): 674—there is no doubt that this barbaric Tamango is patterned after the stereotype of the mean, dangerous, and brutal black rebel who had succeeded the romanticized, heroic one of popular literature prior to the slave revolution of 1791. In her analysis of Victor Hugo's second version of *Bug-Jargal* (1826), Yvette Parent alludes to this new, negative image of the black protagonist. Parent argues that Hugo, in his fictionalization of the Haitian revolution, omits whites' exactions while emphasizing blacks' responsibility and cruelty, and ignoring the social sources of the slave uprising. See Parent, "L'esclavage et *Bug-Jargal*: Victor Hugo entre histoire et mémoire dans la version de 1826," *Groupe Hugo* (Université Paris 7; 16 June 2007): online (accessed 11 November 2017).

self-serving mentality of the white man. Trying to convince a distrustful Aiché
of staying with him, Captain Reinker argues:

> you and I, we want the same thing. Those people out there, they'd die for
> their tribe. We don't want to die for anything. We want to live for ourselves.
> Maybe it's not very great or noble, but that's the way we are, both of us.

While a reminder that slave-ship captains were historically driven not by ideology but by greed, this exchange between the captain and Aiché is pivotal, as
the captain's open confession about his love and ethics backfires and helps
Aiché resolve her dilemma. Between a free, comfortable life with the captain
and racial solidarity, Aiché will finally choose the latter and irrevocably embrace the cause. Once released by Tamango at the end of the story, Aiché, *in
omnia paratus*, chooses to stay in the hold and sacrifice herself: she dies with
the others.

   The fact that Aiché is played by the African-American actress Dorothy Dandridge is no coincidence.[30] Aiché is a "tragic mulatto," a role Dandridge would
often come to be associated with, on and off the screen. Like many African
Americans of the 1950s, Aiché has internalized the racist precept of the one-
drop rule. Initially conceived by Southern segregationists to preserve white
purity, the one-drop rule entered the rhetoric of black militancy in the 1950s:
the slightest trace of African ancestry inexorably makes one African American,
and in these times of racially polarized politics, it should be a source of pride.
It is this ideology Tamango advocates when he calls Aiché "white man's trash"
at the beginning of the film. And the story of Aiché, which is central to the film,
is really about a psychological journey from subservience to resistance to the
white master, with racial loyalty as a corollary.

   At the beginning of the movie, the surgeon, upset at Aiché for rejecting his
advances, humiliates her thus: "You may be quite clear skin, but you are still a
black slave." Much later, Aiché turns her supposed liability into a forceful argument. To the captain who begs her to stay with him instead of returning to
the hold with the other slaves, she retorts: "but I can't stay with you. I don't
belong to you. I belong with them." Aiché's transformation into a black militant
also reflects the hardening political stance of the time. Early in the story, Aiché

---

30   Of Dandridge, Donald Bogle writes: "Onscreen and off, in the mass imagination, the tragic
      flaw was her color"; *Toms, Coons, Mulattoes, Mammies, and Bucks: An Interpretive History
      of Blacks in American Films* (New York: Continuum, 2001): 174. Although a civil rights ac-
      tivist, Dandridge had been accused by some blacks "of having gone on the other side"
      because of her relationships with white men; Walter Leavy, "The Mystery and Real-Life
      Tragedy of Dorothy Dandridge," *Ebony* 49.2 (December 1993): 37.

displays the worst kind of accommodationism. Commenting on Tamango's refusal to be servile, she tells the other women: "He's a fool. Any man who tries to
disobey his master is a fool." Aiché's brainwashed attitude is also emphasized
by her cultural isolation. She cannot identify the necklace of one of the African
women as a wedding ornament. Defeatist but also rational, Aiché warns the
tearful young bride that she is not only separated from her fiancé for good, but
will also very likely fall prey to the lust of sailors. Although she is not conscious
of it, Aiché tries to help her fellow Africans, and by and by she will come around
and understand not only that she should help her own people but also that race
loyalty is a natural imperative, something that she has in her. In this perspective, race is the ruling factor in her life. Her identity is racial before all else.

• • •

The crucial episode of the Middle Passage in *Roots* and its adaptation on screen
helps us understand the notion of family as race. Russell Adams responded
positively to Haley's rendition of the Middle Passage:

> Haley assisted us in visualizing the fact that Blacks were delivered to
> these shores on the flat of their backs and in clinking chains, a posture of
> defeat, degradation and abjection.[31]

As for Arnold Rampersad, he put aside his otherwise lukewarm reception of
Haley's *Roots* and conceded that Haley's "recreation of Kunta's Middle Passage
journey in the hold of a slave ship is harrowing, the major place in the book
where facts are incontrovertibly alchemized into vivid narrative."[32] Haley devotes six chapters of *Roots* to the terrifying experience of crossing the Atlantic.
He uses verisimilitude to do so and spares his readers not a single detail: the
darkness and the exiguity, the bewilderment, the fear, the despair, the heat,
the sweat, the vomit, the feces, the blood, the stench, the beatings, the deaths,
the suicides, the sexual violence, the rats, the lice, and the epidemics. At the
time, the literature of the slave trade was scarce. The best-known early descriptions of the Middle Passage are found in Ottobah Cugoano's *Narrative of the
Enslavement of a Native of Africa* (1787) and Olaudah Equiano's *The Interesting
Narrative of the Life of Olaudah Equiano, Or Gustavus Vassa, The African* (1789),
although these survivors' recourse to paraleipsis makes their accounts less
blunt and vivid than the testimony of abolitionists such as Thomas Clarkson

---

31   Russell L. Adams, "An Analysis of the 'Roots' Phenomenon in the Context of American
     Racial Conservatism," *Présence Africaine* 116.4 (1980): 127–128.
32   Arnold Rampersad, "*Roots*, by Alex Haley," *New Republic* 175.23 (4 December 1976): 24.

in *Essay on the Slave Trade* (1789) and Robert Walsh in *Notices of Brazil in 1828 and 1829* (1830). In the field of fiction *sensu stricto*, however, Martin R. Delany's *Blake: or, the Huts of America* (1861–62) is the only text prior to Haley's *Roots* that offers, in four short Chapters (51–54), a truly graphic depiction of the Middle Passage experience.

Haley's *Roots* and its television counterpart, despite the many analyses intent on exposing fundamental differences between them, do not diverge much in terms of their ideological leanings, and this affinity between the works shows in their respective representation of the Middle Passage. Both the original *Roots* and its adaptation feature a failed insurrection aboard the slave ship *Lord Ligonier*. In the novel, Kunta Kinte becomes aware of his racial identity in the hold—a place of extreme confinement where individuals from diverse cultural and linguistic backgrounds are shackled together. Thus, the Middle Passage is the place where a sense of pan-African solidarity emerges, out of both resentment of the toubob (the white man), and the need to survive: "Hear me!" one of the elders in the hold cries out, cutting short an argument about how they should kill their captors: "We must be as one village, together in this place!" (220) This sense of unity has already led to the killing of the slatee on Kunta's level, while the other slatee on the level below will jump overboard to his death.[33] Some have argued that the producers of the miniseries attenuated this afrocentric sensibility by replacing the nameless, depersonalized toubob of the novel with white characters played by popular actors (e.g., Ed Asner, Ralph Waite, and Lorne Greene), whose familiar faces were meant to relieve the anxiety of a predominantly white audience not necessarily inclined to identify with black heroes fighting slavery and its evil white perpetrators.[34] But this prevailing view ought to be qualified.

---

33 In the novel *Roots*, the African slave traders who helped kidnap Haley's ancestor, Kunta Kinte, are referred to as slatees. In *Travels in the Interior Districts of Africa* (1795–97), Mungo Park defines slatees as "negro slave-merchants [...] who, besides slaves, and the merchandise which they bring for sale to the whites, supply the inhabitants of the maritime districts with native iron, sweet-smelling gums and frankincense, and a commodity called shea-toulou, which, literally translated, signifies tree-butter"; Mungo Park, *Travels in the Interior Districts of Africa*, 2 vols. (1795–97; Teddington: Echo Library, 2006): 11.

34 Lauren Tucker and Hemant Shaw, in particular, embrace this theory, reporting how William Blinn, the head writer on the *Roots* miniseries project, justified the creation of the God-fearing, guilt-ridden Captain Thomas Davies (played by *The Mary Tyler Moore Show* star Ed Asner): "For our purposes, he was certainly not a sympathetic man. An understandable man, yes—but it is clearly absurd to have a likable slave-ship captain. It was equally unwise, we thought, to do four hours of television without showing a white person with whom we could identify"; Tucker & Shaw, "Race and the Transformation of Culture: The Making of the Television Miniseries *Roots*," *Critical Studies in Mass Communication* 9.4 (December 1992): 329. And network executives at ABC were as candid as Blinn. *Roots* was a bold step in television entertainment, and in order for *Roots* to be commercially viable,

First, the novel makes clear that the very idea of African solidarity is only circumstantial: the captives stick together by virtue of their common suffering, not because of some alleged cultural or racial affinity. In fact, the hold is a babel of tongues that impairs communication and mutual understanding. Besides, some like Kunta identify not with race but with religion. Kunta calls all non-Muslim captives pagans and places limited trust in them. More importantly, the captives want to rebel but are split into two factions, one following a Foulah leader and the other a Wolof leader. In the end, the Foulah's battle plan prevails but the Wolof warrior, without warning, takes matters into his own hands and kills five sailors before "the flash of a long knife lop[s] off his head cleanly at the shoulders" (228). The Wolof's act of individual bravery undermines group dynamics and greatly jeopardizes further plans for a coordinated attack. Undeterred, the Foulah leader schedules a new insurrection for the following day, but a storm followed by an epidemic of the bloody flux ruins any chance of revolt. In the film, the uprising is a group effort, but it is Kunta, at the instigation of his fellow Mandika tribesman the wrestler, who spurs his fellow captives into action: after hollering a war cry, Kunta casts the sailor with the key at the feet of the other captives so that they can unfetter themselves and fight. Kunta also slays the first mate, Slater, before the latter can shoot the wrestler. And just as in the novel, the rebellion is cut short when a very young sailor, reaching the swivel gun on the upper deck, shoots grapeshot at the insurgents.

Thus, the miniseries is faithful to the novel in likewise featuring the birth of racial consciousness among African captives. The only significant difference between the miniseries and the novel is that the former tends to simplify and smooth out the conflicting nature of the relationship among the captives, thus giving the impression that African solidarity emerges *ex nihilo*, as if it were natural. Admittedly, this difference owes more to the nature of the television

---

traditionally conservative advertisers had to be convinced to invest in the venture, and pleasing a potential eleven-percent market share of black audiences was not their priority. Some four decades later, however, familiarity with these icons of American television is gone, and, with the exception of the Ed Asner character, most white characters in the early episodes, ranging from the brutal first mate Slater, who brings "belly-warmers" to the captain for the night, and the foppish factor John Carrington in Annapolis, Maryland, to the degenerate-looking crowd surrounding the auction block, and Dr William Reynolds and his theories of racial inferiority justifying slavery, are anything but likeable. And there aren't many likeable whites in the novel, either, if one accepts Howard Stein's view that Haley's *Roots* constitutes "a reversal of white stereotypes, popular and sociological, [which] obscures much of the interpersonal complexity and internal anguish in those both Black and White caught *together* in the 'American Dilemma'"; Howard F. Stein, "In Search of 'Roots': An Epic of Origins and Destiny," *Journal of Popular Culture* 11.1 (Summer 1977): 14.

medium than to a discursive strategy. For a simple matter of length, the mini-series shortened the Middle Passage segment to its essential features, just as it fused several characters into one. Tellingly, none of the critics who deemed the miniseries flawed and racially biased picked up on that particular "distortion" of the original, for it challenges their argument whereby the miniseries curtails the black discourse at the heart of Haley's text. Arguably, the way the minise-ries represents black solidarity leans toward a more essentialist view of black culture than the novel does. But in the end, the representation of the Middle Passage in both Haley's novel and the miniseries is more or less the same: the insurrection fails in both works, thus de-emphasizing notions of race-based solidarity and revolutionary action, and replacing them with notions that the average American reader and viewer of the mid-1970s were more likely to en-dorse: survival, courage in the face of adversity, and capacity to adapt to the new, harsh reality of slavery. In other words, both Haley's *Roots* and its televised version catered to the taste of the white majority by fostering an accommoda-tionist rather than a separatist attitude.

This difference of attitude is crucial, as it resurfaces in the controversy over Haley's political beliefs. In *Malcolm X: A Life of Reinvention* (2011), Man-ning Marable accuses Haley of having spirited away three crucial chapters from his *Autobiography of Malcolm X* (1965) because these chapters revealed a new, un-bigoted, and universalist post-hajj Malcolm X whose strategy of black empowerment across ideological, class, and religious lines promoted an internationalist and pan-Africanist unity that worried the FBI and the CIA. According to Marable, Haley would have edited out these chapters: first, be-cause he was an integrationist who resented the separatist views of the one he called the "fearsome black demagogue," and, second, because he was a sellout eager to enclose "his subject firmly within mainstream civil rights re-spectability at the end of his life." Marable's theory about the missing chapters borders on conspiracy, but his claim that Haley softened the more militant and revolutionary edge of the latter Malcolm X in order to cater to the taste of his liberal, middle-class white readership is credible. Marable's argument that the *Autobiography* "does not read like a manifesto for black insurrection" but, rather, like "a cautionary tale about human waste and the tragedies produced by racial segregation" makes perfect sense. In fact, as Robert Norrell points out, Haley himself suggested to his publisher that the *Autobiography* should read as a book in which whites would find "a non-challenging, palatable, at times even pleasant menu of things they hadn't known concerning Negroes."[35]

---

35   Haley, quoted in Robert J. Norrell, *Alex Haley and the Books That Changed a Nation* (New York: St Martin's, 2015): 79.

In this perspective, one could even see in the Malcolm X of Haley's *Autobiography* a precursor to the fictional Kunta Kinte: initially a rebel against white oppression, Kunta chooses the voice of reason. He may have been subdued into an obedient slave, but he has abandoned neither his strong sense of Muslim identity nor his independence of mind; and he has turned his energy toward more positive goals, doing his best to live by the values he learned as a child in Africa, and pass these values on to his family and descendants.

3   The Perils of Racial Community

All the stories under scrutiny in this chapter feature a slave rebellion, and each rebellion, whatever its outcome, makes authorial ideological positions visible. In Mérimée's *Tamango*, the aftermath of the rebellion brings a new dimension to the story. Tamango, if he is not as dull and gullible as his African brethren, soon reveals his limitations when it comes to mastering white technology. Positioning himself at the helm as he has seen the captain do, he suddenly yanks the wheel, almost capsizing the ship and breaking both masts, thereby ruining any chance of ever returning to Africa. The angry, superstitious blacks immediately blame Tamango for offending "the white men's fetish" (88), and instead of looking for a solution to their desperate situation, they prefer to abandon themselves to a drinking orgy with the brandy they have just discovered on board. It is this image of a childlike, irresponsible people that lingers after the reading. Blacks are not ready for freedom and need the guidance of whites. The example of Haiti, in a state of complete chaos since its independence in 1804, may have been at the back of Mérimée's mind; but, more importantly, this allusion to the incapacity of black people to rule themselves prefigures France's colonial campaigns in Africa, which really took off in 1830, just a year after *Tamango* was published, with the invasion of Algeria. The germs of the French colonial enterprise and its pet dream of a *mission civilisatrice* is an underlying theme in *Tamango*. In fact, there is no incompatibility between Mérimée's abolitionist sympathies and the idea that Africans cannot manage their own destiny. The abolitionists denounced the violence and torture characterizing the slave trade. They did not necessarily object to the white tutelage of Africa. As Victor Hugo, a paragon of human rights activism, famously declared in 1879 at a banquet organized to commemorate the second abolition of slavery: "God offers Africa to Europe. Take it!"[36]

---

36   Quoted in Léon-François Hoffmann, "Victor Hugo, les noirs et l'esclavage," *Francofonia* 16/31 (1996): 82. (My tr.)

As established earlier, Berry's *Tamango* bears little resemblance to its nineteenth-century literary source. It is not that Hugo's well-intentioned racial anthropology has disappeared by the end of the 1950s, but it is being seriously questioned, especially as the notion of racial superiority was one of the tenets of Nazi ideology. Although hailed as daring and groundbreaking in the United States for featuring a few kisses and embraces between a white man and a colored woman, Berry's *Tamango* suffers from a lack of credibility when it does not relay rather conventional ideas. There is very little chance that the captain of a slaver at the beginning of the nineteenth century would take a colored mistress on board and let her strut around the deck in strapless dresses in front of slaves and sailors. But more disturbing is the fact that the plot really hinges on this romance, making the dénouement depend on whether the captain will be strong enough to sacrifice the love of his life in order to salvage his ship and crew.

In other words, the captain is a slave to love, as if that kind of bondage could be paralleled with the fate of the human cargo in the hold. As Doris Kadish observes,

> Berry glorifies [the] revolt, allowing [the insurgents] to die with dignity as martyrs and to stand as models of hope in the future for other oppressed blacks.[37]

No doubt this is what Berry intended. But in the end, the killing of all the blacks by the captain confirms Aiché's initial viewpoint that "the slave can never fight back." As Raymond Borde argues, the dénouement "lends the slave traders an aura of complexity that makes them less obnoxious." And Borde continues: "the social system that spawned the slave trade is pushed into the background."[38] Borde, then, takes his analysis a bit too far by interpreting the plot as a defense of colonialism, as it presents the white colonizer in a compassionate light. It is true that the last shot features the captain alone on deck. The poor man has just lost two essential ingredients for happiness in our modern world: money (his valuable cargo is lost), and love (the woman of his life is dead). But it is an overstatement to interpret such sentimentality as a plea for the colonial enterprise.

Berry's endeavor to address altogether colonialism, racism, and racial solidarity backfires, in that it results in an improbable, if not absurd, romance.

---

37   Doris Y. Kadish, "Mérimée's *Tamango*: Texts, Contexts, Intertexts," paper presented at the "Nineteenth-Century French Studies Colloquium," University of Arizona (October 2003): online (accessed 20 July 2016): 2.

38   Raymond Borde, "*Tamango*," 1905.

Besides, Berry's allegory of a nascent Black Power movement comes across as ingratiating and proves to be both counter-productive (since neither the blacks nor the whites are triumphant) and reactionary, as the promotion of race allegiance inadvertently supports anti-miscegenation values (Aiché and the captain's affair is doomed). It also furthers racial antagonism, since both races are shown as irreconcilable, distinguished by endogenous, and therefore immutable, attributes. Ironically, Mérimée and pro-abolition contemporaries may have embraced such a view: after all, it is in the name of fundamental racial differences that the colonization of Africa was carried out. Hence, Berry, as he tries to reconcile his support of decolonization with his sympathy for the African-American cause, ends up trapped in a discourse of racial essentialism that might have been legitimate at the dawn of the civil rights movement but would prove indefensible in its aftermath as the discourse of race in America started to shift toward the celebration of racial integration, cultural cross-pollination, and inter-ethnic hybridization.

• • •

In the United States, the aftermath of the civil rights movement was characterized by the notion of post-raciality. Great strides had been made in terms of racial equality, and some wanted to believe that Martin Luther King, Jr.'s dream that people should be judged not by "the color of their skin" but by "the content of their character" had come true. But this optimistic view of a color-blind society would soon dissipate, and by the time *Roots* came out in 1976, the conservative onslaught on welfare programs and other political initiatives meant to reduce social and racial inequality had proven frighteningly effective, all the more so as the racial biases that motivated the conservative agenda were concealed behind a discourse of political pragmatism. In fact, the politics of race were back, but not in as blunt and strident a fashion as they once were, and not confined to the claims of minorities.

The white majority in America has never been wholly immune to the effects of the grand narrative of race, if only because it contributed to the construction thereof by simultaneously imposing its norms on, and defending its privileges against, non-white minorities. But the white majority, unlike non-white minorities, never had to protect itself from racism and violence, and as a result it has been less prone than these minorities to conceive of itself as a racialized community. Things changed in the 1960s, however. Although the civil rights movement yielded some improvements, poverty endured, and by the end of the decade the resentment of African Americans at being deprived of job opportunities, decent housing, and education was at its height. The wave of racial violence that ensued left black urban centers in ruins and by the 1970s the white majority, faced with an economic recession and a divisive war in Vietnam, had grown weary of, and even hostile to, social change. In contrast to the so-called "turbulent 1960s," Michael Omi and Howard Winant argue, the 1970s "were years of racial quiescence when the racial minority movements of the previous period seemed to wane."[39] The comfort zone into which racial tolerance seemed to have eased its way was not a complete mirage. The lot of minorities had improved thanks to economic growth and civil rights advances in the 1960s. For instance, "the trend toward smaller racial differences in [educational] attainment persisted in the 1970s,"[40] and while black men still fell behind white men in terms of employment during the lean decade of the 1970s, fewer blacks than ever before were unemployed (196), more had access to better jobs (198), and their earnings had risen faster than those of whites (201), even if discrimination in pay rates still lingered (205). Substantial racial inequalities persisted, but they were less blatant than they once were.

This rebalancing of social status and economic opportunity might well be the source of a malaise that was not yet tangible in the early 1970s. Most whites welcomed the victories of the civil rights movement: the end of *de jure* segregation in the South, and the empowerment of black citizens through the Civil Rights Act of 1964 and the Voting Rights Act of 1965. But these pieces of legislation changed neither *de facto* segregation nor the endemic poverty in which a majority of African Americans were still mired. Poverty and socio-economic inertia among the African-American community led the increasingly popular black nationalists to reject "the assimilationist and integrationist tendencies of the moderates."[41] The Black Power movement would embrace neither passive assimilationism nor the reassuring notion of a "raceless society." In those times of civil rights achievements, such a stance may have come across as unconscionable, but today color-blindness is identified as a discursive strategy meant to turn the issue of race into a taboo to the benefit of the dominant white community. Eduardo Bonilla-Silva compares racism before and after the civil rights movement:

> Much as Jim Crow racism served as the glue for defending a brutal and
> overt system of racial oppression in the pre-civil rights era, color-blind

---

39   Michael Omi & Howard Winant, "Introduction" to Omi & Winant, *Racial Formation in the United States from the 1960s to the 1990s* (New York: Routledge, 2nd ed. 1994): 2.

40   Reynolds Farley, "Trends in Racial Inequalities: Have the Gains of the 1960s Disappeared in the 1970s?" *American Sociological Review* 42.2 (April 1977): 192. Further page references are in the main text.

41   Omi & Winant, *Racial Formation in the United States from the 1960s to the 1990s*, 107.

racism serves today as the ideological armor for a covert and institution-
alized system in the post-civil rights era. And the beauty of this new ideology is that it aids in the maintenance of white privilege without fanfare,
without naming those who it subjects and those who it rewards.[42]

Thus, the Black Power movement had foreseen the conservative backlash that
had started with the electoral realignment of the South in 1964, when Republican presidential nominee Barry Goldwater poached on Democratic turf by
opposing the Civil Rights Act, which he described as an infringement on states'
rights—a term often understood as a code word for opposition to federal initiatives favoring desegregation. Goldwater lost the election, and although his
brand of conservatism would not bear fruit until the election of Ronald Reagan
in 1980, some of his ideas took hold and facilitated the GOP transition toward
the conservative ideology it incarnates today. Omi and Winant illustrate this
very point, explaining that the conservatives, in the 1970s, blamed the defeat of
the Vietnam War and an ailing economy on both welfare and "the liberal inter-
ventionist state."[43] The argument was that too much assistance, in the form of
taxes, as well as state and federal programs, was lavished on the poor, and since
most African Americans were poor, the rest of the nation could connect the
dots and point their finger at black people and other underprivileged minorities for the national ailments.[44] Since America had become a color-blind, egalitarian society, conservatives argued, welfare programs were superfluous and
even un-American, since they encouraged laziness and a culture of dependency that went against the entrepreneurial spirit typifying the American people.

The *Roots* miniseries was innovative only insofar as it brought a black story
into the American living room at peak viewing hours on a major television
network. But by 1977, when *Roots* aired, mainstream America was not ignorant of African-American culture, which had been at the center of national
politics for at least two decades if we consider the 1954 landmark US Supreme
Court case *Brown v. Board of Education* as a starting point for the civil rights
movement. Already by the year 1968 the cutting-edge, black-produced *Soul!*,

---

42   Eduardo Bonilla-Silva, *Racism Without Racists: Color-Blind Racism and the Persistence of
      Racial Inequality in the United States* (Lanham MD: Rowman & Littlefield, 2nd ed. 2006): 4.
43   Omi & Winant, *Racial Formation in the United States from the 1960s to the 1990s*, 115.
44   Russell Adams goes even further back in time, arguing that a "deep current of fatigue
      from efforts to calm the demands of the Blacks and the poor" ("An Analysis of the 'Roots'
      Phenomenon in the Context of American Racial Conservatism," 136) had already started
      in 1963 in the wake of the March on Washington.

"the only nationally televised program dedicated to cultural expressions of the black freedom movement of the late 1960s and early 1970s,"[45] had started its five-year run. In 1971, the African-American musical and variety show *Soul Train*, less avant-garde than *Soul!* but equally eager to promote black culture, was syndicated and watched throughout the nation. Meanwhile, Hollywood, taking its cue from Melvin Van Peebles's independent movie *Sweet Sweetback's Baadasssss Song* (1971), released Gordon Parks's *Shaft* (1971), the first of the mainstream blaxploitation movies. Even slavery had made it to Hollywood before *Roots* with Richard Fleischer's 1975 *Mandingo*.[46] Thus, *Roots* was not so original. In fact, it was slightly behind its time, as the Black Power movement, both in the United States and abroad, was subsiding.

The success of conservative rhetoric with the American middle class from the mid-1960s onward is the consequence of a national effort to address what W.E.B. Du Bois once called the "problem of the color line." Concretely, the achievements of the civil rights movement implied that the United States was finally living up to its founding principle whereby all Americans are equally entitled to the "pursuit of happiness." It also meant that, from then on, the white majority had to share with racial minorities in the prosperity of the nation, and this new order became fertile ground for the rhetoric of reverse discrimination: "During these years," as Omi and Winant point out, "many of the themes of racial reaction, of opposition to the egalitarian ideals of the 1960s, were developed and disseminated."[47] White privileges were being threatened, while the radicalization of the Black Power movement stoked the fires of resentment and xenophobia. In the post-civil rights era, conservatives could no longer be openly racist, but they could argue that it was unfair to favour certain racial minorities when the whole nation had become color-blind and egalitarian. As Omi and Winant show, the conservatives did not oppose the idea of "racial equality but [that of] racial collectivity," and they describe the effect of the neoconservative strategy of undermining the social advances of the civil-rights movement thus:

45   Gayle Wald, *It's Been Beautiful: "Soul!" and Black Power Television*, photos by Chester Higgins (Durham NC: Duke UP, 2015): 1.

46   *Sweet Sweetback's Baadasssss Song* (1971) was written, directed, and independently produced by Van Peebles, who also starred in the film. Parks's *Shaft* (1971), scripted by John Singleton (himself subyequently a director of influential post-blaxploitation films) was produced by Metro-Goldwyn-Mayer; and Richard Fleischer's *Mandingo* (1975) was co-produced by the Dino De Laurentiis Company and Paramount Pictures.

47   Omi & Winant, *Racial Formation in the United States from the 1960s to the 1990s*, 114.

As the 1960s drew to a close and the 1970s began, many ethnicity theorists
felt they had to choose an alliance with the right in order to stem the tide
of radical collectivism which the black movement had set in motion.[48]

Intentionally or not, *Roots* plays into the hands of this conservative agenda,
not only because it extolls basic conservative values but also because it steers
clear of any form of protest. *Roots* does chronicle the dark past of the nation,
and it does celebrate African-American culture. In fact, Haley's countless lectures in white liberal colleges about black pride and the black family in the
late-1960s[49] were welcome alternatives to the more virulent and afrocentric
speeches of more radical speakers; yet, both Haley and these speakers participated in the same desire to celebrate blackness.

Haley was not a revolutionary, but dismissing his work, as Marable did in
an interview, by flatly declaring, "Haley was a Republican"[50]—as if being a
Republican proved Haley's alleged lack of integrity—is a spurious argument.
Haley did come from a long line of southern black Republicans, and his brother George was elected to the Kansas State Senate in 1964 as a Republican. But
that same year, Haley voted for the Democrat Lyndon B. Johnson—not for the
Republican Barry Goldwater.[51] It is likely that Haley was a so-called "Rockefell-
er" or "liberal" Republican: i.e. a Republican who would have supported such
social programmes as Franklin Delano Roosevelt's New Deal, Johnson's civil
rights bills, and even Nixon's Family Assistance Plan—not the plan filled with
Moynihan's biases against African Americans, but the plan that pushed for a
traditional family structure and believed that every able-bodied black man
in the nation should be put to work. The FAP fostered individual autonomy
and promised economic stability through hard work. As a federally controlled
rather than state-supervised plan, it would oppugn the whole southern economy by empowering low-wage black workers, giving them the opportunity
to rise above their station, just as Kunta Kinte's descendants did, all the way
down to Haley and his siblings.[52] But just as *Roots* was akin to a "narrative of

---

48   Omi & Winant, *Racial Formation in the United States from the 1960s to the 1990s*, 131.
49   Robert J. Norrell, *Alex Haley and the Books That Changed a Nation*, 168.
50   Amy Goodman, "The Undiscovered Malcolm X: Stunning New Info on the Assassination,
      His Plans to Unite the Civil Rights and Black Nationalist Movements & the 3 'Missing'
      Chapters from His Autobiography," *Democracy Now: Independent Global News* (21 Febru-
      ary 2005): online (accessed 14 January 2017).
51   Norrell, *Alex Haley and the Books That Changed a Nation*, 84.
52   This is why the South was strongly opposed to the Family Assistance Plan. As Jill Quad-
      agno argues, "For more than a century, blacks had been excluded from welfare in the
      South because the welfare system was an instrument of social control, a part of the local

ascent" comforting a nation frightened by the tragic consequences of its own disparities and injustices, the FAP was an opiate, not a cure. It pledged to help the working poor, especially underpaid black men, with financial incentives, but it had no vision of how to provide them with real opportunities to thrive. The FAP failed to tackle the endemic problems of labor exploitation on which entire sectors of the national economy depended. In a way, the conservative disposition of *Roots* resides in similar shortcomings. *Roots*, by overlooking the causes of economic, social, and racial inequality, not only functions as a conciliatory fairy tale but also inscribes the destiny of African Americans in a wider national narrative, which results in playing down the specificity of the black experience.

4   From Race to Political Consciousness

Tamango and *Roots*, whether on the page or on the screen, remind us that race consciousness is not inborn but instilled. This consciousness does not yet exist in the hold of the slave ship during the Middle Passage, but it becomes the determining factor in the life of the survivors, who, once under the yoke of their masters in the New World, have no choice but to define themselves according to a rigid code of conduct based on a binary opposition between white and non-white. The plots of *Tamango* and *Roots* revolve around this racialized self. Mérimée, his abolitionist credentials notwithstanding, seems unable to refrain from racial stereotyping, and, prefiguring the paternalist rhetoric of the colonial enterprise, suggests that Africans are incapable of ruling themselves and therefore need the benevolent guidance of a civilized nation. Berry, more than a century later, revamps the story to reflect the sensibility of the decolonizing era, making Aiché, the captain's mulatto mistress, an icon of race pride and allegiance. Haley and the TV producers of *Roots* also emphasize racial kinship and solidarity, but they simultaneously water down tropes of black resistance by making Kunta Kinte a pacified warrior who accepts his fate as a plantation slave and turns to the reassuring values of family unity and lineage, thus catering to the taste of the conservative white majority of the 1970s, which was yearning for the normalization of race relations and a discreet transition back to the racial hierarchy of past decades when the social, cultural, and political presence of the African-American community was much more subdued. *Tamango* and *Roots*—the originals and their adaptations—are good illustrations

racial caste system"; Quadagno, "Race, Class, and Gender in the U.S. Welfare State: Nixon's Failed Family Assistance Plan," *American Sociological Review* 55.1 (February 1990): 24.

of how the fictionalization of the transatlantic slave trade reaches far beyond the historical context to become the vehicle of ideological discourses. As the next chapter attests, the slave ship is not only the incubator of the racial divide that still haunts our societies. It can also be reimagined as a microcosm where various groups vie for political power and control. In Charles Johnson's *Middle Passage* (1990), the notion of racial community is still central but much less schematic than in *Tamango* and *Roots* as fundamental questions of democracy, individual freedom, and patriotism emerge and complicate the initial, deceptively simple perception of the slave ship as the site of a tragedy in black and white.

CHAPTER 2

Patriotism and Political Communities: Charles Johnson's *Middle Passage*

A ship is a society, if you get my drift. A commonwealth, Mr. Calhoun.[1]

∵

This chapter places the issue of patriotism at the heart of Charles Johnson's *Middle Passage*. It is in a moment of despair and in the throes of hunger and agony that Rutherford Calhoun, the novel's narrator and central character, concludes a panegyric on the United States with the following piece of banter: "Do I sound like a patriot? Brother, I put it to you: What Negro, in his heart (if he's not a hypocrite), is not?" (179). The remark is unsettling on two counts. First, the story takes place in 1830, a time when people of African descent had no real incentive to love a nation that had systematically marginalized them when it had not enslaved them. Secondly, the Calhoun who opens the story is not endowed with patriotic feelings. A twenty-two-year-old recently manumitted slave, Calhoun prefers to live by his wits in the red-light district of New Orleans than to profit from his superior intellect to pursue professional gains and integration in the community. Calhoun is a defiant, sharp-tongued reprobate who mocks conventions and does not easily socialize. Soon, however, Calhoun stows away on the Africa-bound slaver *Republic* so as to evade Philippe "Papa" Zeringue, a local gangster to whom he owes money, and Isadora Bailey, a besotted schoolmistress bent on marrying him. After a year of tribulations and a near-death experience aboard the sinking *Republic*, the cynical, malcontent Calhoun is eager to embrace the values of American society and set foot again on the shore of what he now calls home.

But the dire circumstances of the shipwreck are not enough to explain Calhoun's turnabout, and the nature of his sudden patriotic élan is perhaps best understood when measured against the three political models to which Calhoun is exposed aboard the *Republic*: first, Ebenezer Falcon, the captain who rules the microcosm of the *Republic* with an iron fist; second, the mutinous

---

1   Charles Johnson, *Middle Passage* (1990; New York: Scribner, 1998): 175. Further page references are in the main text.

© KONINKLIJKE BRILL NV, LEIDEN, 2019 | DOI:10.1163/9789004389229_004

crew, a bunch of rough-hewn seafarers whose sole purpose is to kill the captain
and steal his cargo; and, third, said cargo, a group of forty Allmuseri tribesmen
who successfully rebel, take control of the ship, and impose a race-based order. Each of these three models represents an ideology that will put Calhoun's
ethos of freedom to the test and lead him to forgo his seemingly self-indulgent
and antisocial perspective on life for that of a self-abnegating and socially committed citizen. Before describing these three models against which Calhoun
will forge his own political beliefs, this chapter dwells on the Calhoun character in New Orleans, prior to his involvement in the transatlantic slave trade.
In this early stage of the story, Calhoun's understanding of freedom stands as
a counter-discourse to the institutional discourse of his nation, of which the
slave ship *Republic* is an obvious metaphor.

Falcon, as the skipper of the *Republic*, appears to be an extension of what the
United States stands for, but the parallel is deceptively evident. Calhoun does
define Falcon as a man of Manifest Destiny and a fervent patriot who has embraced the values of his conquering nation, but Falcon, as the second section of
this chapter will show, is anything but a blind follower of the dominant ideology.
As for the crewmen, they are much less developed than Falcon and the Allmuseri
as characters, but they constitute major political players, as they represent revo-
lutionaries plotting to overthrow the tyrannical Falcon. Finally, the Allmuseri,
presented as pacifist and egalitarian, prove as bellicose and self-serving as their
oppressors once in control of the ship, and it becomes clear that the Allmuseri
utopia is not so different from the Puritan utopia that spawned the likes of Falcon and the world of ruthless competition and antagonism the latter inhabits.

While Calhoun's decision to reject each of these three flawed models appears eminently sensible, his decision to embrace the values of a nation where
de facto and *de jure* negrophobia is endemic remains a perplexing alternative.
But Calhoun's experience aboard the *Republic* has helped him refine his earlier conception of freedom and reconsider the role he should play as a citizen.
Likening the character Calhoun to the unnamed narrator of Ralph Ellison's
Invisible Man (1952), the final section of this chapter argues that patriotism—
broadly construed as the attachment to, and fostering of, the values of one's
nation—can impose itself not only as an act of generosity and courage but
also as a necessity. Ultimately, this chapter suggests that both Calhoun and his
illustrious literary predecessor decide to become patriots because of, and in
spite of, discrimination.

1   Calhoun, Freedom, the *Republic*, and Manifest Destiny

In order to grasp the changes Calhoun went through during his transatlantic
journey, one ought to understand who Calhoun was when he arrived in New

Orleans in 1829. Calhoun introduces himself as a "randy" country boy from southern Illinois who has chosen to start his life as a free man in New Orleans because it is a city "tailored to [his] taste for the excessive, exotic fringes of life" (1); a city "devoted to an almost religious pursuit of Sin" or at least "to a steamy sexuality" (2). As an antidote to his tedious youth in the care of his benevolent but austere former master, Reverend Peleg Chandler, Calhoun is eager for thrills. Confined to what was known as the colored quarters of the city, Calhoun is denied access to a decent job and resorts to what he does best—petty thievery. But Calhoun is not sorry for himself; his new way of life is a calculated response rather than hardship endured. Although raised by Chandler as a son and never really subjected to the hardships of slavery, Calhoun still grew up a bondsman, and he intends to experience his newly acquired freedom to the full: emancipation from slavery—yes—but also emancipation from any other kind of restriction, authority, or social control. Calhoun's understanding of freedom is radical: he absolves himself of moral, social, and professional responsibility, making his freedom contingent on his marginality and thus on his criminal activities.

In spite of this bold stance, Calhoun feels the need to justify his unsavory métier by stigmatizing "cityfolks [who] lived by cheating and crime" (3); and he dismisses cardinal American values, longing for a faraway land "where a freeman could escape the vanities cityfolk called self-interest, the mediocrity they called achievement, [and] the blatant selfishness they called individual freedom" (4). Although Calhoun avoids any commitment, his mordant criticism of the corruption and hypocrisy around him suggests an acute awareness of injustice and makes his recusant attitude look more level-headed and laudable than servile compliance with a system in which his rights as a citizen are flouted on both the local and the national level.[2] Thus, as the concluding

2 Barely a decade before Calhoun starts as a free man in New Orleans, the nation was caught up in the Missouri controversy opposing antislavery advocates and slavery proponents on the very practical question of whether new slave states should be added to the Union, and on the more fundamental question of whether or not the Founding Fathers had been opposed to slavery in principle when they claimed, in the preamble to the Declaration of Independence, that "all men are created equal." The Missouri Compromise of 1820, obliging free states to return fugitive slaves to their Southern masters, had the effect of reinforcing slavery in the South and accelerating disenfranchisement of blacks elsewhere. In addition, Denmark Vesey's failed conspiracy a couple years later threw North Carolina and the South into a panic, resulting in stricter control and oppression of both slaves and free citizens of color by the slaveholding class and their supporters. Things were not much better in the northern states: in 1824 Hard Scrabble and Snow Town, two African-American neighborhoods in Providence, Rhode Island, were attacked by working-class whites. In 1829 (the year Calhoun arrives in New Orleans), riots erupted in Cincinnati, Ohio, between African Americans and Irish immigrants over employment opportunities. And that same year, David Walker, a free man of color, published the first version of his inflammatory *Appeal*, in which he argues: "America is more our country than it is the whites—we have enriched it with our blood and

part of the chapter will show, Calhoun is more than a mere nihilist, and his apparent passivity should not be interpreted as insouciance. On the contrary, Calhoun's quiet but deliberate rejection of norms, doctrines, and biased laws as well as his reluctance to wallow in the bourgeois existence of New Orleans's Creoles of color mark him as a perfect illustration of rebellion as defined by Albert Camus in his essay *The Rebel* (1951): "Rebellion is born of the spectacle of irrationality, confronted with an unjust and incomprehensible condition."[3] This chapter will return to that theme in its last segment, once the political maturation and psychological evolution of the Calhoun character have been described, for, at the beginning of the story, Calhoun is not yet a *frondeur*. Rather, he is an apolitical individual, and his decision to ignore current affairs stems from his belief that freedom can be exercised on the margins of society and outside the realm of politics. His escape on board the *Republic*, however, will dispel such a misconception.

Between the plantation in Illinois and the deck of the slave ship *Republic*, Calhoun's hedonistic episode in New Orleans is a mere hiatus. On the plantation, Calhoun was schooled in the classics and learned a bitter lesson in Proudhonian economy when his brother, Jackson, redistributed equally among all the slaves the property the late Chandler had bestowed on the two of them. In New Orleans, he learned the limits of his freedom once "Papa" Zeringue demanded his money back, and the infatuated Isadora decided it was time to get married. It is on the slave ship, however, that Calhoun is to polish his understanding of the world in which he lives, while also fashioning his own beliefs and defining his political values against those of the skipper, the crew, and the cargo.

When it comes to the slave ship, the text does not shy away from metaphors. The aptly named *Republic* is like the country it incarnates: still in its infancy, and unsafe. Its lowest deck is separated from the bottom of the sea by "only an inch of plank" (35) and its crew "spent most of the time literally rebuilding [it] as we crawled along the waves" (36). Also, the *Republic* is not free from financial interests, underwritten as it is by "powerful families in New Orleans" (48). Nature itself rages against the *Republic*. On the way back from Africa, "gusts of strong, skirling wind galed and swung the *Republic* broadside to windward,

---

tears"; Walker, *David Walker's Appeal, In Four Articles; Together with a Preamble, To The Coloured Citizens Of The World, But In Particular, And Very Expressly, To Those Of The United States Of America* (1829; Baltimore MD: Black Classic, 1997): 84.

3   Albert Camus, *The Rebel: An Essay on Man in Revolt*, tr. Anthony Bower, foreword by Herbert Read (*L'homme révolté*, 1951; tr. 1956; New York: Vintage, rev. ed. 1992): 10.

pointing her *back* the way we had come" (79). The *Republic* is not going back, however, and becomes a "shrinking casket" (81). Later, the *Republic* seems to implode in a blast during the crew's failed insurrection, as a result of which its walls "buckled from a tremendous rolling crash and rumbling that smashed the beams of the ceiling and threw us to the floor" (128). At the end of the story, as a survivor aboard the *Juno*, Calhoun thinks he has become impotent and calls himself "a wreck of the *Republic*" (190). Clearly, the *res publica* is not yet a government "made for the people, made by the people, and answerable to the people," as Senator Daniel Webster had defined it in a speech to the American Senate in 1830, the very same year the *Republic*, in the story, founders.[4]

The text extends the metaphor of the young American republic through Captain Ebenezer Falcon. His last name evokes the American eagle, and his year of birth, 1776, coincides with that of the nation. Furthermore, the republic Falcon embodies is in his image: brazen and bellicose, but also confident and purpose-driven. A pedophile dwarf who has traveled the world to plunder the treasures of distant tribes and cultures, Falcon is also a polymath and a self-made man in the purest American tradition. In the words of Calhoun, Falcon

> possessed a few of the solitary virtues and the entire twisted will of Puritanism: a desire to achieve perfection; the loneliness, self-punishment, and bouts of suicide this brings; and a profound disdain for anyone who failed to meet his nearly superhuman standards.[5]
>
> *Middle Passage* 51

And when Calhoun calls Falcon a patriot, he does not do so in a flattering way: "He [Falcon] was a patriot whose burning passion was the manifest destiny of the United States to Americanize the entire planet" (30).

The term Manifest Destiny had not yet been coined at the time of the story, but the territorial expansion of the nation, with its attendant subjugation,

---

4   Webster's words are paraphrased a few decades later in Abraham Lincoln's 1863 Gettysburg Address. Honoring the soldiers who died at the battle of Gettysburg, Lincoln exalts the Union and concludes his speech thus: "we here highly resolve that these dead shall not have died in vain—that this nation, under God, shall have a new birth of freedom—and that government *of the people, by the people, for the people,* shall not perish from the earth" (emphasis added).

5   According to the book critic Eleanor Blau, Falcon "is based loosely on Sir Richard Francis Burton, whose contradictions fascinated the author. 'He was an explorer, an imperialist, a translator, a quasi-genius,' [Johnson] said, 'and also the biggest bigot in the world'"; Blau, "Charles Johnson's Tale of Slaving, Seafaring and Philosophizing," *New York Times* (2 January 1991): C9+.

removal or decimation of indigenous peoples, was well under way.[6] From the
Treaty of Paris in 1783 to the Louisiana Purchase of 1803 and the Indian Removal Act of 1830, the young republic of Falcon, through diplomatic maneuvers,
business deals, and military campaigns, had relentlessly pursued its goal of
controlling the vast expanse of land stretching from the Atlantic to the Pacific.[7]
Thus, when it appeared in 1845, the term "manifest destiny" did not mark the
beginning of a national policy. Rather, it encapsulated a mood and ideology
harkening back to the beginnings of the Massachusetts Bay Colony. The first
Puritans, for all their declared intention to build a shining "city upon a hill,"[8] a

---

6   The term "Manifest Destiny" was coined in the summer of 1845 by John L. O'Sullivan, the edi-
    tor for the *United States Magazine and Democratic Review*. In "Annexation," an article cham-
    pioning the integration of the young Republic of Texas into the Union, O'Sullivan wrote that
    it was the "manifest destiny" of the United States "to overspread the continent allotted by
    Providence for the free development of our yearly multiplying millions"; quoted in Anders
    Stephanson, *Manifest Destiny: American Expansionism and the Empire of Right* (New York:
    Hill & Wang, 1995): xi. And O'Sullivan used that same term again on 27 December 1845 in an
    editorial for the *New York Morning News*. On that occasion, O'Sullivan supported the United
    States's claim to the Oregon country and that claim, he argued, "is by the right of our manifest
    destiny to overspread and to possess the whole of the continent which Providence has given
    us for the development of the great experiment of liberty and federated self-government
    entrusted to us"; quoted in Richard White, *"It's Your Misfortune and None of My Own": A New
    History of the American West* (Norman: U of Oklahoma P, 1991): 73. Manifest destiny is thus
    associated with the presidential terms of John Tyler (1841–45) and James Knox Polk (1845–49)
    during which Texas and the Oregon country, along with California and other territories relin-
    quished by Mexico, were integrated into the Union, thus completing the continental United
    States as we know it today.
7   The Treaty of Paris (1783) marked the end of the American Revolution and made official the
    acquisition by the United States of all British territories south of Canada and east of the Mis-
    sissippi River. Twenty years later, President Thomas Jefferson doubled the size of the nation
    with the Louisiana Purchase (1803). In 1819, Spain ceded Florida to the United States, and the
    Monroe doctrine prohibiting European interference on the American continent was set up
    in 1823. At the time of the story, while Falcon is crossing the Atlantic to bring back slaves for
    the plantations of the South, President Andrew Jackson signs the Indian Removal Act (1830)
    that will force the Five Civilized Tribes (Cherokees, Chickasaws, Choctaws, Creeks, and Semi-
    noles) to move west of the Mississippi River.
8   The "city upon a hill" metaphor is from "A Modell of Christian Charity," a sermon delivered
    aboard the ship *Arabella* in 1630 by John Winthrop, a Puritan leader and one of the founders
    of the Massachusetts Bay colony. With this image, Winthrop exhorted his flock to build an
    ideal society that would be looked upon across the world as a model to emulate: "For wee
    must consider that wee shall be as a citty upon a hill. The eies of all people are uppon us. Soe
    that if wee shall deale falsely with our God in this worke wee haue undertaken, and soe cause
    him to withdrawe his present help from us, wee shall be made a story and a by-word through
    the world"; Winthrop, "A Modell of Christian Charity (1630)," *Collections of the Massachusetts
    Historical Society*, 3rd series 7 (1838): 47.

Christian utopia fostering exemplary moral conduct, frugality, solidarity, and equality, were quick to deem the natives benighted heathens, ban them from their towns and villages, and finally drive them out of their ancestral land. The Puritans might not have suspected what their messianic zeal was going to unleash, and after the dissension and turmoil of the early decades, their relative prosperity reinforced their belief that God had chosen them and that the wilderness of the American continent was the place where a God-blessed, perfect society was to flourish.

In the years leading up to the American Revolution, this rhetoric of predestination had made its way into political speeches and strengthened the desire to be free of the yoke of England. By then, the harsh Calvinist doctrines of permanent and irredeemable sinfulness, as well as random, divine Election, had long faded into the more worldly values of piety and hard work as a way to attain salvation. Thus, Americans of the late eighteenth century were more secular and materialistic than their forefathers, but their victorious revolution had also convinced them of their sacred destiny, which had become fused with feelings of racial and political superiority—a sentiment that found a practical application in the ruthless conquest of the West. The character Ebenezer Falcon must be understood against this backdrop of religious and national self-righteousness; and so, Calhoun's depiction of Falcon as a patriot and a man of manifest destiny ought to be qualified.

2   Political Models: Ebenezer Falcon, the Crew, and the Allmuseri

For one thing, Falcon does not share in the religious fervor of his time, and when he tells Calhoun that he believes in "Christian decency and doing right as much as the next man" (32), it is only to exculpate himself from once resorting to cannibalism in a life-and-death situation. Falcon's position on race is also less predictable than one would expect: upon meeting Calhoun, Falcon tells him that, "generally speaking, [he doesn't] like Negroes" (30), seemingly because he finds them clueless. Yet, by the end of the conversation, Falcon tells Calhoun that he doesn't "hold it against [him] for being [...] black" (31). Falcon's creed is excellence, and while he believes that helping disadvantaged "minorities" (31) spawns mediocrity, he acknowledges that "discrimination denied [minorities] the training that makes for true excellence" (31). In other words, Falcon does not buy into the racialist rhetoric of his time. He knows that the so-called inferiority of minorities is not innate but results from unfavorable conditions. Yet Falcon takes injustice for granted, for it is this injustice that underlies his success as a slaver.

Falcon is an opportunist and his political views owe more to rationality than to deep-seated values. Falcon is anti-British because he hates "men like George III" (50) and the monarchical system they embody; and he is anti-Jeffersonian because the Embargo Act of 1807 "threw seamen and shipbuilders out of work" (50).[9] Furthermore, Falcon joined the slave-trading industry (even though his government banned it in 1808) in order to avoid both conscription in the under-requipped national fleet and impressment into the Royal Navy. As for Falcon's dream to "divide the western region of the continent into empires separate from the United States, one of which [he] hoped to shape himself" so as to establish "a true American Utopia" (50), it is reminiscent of the attempt by Aaron Burr, Jr., Jefferson's first Vice-President, to raise a private army and appropriate a large swathe of land out of the Louisiana Territory.[10] Falcon is no more motivated than Burr by the purported ideals of his nation to bring freedom, democracy, and prosperity to whomever Americans subdue in their move westward, and, judging by his repressive conduct at the helm of the *Republic*, his "true American Utopia" would be every bit as despotic as the regimes of Europe he so abhors.

The mere thought of a country ruled by Falcon is preposterous, but Falcon's fantasy is nonetheless evocative of the Puritan heritage of the United States. Like any other utopia, the society the Puritans wanted to build in the New World quickly degenerated into a national agenda of religious exclusivism, racial discrimination, expropriation, and extermination. Falcon inherited from the Puritans neither their sense of mission nor their religious zeal, and if he believes in any kind of exceptionalism, it is more his own than that of the nation. As for his fixation on excellence, it has little to do with the Puritan notion of moral excellence, unless that moral excellence is considered to be a determining factor in the development of the American work ethic. But even on that particular issue, the parallel between Falcon and the Puritans is limited, for the Puritans saw hard work and thrift as a contribution to the commonwealth

---

9   The Embargo Act of 1807 was Thomas Jefferson's punitive measure against France and England's interference with American trade. The embargo "forbade all international trade to and from American ports, and Jefferson hoped that Britain and France would be persuaded of the value and the rights of a neutral commerce." Instead of the expected effect on the two European powers, the measure stifled American trade, depriving merchants, sea captains, and sailors of a job. The embargo was a failure, and it is easy to see why Falcon, a warmongering seaman, would resent Jefferson's weak and misguided response to the Europeans' hawkish posture.

10   Aaron Burr is also known for killing his political rival Alexander Hamilton in a duel during his vice-presidency under Jefferson. The parallel with Falcon is all the more appropriate as Burr's attempt to create an empire for himself may be interpreted as the desperate gesture of a man who had lost all political credibility and support as well as financial resources.

rather than in terms of personal gain. By contrast, Falcon works essentially for his personal benefit and cares little about the welfare of others. It is hard to see a connection between the microcosm of the fictional *Republic* and that of the historical Massachusetts Bay Colony, and yet both places are autocracies governed by absolute rulers. Falcon is the skipper of a slave ship—a floating penitentiary, as it were—and behaves accordingly. The Puritan leaders based their success on strict observance of their religious precepts, which was also a way of asserting their relative independence from both the Crown and the Church of England.[11] The Puritans were sectarian in the sense that they tolerated no other creed, and authoritarian in the sense that they were self-appointed, restrained freedom of speech, and controlled people's behavior.[12] What Falcon has inherited from his forefathers is absolute self-confidence and grim determination—two virtues which, together with the expansionist disposition of his nation, help him shape a cynical view of the world he inhabits.

Just as Calhoun's depiction of Falcon as a man of manifest destiny is both anachronistic and somewhat conjectural, his association of Falcon with that "special breed of empire builder, explorer, and imperialist" (29) is slightly off the mark. While it is true that Falcon's models are the conquistador Pizarro and the navigator Magellan, American imperialism: i.e. the extension of American political and economic influence around the globe, did not start before the Mexican–American war of 1846 under the presidency of James K. Polk (unless one considers the involvement of individuals like Falcon in the transatlantic slave trade to be a forerunner of American imperialism). Calhoun is accurate,

---

11   The Puritan leaders saw the Massachusetts Bay Colony as "a commonwealth owing allegiance to no higher political authority than its charter" (Paul R. Lucas, "Colony or Commonwealth: Massachusetts Bay, 1661–1666," *William and Mary Quarterly* 24.1 [January 1967]: 90)—meaning that Massachusetts was a commonwealth under God rather than a colony bound hand and foot to the Crown of England and its Anglican church. Regarding the "commonwealth faction" of the Massachusetts Bay at the time of the Restoration when Charles II reclaimed the crown of England after the Interregnum of Oliver Cromwell (1649–60), Paul Lucas writes that many in the Massachusetts Bay Colony supported the idea that "the colony's charter was a compact between King and colonists in which the King granted autonomous self-government in return for an annual payment of one fifth of all gold and silver discovered by the inhabitants" ("Colony or Commonwealth," 90).

12   In 1636 John Cotton, for instance, stated: "Democracy, I do not conceyve that ever God did ordeyne as a fitt government eyther for church or commonwealth"; quoted in *The Correspondence of John Cotton*, ed. Sargent Bush, Jr. (Chapel Hill: U of North Carolina P, 2001): 245. And in 1648, John Winthrop discussed the government and the concept of true liberty in the following terms: "This liberty is maintained and exercised in a way of subjection to authority; it is of the same kind of liberty wherewith Christ has made us free"; quoted in Michael W. Kaufmann, *Institutional Individualism: Conversion, Exile, and Nostalgia in Puritan New England* (Middletown CT: Wesleyan UP, 1999): 22.

however, in his assessment of Falcon as a mere soldier of fortune working for wealthy entrepreneurs eager "to stock Yankee museums and their homes with whatever of value was not nailed down in the nations he visited" (49). Falcon is a pawn, and he acknowledges as much to Calhoun shortly before passing away. The ship, he tells Calhoun,

> wasn't *our* ship from the start [...] Every plank and piece of canvas on the *Republic*, and any cargo she's carrying, from clew to earring [...] belongs to the three blokes who outfitted her in New Orleans and pay our wages. See, someone has to pay the *bill*. I'm captain'cause I knew how to bow and scrape and kiss rich arses to raise money for this run.
>
> *Middle Passage* 147

Falcon's candid confession is a stark reminder that greed, rather than politics, race, or ideology, was the prime motive in the slave trade—or any other trade. At the time of the story, the American industrial revolution was underway and the pious, thrifty, and hardworking original Puritan settlements had morphed into a ruthless, compulsive mercantile economy. The claim that each and every individual, regardless of his origins, was entitled to his share of the loot was anchored in the national rhetoric, even though slaves, indentured servants, Native Americans, and non-European immigrants were denied access to it by law and by force. For others, bootstrapping and resilience are promises of success, and Falcon's fanatical self-discipline, ambition, and overall philosophy of "Never Explain and Never Apologize" (143) make him the archetype of what the young republic stood for.

In Falcon's journal, Calhoun discovers that the captain has devised for himself a series of exercises that he calls "Self-Reliance" (51). Falcon would thus precede Ralph Waldo Emerson, whose paternity of the term, for that matter, has been contested.[13] Humor notwithstanding, Falcon is a dreadful perversion of the philosophy of the self that Emerson elaborated in his seminal essay of 1841. On the surface, Falcon corresponds to what Emerson defines at the beginning of "Self-Reliance," as genius: "To believe your own thought, to believe that what is true for you in your private heart is true for all men—that is genius."[14]

---

13   Seth Lobis, in an entry for the online journal *In Character*, writes: "The *Oxford English Dictionary* credits not Emerson but John Stuart Mill with the first use of 'self-reliance,' which appears in a letter dated 25 November 1833 that Mill wrote to Thomas Carlyle." Arguably, this would still put Falcon ahead of Mill, which reveals yet another anachronism in *Middle Passage*.

14   Ralph Waldo Emerson, "Self-Reliance" (*Essays, First Series*, 1841), in Emerson, *Essays & Lectures*, ed. Joel Porte (New York: Library of America, 1983): 259.

Perhaps because he wants to reduce his dependence on his financial backers with independence of mind, Falcon trusts no one but himself, and never tries to justify his questionable deeds with the religious and political rationales of his time. He has also developed his own theory of the human psyche, which he expounds to a skeptical Calhoun:

> For a self to act, it must have somethin' to act *on*. A nonself [...] that resists, thwarts the will, and *vetoes* the actor. [...] Well, suppose that nonself is another self? What then? As long as each sees a situation differently there will be slaughter and slavery and the subordination of one another 'cause two notions of things never exist side by side as equals. Why not [...] if both are true? The reason—the irrefragable truth is each person in his heart believes *his* beliefs is best.
>
> *Middle Passage* 97

At this stage, Falcon's view of the world deviates from Emerson's, for Emerson believes in God-given inborn knowledge that each and every individual ought to discover in order to achieve moral truth: "A man should learn to detect and watch that gleam of light that flashes across his mind from within, more than the lustre of the firmament of bards and sages."[15] In other words, we have it in us, through divine mediation, to strive toward integrity and help build a better society rid of greed and materialism. To this inherent goodness of humankind Falcon opposes the inherent evilness thereof. According to Falcon, "no man's democratic" (97) and "the final test of truth is war on foreign soil. War in your front yard. War in your bedroom" (97), and, as though to mock the Emersonian virtue of solitude: i.e. the capacity to remain immune to dominant views, Falcon adds that "war [will rage] in your own heart, if you listen too much to other people" (97). On the personal level, Falcon's nihilistic convictions have turned him into a paranoid megalomaniac. On a general level, his belief that we are in a state of permanent conflict within ourselves and with others absolves him of the crimes he has committed and accounts for his nation's acts of aggression both on the continent and abroad. Closing his disquisition on the binary oppositions that constitute the structure of the mind, Falcon, as if distorting the principles of Transcendentalism even before they were formulated, tells Calhoun that these binary oppositions "are signs of the transcendental Fault, a deep crack in consciousness itself" (98). Falcon's theory of dualism reinforces the image of the United States as a war-mongering nation, but war, to Falcon, is more than a pretext to invade foreign lands or protect the nation from

---

15   Emerson, "Self-Reliance," 259.

implausible enemies.[16] War, for Falcon, is inherent in human nature; therefore, it would be futile to either ignore the fact of it or believe there is a way around it.

The emphasis on the ideology of war, as well as the critical view of Manifest Destiny in *Middle Passage*, must also be understood in relation to Johnson's own historical context. Arguably, the military involvement of the United States in various Cold War-related conflicts over the postwar years had a strong influence on Johnson, who completed *Middle Passage* during the Reagan years, a time when the idea of American exceptionalism was forcefully revived. Just a few years after the debacle of the Vietnam War, President Ronald Reagan rekindled American pride and confidence by increasing the military budget, beefing-up anti-Soviet rhetoric, and backing anti-Marxist insurgents around the world. What makes the Reagan Doctrine a modern echo of Manifest Destiny is not only its ambition to impose American ideological and military domination everywhere, but also its religious undertones: Reagan labeled the Soviet Union the "evil empire"[17] and saw the United States as the "leader of the free world" sent on a divine mission to bring others the gifts of American democracy, prosperity, and freedom.[18]

---

16   In addition to the two-decades-long war in Afghanistan (2001–2014), one of the most recent displays of American military might is, of course, the controversial invasion of Iraq launched by the George W. Bush administration in March 2003 as part of the War on Terror. In the two or three years preceding the release of Johnson's *Middle Passage*, the United States, under the presidencies of Ronald Reagan (1981–89) and George H.W. Bush (1989–93), had been involved in the Iran–Iraq War (1987–88), had orchestrated the invasion of Panama (1989), and had led an international coalition in Operation Desert Storm against Iraq for its invasion of Kuwait (1990).

17   Significantly, Reagan used the phrase for the first time on the occasion of a speech to the National Association of Evangelicals in Orlando, Florida on 8 March 1983. Worried that Congress would help ban the deployment of U.S. cruise and Pershing II missiles in Europe, Reagan warned his countrymen: "I urge you to speak out against those who would place the United States in a position of military and moral inferiority. You know, I've always believed that old Screwtape reserved his best efforts for those of you in the church. So, in your discussions of the nuclear freeze proposals, I urge you to beware the temptation of pride—the temptation of blithely declaring yourselves above it all and label both sides equally at fault, to ignore the facts of history and the aggressive impulses of an *evil empire*, to simply call the arms race a giant misunderstanding and thereby remove yourself from *the struggle between right and wrong and good and evil*"; in *Cold War: The Essential Reference Guide*, ed. James R. Arnold, & Roberta Wiener (Santa Barbara CA: ABC–CLIO, 2012): 347. (Emphasis added).

18   President Reagan made his views about the role of the United States in the world clear in his State of the Union Address on 6 February 1985: "Our progress began not in Washington, DC but in the hearts of our families, communities, workplaces, and voluntary groups which, together, are unleashing the invincible spirit of *one great nation under God* [...] And tonight, we declare anew to our fellow citizens of the world: *Freedom is not the sole*

Freedom is a very slippery concept, but in Reagan's mind it was strongly associated with the free-market economy—a system free of government control,
regulated by the law of supply and demand, and, by extension, supportive of
individual initiative and the accumulation of wealth. Incidentally, Ebenezer
Falcon would not have disapproved of so-called Reaganomics and its onslaught
on social welfare, as it fits his creed of excellence and the related components
of hard work and self-improvement. As demonstrated earlier, however, Falcon
is well aware that the system on which he thrives is blatantly unfair. By contrast,
Reagan blindly adhered to that system, and this may explain why Charles Johnson sounded the alarm and felt the urge to suggest that there was nothing *new*
about *neo*-liberalism, that beneath the veneer of economic dynamism and the
tale of prosperous communities lies a deeply inequitable system in which the
more virtuous and talented are not necessarily the most successful. Through
his recurrent use of John Winthrop's metaphor of the "city upon a hill," Reagan
depicted a world of God-fearing, close-knit communities made prosperous by
the miracle of capitalism, thus consolidating the misguided belief that capitalism and freedom are interchangeable notions.[19] However, when Winthrop
spoke of freedom, he did not have the free-market economy in mind. Rather,
he envisioned a commonwealth of self-sacrificing people whose liberty was
limited by the rule of God and the theocrats who enforced it. Winthrop and his
flock, like the rest of the counter-Reformation, welcomed commerce and social mobility, but their world remained self-contained, controlling, and closer
to a socialist than a capitalist utopia. It is not the world of John Winthrop about
which Reagan was nostalgic; it is the world of Falcon, a world in which the
original purpose of the Puritans (building the New Jerusalem) and their values

---

prerogative of a chosen few; it is the universal right of all God's children"; quoted in Lamont
C. Colucci, *The National Security Doctrines of the American Presidency: How They Shape
Our Present and Future* (Santa Barbara CA: Praeger, 2012) 649. (Emphasis added).

19   Ronald Reagan's amalgamation of capitalism and freedom appears clearly in his Farewell
Address on 11 January 1989: "The past few days when I've been at that window upstairs,
I've thought a bit of the 'shining city upon a hill.' The phrase comes from John Winthrop,
who wrote it to describe the America he imagined. What he imagined was important
because he was an *early Pilgrim, an early freedom man*. He journeyed here on what today
we'd call a little wooden boat; and like the other Pilgrims, he was looking for a home that
would be free. I've spoken of the shining city all my political life, but I don't know if I ever
quite communicated what I saw when I said it. But in my mind it was a tall proud city
built on rocks stronger than oceans, wind-swept, *God-blessed, and teeming with people
of all kinds living in harmony and peace, a city with free ports that hummed with commerce
and creativity*, and if there had to be city walls, the walls had doors and the doors were
open to anyone with the will and the heart to get here. That's how I saw it and see it still";
in *American Presidents: Farewell Messages to the Nation, 1796–2001*, ed. Whitney Gleaves
(Lanham MD: Lexington, 2003) 459–460. (Emphasis added).

(thrift, hard work, and good morals) have become an excuse for conquest and personal advancement.

••••

Although not a prominent player in the novel, the crew remains one of the three forces that shape Calhoun's political ideas during the crossing of the Atlantic. Historically, slave-ship sailors were recruited from among the lowlife of port cities, a reality Calhoun reports in his usual sardonic tone: "We [the crew] were forty of a company":

> we were, to tell the truth, all refugees from responsibility and, like social misfits ever pushing westward to escape citified life, took to the sea as the last frontier that welcomes miscreants, dreamers, and fools.
>
> *Middle Passage* 39–40

Calhoun's comparison of his disreputable crewmates to frontiersmen is, of course, a critical allusion to the American myth of the courageous, God-fearing pioneers settling in the wilderness. But beyond the sarcasm, sailors, like frontiersmen, were poor and in search of a better life. Of the typical jack tar, Marcus Rediker writes: "his motivations in seeking a berth would be fundamentally economic"; as a proletarian, "he depended on the money wage. He would go back to sea when his pockets were empty."[20]

Calhoun's portrayal of his shipmates and himself echoes Karl Marx's description of a segment of the working class that Marx called the lumpenproletariat.[21] Marx deemed the lumpenproletariat worthless because such workers would never rise against their capitalist oppressors with the goal of achieving a classless society. It is true that the crew of the *Republic* is not characterized by a strong political consciousness, yet the men suffer at the hands of Falcon and have resolved to change their lot: "A crew has to trust the captain" (86), the first

---

20   Marcus Rediker, *The Slave-Ship: A Human History*, 227.

21   In *The Eighteenth Brumaire of Louis Napoleon* (1852), Karl Marx describes what he calls the "slum-proletariat of Paris" manipulated by Bonapartist agents thus: "Along with the ruined roués of questionable means of support and questionable antecedents, along with the foul and adventures-seeking dregs of the bourgeoisie, there were vagabonds, dismissed soldiers, discharged convicts, runaway gallery slaves, sharpers, jugglers, lazzaroni, pickpockets, sleight-of-hand performers, gamblers, procurers, keepers of disorderly houses, porters, literati, organ grinders, rag pickers, scissors grinders, tinkers, beggars—in short, that whole undefined, dissolute, kicked-about mass that the Frenchmen style 'la Bohème'"; Marx, *The Eighteenth Brumaire of Louis Napoleon* (1852; Chicago: Charles H. Kerr, 1907): 41.

mate Peter Cringle tells Calhoun on the occasion of the first mutineers' secret
meeting, and "we think it's time to change leadership" (86)—by which Cringle
means disposing of Falcon and selling the cargo in the New World. In spite of
Calhoun's musing that "no less than the blacks in the hold these sea-toughened
killbucks were chattel" (87), the sailors never think of the captives as their
equals in misery; rather, they see them as valuable goods from which they can
make a profit. The sailors are mere cogs in the globalized market economy, and
their freedom is contingent both on emancipation from their cruel skipper
and on continued oppression of those below deck—a paradox Emma Christopher explains in "The Bloody Rise of Western Freedom," the third chapter
of her *Slave Ship Sailors and Their Captive Cargoes*, in which she argues that
slave-ship sailors had a unique perspective on freedom, since they "asserted
their own claims to liberty, while holding the musket or whip of repression
firmly in their hands."[22]

The crew aboard slavers usually formed a tight bunch. Christopher talks
of "ersatz kinship" among sailors,[23] and Rediker says that such solidarity was
meant to "incorporate workingmen of many different national, cultural, and
racial origins. The motley crew found unity in their work. They were 'brother
tars.'"[24] Rediker argues that a sailor would find "two overlapping and conflicting communities" on the ship:

> the first was a corporate community linking the entire crew from the top
> of the laboring hierarchy to the bottom [...] The second was a class com-
> munity, in which he would have been arrayed alongside other common
> sailors against the captain and officers.
>
> *The Slave-Ship: A Human History* 262

Calhoun's African ancestry is never questioned among his crewmates aboard
the *Republic*. Rediker argues that any crew member would become "white"
once aboard the slaver:

> It was the common practice for everyone involved in the slave trade,
> whether African or European, to refer to the ship's crew as the 'white
> men' or the 'white people,' even when the crew was motley, a portion of it
> 'colored' and distinctly not white.
>
> *The Slave-Ship: A Human History* 263

---

22   Emma Christopher, *Slave Ship Sailors and Their Captive Cargoes, 1730–1807* (Cambridge:
      Cambridge UP, 2006): 94.

23   Christopher, *Slave Ship Sailors and Their Captive Cargoes*, xvi.

24   Marcus Rediker, *The Slave-Ship: A Human History*, 231.

But Calhoun's complicated relation to Falcon and his status as a member of the crew put him in an ambiguous, if not dangerous, position.

Calhoun does experience difficulties with the mutineers, but not because of the color of his skin—rather, because of his closeness to Falcon. McGaffin, the most hot-tempered of the mutineers, is distrustful of Calhoun and devises a plan in which Calhoun, to prove his loyalty, will play a key role in the plot against Falcon. McGaffin is a ruffian, but he is also a family man aware of the stakes, and candid when sending back to Calhoun the image he has given of himself. McGaffin tells Cringle and their accomplices:

> If we poach this ship, it's plain we'll swing for piracy. The brokers Falcon works for will have us hunted from Chesapeake Bay to the South Sea China. Our wives'll be widowed. Our sisters [...] will have to go out on the twang to turn a coin. And our wee li'l ones? They'll be orphaned [...] or sold to the workhouse.
> *Middle Passage* 88

The way to avoid such an outcome, McGaffin contends, is to designate Calhoun, a stowaway, as the culprit. Thus, the mutineers would be exculpated of any misdeed and free to sign on with other ships, while

> Calhoun'll go his own way, like he's always done, believin' in nothin,' belongin' to nobody, driftin' here and there and dyin,' probably, in a ditch without so much as leavin' a mark on the world.
> *Middle Passage* 88

The brand of absolute freedom Calhoun was trying to sell at the beginning of the story is now turning against him, as it has become the linchpin in McGaffin's argument: since Calhoun has no ties to anyone or any place, since he can disappear as easily as he appeared, he may as well be held responsible for disposing of Falcon.

Falcon's demand that Calhoun be his "eyes and ears" (57) on the ship is less onerous than that of the mutineers who set Calhoun the task of neutralizing all wires and security devices in Falcon's cabin so as to facilitate their operations. Calhoun is now compelled to do what he has been avoiding all his life: take responsibility for his deeds and, in this case, prove his allegiance to one of two sides, each as greedy and evil as the other. "I could no longer find my loyalties" (92), Calhoun laments before deploring the corruption typifying human interaction:

> All bonds, landside or on ships, between masters and mates, women and
> men [...] were a lie forged briefly in the name of convenience and just as
> quickly broken when they no longer served one's interests.
>
> *Middle Passage* 92

Just a few weeks earlier, Calhoun had been celebrating his freedom by trying
to remain immune to any sort of social commitment: i.e. by unconsciously recreating the kind of comfort zone he enjoyed under the yoke of Master Chandler without realizing that, once free, he must negotiate his integration into
society. He thus wonders where his interests lie and realizes the consequences
of his asocial attitude:

> No question that since my manumission I'd brought a world of grief on
> myself but [...] I wished like hell I had someone to blame—my parents,
> the Jackson administration, or white people in general—for this new
> tangle of predicaments.
>
> *Middle Passage* 92–93

Calhoun's worries are far from over—the Allmuseri are about to rebel and take
control of the ship, confronting him with yet more questions and more choices
to make. However, before delving into the Allmuseri world and understanding
the significance of their rebellion, *Middle Passage* must be put in dialogue with
its literary antecedents.

• • •

The rebellion of the Allmuseri aboard the *Republic* evokes the rebellion of Babo
and his fellow captives aboard the *San Dominick* in Herman Melville's *Benito
Cereno* (1855). Johnson acknowledges the rich intertextuality between *Middle
Passage* and *Benito Cereno* in various ways, including transferring names—
Melville's Babo, Atufal, Francisco, Ghofan, Akim, and Diamelo have become
characters in Johnson's novel, albeit in different roles. For instance, Babo and
Atufal, respectively the mastermind of the rebellion and the haughty, regal slave
in Melville's novella, are now hatchet-sharpening henchmen at the beck and
call of the new ruler of the *Republic*, Diamelo, who is mentioned only once as the
dead son of a dead old Negro in Melville's original. Allusions and similarities are
numerous, but *Middle Passage* is much more than a pastiche of *Benito Cereno*.

Johnson gives a hint of his authorial agenda when he has Cringle rant
about the historical figure on whose memoir Melville based *Benito Cereno*:

"'tis scandalous how some writers such as Amasa Delano have slandered black rebels in their tales" (173). For Cringle to make such an incongruous statement just before offering his body in sacrifice to his starving companions cannot be fortuitous: Johnson, like Melville before him, urges his readers to ponder racial biases and their consequences. Melville, in his novella, depicts Delano as a right-thinking, guilt-free New Englander whose belief in the natural servility of Africans prevents him from seeing the obvious: that the African captives have overthrown their European captors. As William Nash puts it, "the tension of 'Benito Cereno' arises from the disconnect between actual events aboard the *San Dominick* and Captain Delano's persistent misinterpretation of them"[25]— a view shared by Andrew Delbanco: "Delano's capacity for self-deception is limitless."[26]

Taking up Nash's opinion that "Johnson concerns himself with [Melville's] views on perception and freedom" (146), Tuire Valkeakari argues that both *Middle Passage* and *Benito Cereno* "examine the dynamics of influence among perception, culture, politics, and individual integrity,"[27] and she expands on the dangerous consequences of Delano's cultural myopia:

> Once Delano's adventure is over, the "good captain" symbolizing American democracy is unwilling to dwell on any political implications of his encounter with an intelligently orchestrated black revolt. Although Delano, a Northerner, believes himself to be racially progressive, he refuses to let his life be impacted by this potentially transformative encounter. Instead, he remains an uncommitted individual on the *Bachelor's Delight*, a carefree sea-wanderer whose whaleboat is aptly named *Rover*.[28]

Valkeakari emphasizes the difference between Delano's crass ignorance, which Babo exploits to perfection on the occasion of the latter's initial visit aboard the *San Dominick*, and Delano's willful ignorance, which is revealed after the dramatic events in which he took part aboard the ship. Valkeakari's argument is a reminder that, despite the rise of abolitionist sentiment in the North in the nineteenth century, many turned a blind eye to the "Peculiar Institution" because they either had no real objection to it, or resented radical abolitionist positions, or refused to antagonize the South lest its cotton-reliant economy

---

25   William R. Nash, *Charles Johnson's Fiction* (Urbana–Champaign: U of Illinois P, 2002): 149.
26   Andrew Delbanco, *Melville: His World and Work* (New York: Alfred A. Knopf, 2005): 238.
27   Tuire Valkeakari, *Precarious Passages: The Diasporic Imagination in Contemporary Black Anglophone Fiction* (Gainesville: UP of Florida, 2017): 40.
28   Valkeakari, *Precarious Passages*, 41.

collapse, drawing Northern textile mills and probably the rest of the nation into its fall.[29]

In *Middle Passage*, the role of the unmindful, self-serving pleasure seeker is fulfilled by the early Calhoun, the *jouisseur* who deliberately evades issues of race and politics for the decadent gratification of the Crescent City. However, once aboard the *Republic*, Calhoun cannot afford to be callous. Like Olaudah Equiano, Calhoun is compelled to take part in a trade whose exchange currency is black people like himself.[30] Hence, Calhoun, unlike Delano, undergoes a drastic transformation of personality in the aftermath of the mutiny, and, as the final section of this chapter shows, he determines to take matters into his hands and become the agent of personal, communal, and national change. Calhoun's undertaking, which is rooted in the most cherished principles of his young nation, aims to resolve the discrepancy between the national rhetoric of freedom and equality and the tacit and explicit endorsement of racial discrimination.

Frederick Douglass's *The Heroic Slave* (1855), although not a direct template for Johnson's *Middle Passage*, addresses similar issues of racial prejudice and democratic principles in the United States. Douglass's story is based on Madison Washington, a slave who, in 1841, led a rebellion aboard the *Creole*, a

---

29   In *Proslavery: A History of the Defense of Slavery in America, 1701–1840* (Athens: U of Georgia P, 1987), Larry Tise shows how, in the early nineteenth century, the United States transitioned from a mercantilist to a laissez-faire economy: "No sooner was the [economic] revolution under way," Tise writes, "when a host of political economists set about assessing the viability of slavery as a socio-economic institution, the relationship between slave and free labor in an agricultural economy" (65). While some economists remained critical of slavery as detrimental to the development of the South, others justified it by invoking either the free-market economy, state rights, the bondage/freedom dichotomy as a positive factor in the establishment of a well-ordered civilization in the New World, or the fact that plantation slaves in the South were better-off than poor workers in the North. There was no consensus on slavery among the new economists, but there was no dearth of justification for it, either.

30   Toward the end of his *Interesting Narrative*, Equiano becomes the slave of the Philadelphia-based Quaker merchant Robert King, who occasionally loans Equiano out to other masters doing business in the Caribbean. It is on the occasion of such assignments that Equiano ends up being involved in slave-trading activities: "While I was thus employed by my master I was often a witness to cruelties of every kind, which were exercised on my unhappy fellow slaves. I used frequently to have different cargoes of new negroes in my care for sale; and it was almost a constant practice with our clerks, and other whites, to commit violent depredations on the chastity of the female slaves; and these I was, though with reluctance, obliged to submit to at all times, being unable to help them." Olaudah Equiano, *The Interesting Narrative of the Life of Olaudah Equiano, or Gustavus Vassa, The African, Written by Himself*, ed. Werner Sollors (1789; Norton Critical Editions; New York: W.W. Norton, 2001): 42.

brig involved in the coastwise slave trade. Helen Lock, in her comparative analysis of Douglass's novella alongside *Benito Cereno* and *Middle Passage*, focusses on the character of Tom Grant, the former first mate aboard the *Creole,* who, while in a tavern in Richmond, must face the criticism of Jack Williams, an old patron who argues that Negroes are cowards easy to scare into submission. Grant flatly denies his detractor's argument, and eager, to cut the taunt short, exclaims: "this whole slave-trading business is a disgrace and scandal to Old Virginia"[31]—a stance that prompts his hostile audience to call him an abolitionist. Grant resents the accusation and tries to justify his debacle by blaming the loss of the *Creole* on "what he regards," Lock observes rather sardonically, "as the imposture of Washington" (64). Grant describes the events thus:

> In the short time [Washington] had been on board, he had secured the confidence of every officer. The negroes fairly worshipped him. His manner and bearing were such, that no one could suspect him of a murderous purpose. The only feeling with which we regarded him was, that he was a powerful, good-disposed negro. He seldom spake to any one, and when he did speak, it was with the utmost propriety. His words were well chosen, and his pronunciation equal to that of any schoolmaster. It was a mystery to us where he got his knowledge of language; but as little was said to him, none of us knew the extent of his intelligence and ability till it was too late.
>
> *The Heroic Slave* 47

From Grant's point of view, the *Creole* was taken over by the slaves because Washington did not behave as a black individual is supposed to behave. As Grant confesses to his audience, "I forgot his blackness in the dignity of his manner, and the eloquence of his speech" (49). Grant and the rest of the crew, like Captain Delano in *Benito Cereno*, were duped by their own racist assumptions, but Grant, unlike the latter, is able to recognize his lack of judgment. In that regard, Grant's attitude is akin to that of Falcon, who, in the aftermath of the Allmuseri rebellion, admits to Calhoun that he has misjudged the Allmuseri: "Then we underestimated the blacks? They're smarter than I thought?" (146). The irony, of course, is that Falcon alone underestimated the Allmuseri. Calhoun and the rest of the crew overestimated them by forming too high an opinion of them.

---

31   Frederick Douglass, *The Heroic Slave*, ed. John R. McKivigan, Robert S. Levine & John Stauffer (1853; New Haven CT: Yale UP, 2015): 45.

• • •

Within the internal structure of the novel, the philosophy of the Allmuseri tribe is the antithesis of Falcon's theory of the dualism of the mind and its correlate of infinite conflict and the might-makes-right mentality. In Falcon's Manichean view of the world, the victor imposes history on the vanquished. By contrast, the Allmuseri believe that reality is not imposed from outside but, rather, revealed from inside through a process they call outpicturing. According to this belief,

> Each man outpictured his world from deep within his own heart [...]
> As within, so it was without. More specifically: what came out of us, not
> what went in made us clean or unclean. Their notion of "experience" [...]
> held each man utterly responsible for his own happiness or sorrow, even
> for his dreams and his entire way of seeing.
>
> *Middle Passage* 164

Outpicturing, as Barbara Thaden has shown, resonates with the Buddhist idea of karma.[32] But outpicturing is also related to self-reliance, as it holds each person accountable for the way they lead their life instead of measuring that life by a series of external criteria. In such a system, Falcon would be able to justify his deeds neither on the ground of humankind's innate corruption nor by claiming that he ought to satisfy the demands of wealthy people above him. Furthermore, outpicturing is an implicit denial of the Protestant notion of chosenness, whereby the United States so often justified its territorial expansion and extermination of people deemed inferior. Admittedly, Allmuseri would never engage in hostile activities against non-Allmuseri, as they are of a pacifist disposition. And they would never deem other people inferior, as they form an egalitarian society that need not measure itself against others; their polity is perfectly harmonious and self-contained. At least, such is the view of the first mate, Peter Cringle, who is the main provider of Allmuseri lore to the narrator Calhoun.

---

32 Barbara Z. Thaden argues: "Johnson has inscribed into the Allmuseri mindset many classical Buddhist beliefs, such as the belief that even though we are inherently inclined to divide our entire experience into two parts, what we do and what happens to us, this belief is the greatest illusion. Buddhists hold that what happens to us is our 'karma,' and 'karma' is a Sanskrit word which means 'doing.' Therefore, according to the doctrine of the Buddha, what happens to us, as well as what we do, is fundamentally our doing"; Thaden, "Charles Johnson's *Middle Passage* as Historiographic Metafiction," *College English* 59.7 (November 1997): 761.

Ashraf Rushdy, in his meticulous "Phenomenology of the Allmuseri," speaks of "accumulatedness"[33] to define what Calhoun calls a "remarkably *old* people," which seems to "have run the full gamut of civilized choices, or played through every political and social possibility" (61). Physically, the Allmuseri seem "a synthesis of several tribes [...] a clan distilled from the essence of everything that came earlier" (61); and, according to Cringle, the Allmuseri "might have been the Ur-Tribe of humanity itself" (61)—a belief that Ngonyama, the charismatic leader of the Allmuseri, will corroborate at a time when, still in chains, he is trying to inveigle Calhoun into teaching him how to steer the ship. It is easy to imagine how those Calhoun calls the "ragtag crew" of the *Republic,* those "refugees from responsibility" who, Calhoun continues, "took to the sea as the last frontier that welcomed miscreants, dreamers, and fools" (40),[34] would idealize the world of an exotic tribe in order to cope with their own:

> According to legend, Allmuseri elders took twig brooms with them everywhere, sweeping the ground so as not to inadvertently step on creatures too small to see. Eating no meat, they were easy to feed. Disliking property, they were simple to clothe. Able to heal themselves, they required no medication. They seldom fought. They could not steal. They fell *sick* [...] if they wronged anyone.
>
> *Middle Passage* 78

This world, seemingly organized around such traditional Buddhist values as compassion for all living creatures, vegetarianism, detachment from worldly possessions, and non-violence, is antipodal to the world that has evolved from

---

33   Ashraf H.A. Rushdy, "The Phenomenology of the Allmuseri: Charles Johnson and the Subject of the Narrative of Slavery," *African American Review* 26.3 (Summer 1992): 373.

34   Calhoun's farcical tone aside, the definition he gives of his shipmates is rather close to reality: historically, slave-ship crew were recruited among the lumpenproletariat of slave ports. Their prospects were scant and their mortality rate at sea often as high as that of their human cargo. Comparing crew and cargo death rates on slavers isn't new since it had already been "made familiar by Thomas Clarkson in his first major attack on the slave trade"; Herbert S. Klein, Stanley L. Engerman, Robin Haines & Ralph Shlomowitz, "Transoceanic Mortality: The Slave Trade in Comparative Perspective," *William and Mary Quarterly* 58.1 (January 2001): 99. In his introduction to *The Slave-Ship: A Human History*, Marcus Rediker argues that, "for sailors in the slave trade, rations were poor, wages were usually low, and the mortality rate was high—as high as that of the enslaved" (7). In "New Evidence on the Causes of Slave and Crew Mortality in the Atlantic Slave Trade," *Journal of Economic History* 46.1 (March 1986): 57–77, Richard Steckel and Richard Jensen show that mortality on slavers was contingent on a great number of criteria, and overall their minute study confirms Rediker's view.

European greed.[35] Europeans, in Allmuseri mythology, illustrate the fall of man. Europeans, the myth goes,

> fell into what was for these people the blackest of sins. The failure to experience the unity of Being everywhere was the Allmuseri vision of Hell. And that was where we lived: purgatory. That was where we were taking them—into the madness of multiplicity.
>
> *Middle Passage* 65

According to Rushdy, "The Allmuseri believe in a form of intersubjectivity so basic that their ideas of failure and hell are represented by division, individuality, or autonomy."[36] Rushdy's use of the intensifier "so" to emphasize the elemental nature of Allmuseri intersubjectivity is meant as an objective observation, but it also suggests that Charles Johnson endowed his ideal tribe with attributes that leave little room for ambiguity or interpretation. Thus, the uncomplicated system of communication among Allmuseri tribesmen indicates that the reality of Allmuseri life has been simplified so that the Allmuseri, by Johnson's own admission, epitomize "the complete opposite of Capt. Ebenezer Falcon's conflict-based, Western vision of the world."[37] Rushdy's intention, however, is not to ponder but, rather, to describe Johnson's creation; thus, Rushdy proceeds further with his dispassionate description of the Allmuseri,

> According to Allmuseri phenomenology, the individual subject's ideal condition involves the renunciation of being situated in the material world. In other words, the ideal of intersubjectivity includes the condition of the individual's being "unpositioned" in the world, of each person's having a relationship with the tribal community that is so integral that the individual is rendered "invisible" in the "presence of others."
>
> "The Phenomenology of the Allmuseri" 377

---

35   In *An Essay on the Inequality of the Human Races* (1853–55), Count Arthur de Gobineau devised a racial ladder, at the bottom of which he put the "negroid variety" and at the top the Aryan family. The essay was particularly influential, in that Gobineau posited a connection between race and civilizational achievement, which inspired subsequent generations of white supremacists, from proslavery advocates to Nazi ideologues. In *Middle Passage*, the creation of the notably superior Allmuseri tribe can be read as Johnson's way of toying with Gobineau's dangerous theories.

36   Rushdy, "The Phenomenology of the Allmuseri," 373.

37   Charles Johnson, in Ethelbert Miller, "All You Need to Know About the Allmuseri," *The E-Channel* (17 April 2011): online (accessed 24 July 2014).

Here again, Rushdy feels compelled to use the intensifier "so" in order to describe the attachment of Allmuseri individuals to their tribe, perhaps because that attachment is more coercive than volitional. The state of plenitude that the unity of Being confers on the individual is not one of harmony, cooperation, and solidarity with others, since the very idea of otherness, which presupposes two interactive subjects, is erased from such a system. Nor are the Allmuseri a tribe that draws its strength from heterogeneity, differences, and negotiations among its members. Instead, the unity of Being implies a willful and complete surrendering of the self to the community, which suggests that the Allmuseri can conceive of freedom only through the dilution of the self in the wider community. Thus, the Allmuseri community is indeed the opposite of the traditional Western community characterized by a balance between individualism and communal fraternity.

Such a community as that of the Allmuseri, however, is only conceivable in the case of a highly self-enclosed entity such as a monastery (where consensus is both the rule and a disembodied notion transcended by love of God) or an isolated group of human beings that would have been living in autarky for generations. Such societies can only operate if preserved from any contact with the outside world, and the Allmuseri, if we are to believe Cringle, seem to have fiercely defended their freedom from interference, since Europeans who "had been to their village [never] lived to tell the tale" (43). However, this story about the Allmuseri's hard-line policy toward outsiders is later tempered by Calhoun, who reports that "the Allmuseri spat at the feet of visitors to their village" in deference to "the stranger's feet [that] must be hot and tired after so long a journey and might welcome a little water on his boots to cool them" (124). Stories about Allmuseri culture abound and are evidence of a wide array of emotions from dread to veneration, but they are mostly the fruit of the crew's imagination. Such stories are the stuff of a fantasized world, and all the myths and legends that had made their way in the hearts and minds of the crew do not stand the test of reality when circumstances compel the Allmuseri, all-forgiving and pacifist as they are, to resort to violence in order to wrest control of the ship.

Describing the state of mind of the Allmuseri in the wake of their successful rebellion, Calhoun writes that, from their perspective, "the captain had made Ngonyama and his tribesmen as bloodthirsty as himself" (140). We are given to understand that the Allmuseri, because they have slain a good number of the crew, experience their victorious rebellion as a lapse into a state of irreparable sin. Ngonyama, Calhoun explains, "had fallen [and] was now part of the world of multiplicity, of *me* versus *thee*" (140). The clash of the deeply traditional and endogenous Allmuseri world with a world of chaos where one has to vie for power and domination has damaged their self-esteem, and so corroded their sense of communal harmony that they have split into rival factions—one led by the magnanimous Ngonyama, and the other by the malevolent Diamelo. The general tone of the story invites readers to impute the dramatic transformation of the Allmuseri to some sort of Western contamination, which is most likely the response Johnson wanted to elicit. Yet, Johnson has also left subtle cues for readers to step outside the consensus and discern unmistakable cracks beneath the veneer of perfection and harmony that coats Allmuseri society.

A comparative analysis of the narrative strategies implemented in *Middle Passage* with those of *Benito Cereno* and *The Heroic Slave* helps understand Johnson's intentions. Melville's text owes its tremendous impact on readers to a mode of unreliable third-person narration drawing almost exclusively on Delano's point of view. It is only in hindsight that readers must reconsider the events of the day and reassess their own assumptions about racial differences. By contrast, Douglass's narration is less slippery, as the story is told through a conventional third-person point of view. The narration includes what Mr. Listwell, an archetypal abolitionist, saw and heard (Section 1), as well as dialogues between Washington and Listwell (Sections 2 and 3). In the fourth and last section, however, the narration shifts to the point of view of Grant, who, goaded by Williams's aspersion, loses his temper and grudgingly divulges that Washington's heroic deeds changed his view of the slave trade and the black race. Grant candidly exposes the self-contradictory discourse of the United States by quoting Washington after the latter has rebuffed him for calling him a "black murderer":

> You call me a black murderer. I am not a murderer. God is my witness that LIBERTY, not malice, is the motive for this night's work. [...] We have struck for our freedom, and if a true man's heart be in you, you will honor us for the deed. We have done that which you applaud your fathers for doing, and if we are murderers, so were they.
> *The Heroic Slave* 48

Through Washington, Grant invokes the Spirit of '76 to reveal the fallacy of a national discourse that celebrates self-determination and individual liberty while denying basic freedoms to part of its population in order to secure economic prosperity for a few.

Not unlike Melville, who lulls his readers into a false sense of moral satisfaction, only to jolt them back into confronting their own racial prejudices, Johnson toys with his readers' eagerness to idealize the Allmuseri along with Calhoun and his shipmates by making Calhoun a seemingly reliable first-person narrator. But Calhoun's narration is in his own image, neither reliable nor conventional. As Daniel Scott notes,

The narrative establishes a chaos of contradictory justifications, motivations, explanations, revelations, and denials against which the story
struggles, [and it] oscillates between naturalistic representation and a
super-real representation of a self-conscious (anti-mimetic) telling. Johnson uses parenthetical intrusions which promise, withhold, delay, betray,
falsify, and verify the narrative, and finally reveal it as performance.[38]

Two-thirds of the story have already been told when Calhoun reveals that
Falcon, now a dying man, has made him responsible for keeping the logbook
of the voyage back to America. Calhoun reluctantly complies, but "promised
[himself] that even though [he]'d tell the story [...], it would be, first and foremost, as [he] saw it since [his] escape from New Orleans" (146). Thus, the novel
Middle Passage is presented as a narrative over which Calhoun assumes complete agency, choosing and discarding information as he sees fit, and at the
pace that suits him best. Calhoun's, however, is not the only layer of narration
in the story—the Allmuseri, especially through Ngonyama, have been particularly good at fueling the crew's utopian longings with Allmuseri lore.

Calhoun, who tells the story retrospectively, has had time to mull over his
ordeal aboard the *Republic*, and even though he may still be in awe of Allmuseri culture, he is well aware that his knowledge of it consists mostly of fables.
Yet, he only imparts this insight in a casual way, in the fourth of nine logbook
entries comprising the entire narrative, when he tells readers that Ngonyama
"unfolded before me like a merchant's cloth his tribe's official history, the story
of themselves they stuck by" (76). The remark is crucial to the present argument, insofar as it normalizes the Allmuseri, who, like any other community,
Calhoun implies, have fashioned their own version of the past. Yet, this remark
is hidden in plain sight, as it follows and precedes scenes and descriptions emphasizing the extraordinariness of Allmuseri cutlure.

This feeling of discrepancy comes from Calhoun's constant to-and-fro between two levels of narration, which narratologists, after Gérard Genette, call
metalepsis, a process whereby the diegetic level (the level of the characters and
action) intrudes on the extradiegetic level (the level of the narrative) and vice
versa.[39] Thus, as events unfold on the *Republic*, Calhoun, like his shipmates,

---

38   Daniel M. Scott, "Interrogating Identity: Appropriation and Transformation in *Middle Pas-
      sage*," *African American Review* 29.4 (Winter 1995): 649.

39   The above description paraphrases Genette, who coined the term "metalepsis" and
      defined it as "any intrusion by the extradiegetic narrator or narratee into the diegetic
      universe (or by diegetic characters into a metadiegetic universe, etc.), or the inverse"; Ge-
      nette, *Narrative Discourse: An Essay in Method*, tr. Jane E. Lewin, foreword by Jonathan
      Culler, ("Discours du récit," in *Figures III*, 1972; Ithaca NY: Cornell UP, 1980): 234–235.

must wait for the successful Allmuseri insurrection to fully come round and accept that the "ageless culture" he "wanted to be his own" (78) is as iniquitous as any other. But, in retrospect, Calhoun has clearly dismissed such beliefs as those Rushdy takes for granted throughout his essay:

> The Allmuseri [...] are a tribe who have developed their own concepts of history, identity, the performance of doubles, nonlinear and nonbinary modes of mentation, and their own theory of subjective and intersubjective being.
>
> "The Phenomenology of the Allmuseri" 377

These narrative acrobatics are where Johnson's agenda is at once best camouflaged and most salient. In an interview, Johnson explains that, when writing *Middle Passage*, his "guiding principle was to make [the Allmuseri] the most spiritual tribe in the world, a whole tribe of Mother Theresas and Gandhis."[40] And so Johnson did: through Calhoun's panegyric, the Allmuseri come across as a flawless, unique people. Yet, Johnson has left clues for the reader to take a critical stance and understand that the Allmuseri do not constitute a civilization apart from other civilizations, and that their model of a homogeneous society free of discord is more conceptual than factual, and more coercive than liberating.

Once Diamelo has put most survivors on the ship under his yoke, Ngonyama confides to Calhoun that the reality of everyday Allmuseri life is a far cry from what he had been telling him so far. The Allmuseri legal system is rudimentary and expeditious, and theirs is a class-based society: "'You know,'" Ngonyama tells Calhoun, "'in our village I was a poor man, like you, but [Diamelo's] father was well-to-do [and] Diamelo is used to getting his way'" (137). Thus, Diamelo's influence over his people is the result not of charisma but of inherited social status. Ngonyama tells Calhoun that before they were captured, "Diamelo had been a soger who drank palm wine and drifted indifferently from one occupation to another" (153). He had been "the village wastrel," Ngonyama continues:

> the bully who proved himself on smaller boys [...] contemptuous of the doddering elders, [and] impatient with the painstaking years required to master one of the complex Allmuseri crafts.
>
> *Middle Passage* 153–154

---

40   Charles H. Rowell, "An Interview with Charles Johnson," *Callaloo* 20.3 (Summer 1997): 545.

Prior to his capture, Diamelo cared little about his culture, but he found in his fellow tribesmen's shared hatred of Ebenezer Falcon a catalyst for self-aggrandizement. And what better instrument of power than the very discourse of racial differences with which his former oppressors justified the enslavement of the Allmuseri?

Diamelo's attitude, as the undisputed ruler of the *Republic*, gives credence to Lock's argument about the use of the paradox as a "key rhetorical strategy"[41] in slave trade literature. According to Lock, slave mutinies are paradoxical, as they reveal that the captor and the captive are "opposed figures [that] mirror each other, [and] are mutually dependent for self-definition" (61). Mutinies create a topsy-turvy world in which "each side reveals characteristics of the other, for better and worse, until [...] there is no discernible distinction" (59). The trope of the slave mutiny, Lock implies, dispels the preconceived notion that the power relationship aboard the slave ship is the result of a natural order reflecting an immutable racial hierarchy.

Lock's theory of the slave mutiny as paradox applies with equal force to *Benito Cereno*, *The Heroic Slave*, and *Middle Passage*, but the latter explores further the consequences of such a power reversal. Diamelo's methods are no less oppressive than are Falcon's, and his ideology is simple: racial purity. Accordingly, Diamelo imposes a very rigid program of acculturation: "Only Allmuseri [is] to be spoken by the crew when in contact with the newly empowered bondmen" (154); furthermore, the crew are not allowed to sing in English while working; they must also learn Allmuseri stories, "nurture [the Allmuseri] god," use Allmuseri medicine, and "lower their eyes" in respect when in the presence of Allmuseri people (155). Finally, Diamelo has become so obsessive about race that he "never spoke to the Americans except through a third person" (153) and "continued to wash himself in salt water whenever Cringle's shadow fell upon him" (155). Diamelo's racial order, although excessive and preposterous, is proportionate to Falcon's order in which the Allmuseri were mere merchandise on account of their African identity. In this sense, the inversion of power generated by the mutiny prevents readers from interpreting the transatlantic slave trade as a binary opposition between evil Westerners and good Africans, which would be historically inaccurate and demeaning to the Africans. Furthermore, Diamelo's discriminatory policies anticipate, albeit in reverse, the rules of European colonizers in Africa and the theories of racial purity and

---

41   Helen Lock, "The Paradox of Slave Mutiny in Herman Melville, Charles Johnson, and Frederick Douglass," *College Literature* 30.4 (Fall 2003): 54.

hygiene developed by such theorists as Arthur de Gobineau at the end of the nineteenth century.[42]

When *Middle Passage* was published in 1990, racism had not disappeared, but it now differed greatly from the type of racism Melville and Douglass were dealing with in the mid-nineteenth century. Accordingly, Johnson turned his story of a slave mutiny into a cautionary tale about late-twentieth-century Amasa Delanos. *Middle Passage* invites the reader to desacralize the Allmuseri tribe and recognize that their world—neither more nor less than the Western world—grapples with issues of individual and collective freedom, social inequality, and violence. Failing to deconstruct the Allmuseri reduces the tribe (and through them all Africans) to the sole status of meek and pitiable victims. To disregard the complexity of Africans and see them as perfect people who were wrested from their paradise is to take their humanity away. *Middle Passage*, by showing that the Allmuseri are not as good as they appear to be, humanizes them and maintains them within the fold of humanity with all its imperfections and injustices.

Diamelo's politics of reverse discrimination may also be read in light of this endeavor to make the Allmuseri a civilization among others. By turning the power structure of the *Republic* on its head, Diamelo and his followers appropriate a power only their god could grant them through a session of outpicturing. Indeed, Falcon had once explained to Calhoun that the Allmuseri god could create "alternate universes, parallel worlds and counterhistories" (100); but this turning of the social order upside down remained confined to a ritual and may be construed as a device to come closer to tolerance and wisdom. Experiencing counter-history under the spell of the Allmuseri god may teach humility and boost one's karma, but experiencing counter-history under the yoke of Diamelo amounts to a mere role reversal, the sort featured in the folktales of yore in which the poor suddenly became the wealthy—a relief mechanism whereby those who had nothing could, if only in their imagination, fill the shoes of those who ruled them. In this perspective, counter-histories suggest that Allmuseri are as subject to division and dualism as Westerners are, for what would be the purpose of such a mechanism if there were no injustice or no need to ever right a wrong in the world of the Allmuseri?

---

42   This argument echoes that of Richard Hardack, who uses the concept of the unity of Being to discuss issues of racial identity and the riddance therefrom, arguing, especially, that, "for Johnson, the transcendence of particularity or relativism is equivalent to the transcendence of race itself"; Hardack, "Black Skin, White Tissues: Local Color and Universal Solvents in the Novels of Charles Johnson," *Callaloo* 22.4 (Fall 1999): 1029.

The novel does not elaborate on the role counter-histories play in Allmuseri culture, but—to go back to Michel Foucault's original concept—the advent of counter-history marks the end of a historical discourse whose function was "to speak the right of power and to intensify the luster of power."[43] According to Foucault, history before the sixteenth century was markedly linear and served to reinforce sovereignty by binding the history of the nation and its subjects to the history of the monarch. The new discourse, from the sixteenth century on, disrupted such a pattern by revealing the protean nature of history and establishing that "one man's victory is another man's defeat."[44] Foucault argues that the unifying function of history was thus replaced by a principle of heterogeneity—a principle that would contradict the principle of homogeneity typifying Allmuseri society. When Calhoun remarks, prior to the insurrection, that "the Allmuseri seemed less a biological tribe than a clan held together by values" (109), he is too much in awe to realize that he is trying to realize the American motto of his age, *E Pluribus Unum* (out of many, one), through Allmuseri society, which seems to have evolved beyond a race-based identity and rallied under a set of unifying values applicable to all members of society irrespective of biological differences.[45] But Calhoun has overlooked a detail: the homogeneity of the Allmuseri tribe extends to physical sameness. By virtue of their geographical isolation and absence of biological diversity, the Allmuseri could have never developed their own brand of scientific racism, which is based on difference and alterity. It does not mean, however, that Allmuseri people never feel the need to discriminate, if only among themselves, as the foregoing difference of social status between Diamelo and Ngonyama shows. And this is what Calhoun finds out, for the much-admired Allmuseri society, like any other, is riddled by dissent that only a series of communal rules and values manage to keep in check.

Counter-history, José Médina observes, "blocks the unifying function of the official history by bringing to the fore the oppositions and divisions in the political body."[46] The conflict that has arisen between the partisans of Diamelo, on the one hand, and those of Ngonyama, on the other, is evidence that the

---

43   Michel Foucault, *Society Must Be Defended*, tr. David Macey (Lectures at the Collège de France 1975–1976; New York: Picador, 2003): 66.

44   Foucault, *Society Must Be Defended*, 69.

45   Asked in an interview for *Callaloo* about the traditions that have influenced him, Johnson replies: "Well, Hinduism, Buddhism, and Taoism have always been very attractive to me. I've studied those religions since my late teens, and they permeate my short fiction and novels"; Charles H. Rowell, "An Interview with Charles Johnson," *Callaloo* 20.3 (Summer 1997): 545.

46   José Médina, "Toward a Foucaultian Epistemology of Resistance: Counter-Memory, Epistemic Friction, and Guerilla Pluralism," *Foucault Studies* 12 (October 2011): 14.

legendary harmony of the Allmuseri before their deportation was precarious at best. It is hard to query a culture that has instituted a monthly "Day of Renunciation," a day of rejoicing on the occasion of which one "[gives] up a deep-rooted, selfish desire" (180). The Day of Renunciation is a striking example of the tribe's self-fashioned narrative of communality, and it constitutes a distant echo of the system of taxation found in any welfare state and democracy worthy of the name. However, the Day of Renunciation can also be seen as a means of control whereby each and every citizen is bound to do what others do, thus forcing rather than promoting consensus and solidarity. In Foucauldian terms, the Day of Renunciation could be called a heterotopia.

In "Different Spaces," the only text in which Foucault expands on the concept of heterotopia, the latter are defined thus:

> real places, actual places, places that are designed into the very institution of society, which are sorts of actually realized utopias in which the real emplacements, all the other real emplacements that can be found within the culture are, at the same time, represented, contested, and reversed, sorts of places that are outside all places, although they are actually localizable.[47]

While heterotopia is most often understood as a physical space (prisons, schools, gardens), it can also refer to a non-physical space or, in the words of Foucault, "temporal discontinuities" (182). In the fourth principle of his "heterotopology" (179), Foucault describes what he calls "heterochronia," a phenomenon in which "the heterotopia begins to function fully when men are in a kind of absolute break with their traditional time" (182). Foucault gives museums and libraries as examples of "heterotopias of time that accumulates indefinitely," but he also talks of heterotopias "that are linked [...] to time in its most futile, most transitory and precarious aspect, and in the form of the festival" (182). These heterotopias, Foucault argues, are "absolutely chronic" (182), and he illustrates his point with fairs,

> those marvelous empty emplacements on the outskirts of cities that fill up once or twice a year with booths, stalls, unusual objects, wrestlers, snake ladies, fortune tellers.
>
> "Different Spaces" 182–183

---

47   Michel Foucault, "Different Spaces" ("Des Espaces Autres," 1967), tr. Robert Hurley, in *Essential Works of Foucault, 1954–1984*, vol. 2: *Aesthetics, Method, and Epistemology*, ed. James D. Faubion (New York: The New Press, 1998): 178. Further page references are in the main text.

Foucault's words find an echo in Calhoun's description of the Day of Renunciation in *Middle Passage*. According to Calhoun, the Allmuseri made the Day of Renunciation "a celebration, a festive holiday [...] with dancing and music and clowning magicians everywhere" (180). Yet, the Day of Renunciation should not be construed merely as a fair, let alone as a carnival in the sense Mikhail Bakhtin gives this notion.[48] While the Day of Renunciation is akin to an annual jubilee on the occasion of which the Allmuseri celebrate their culture, it is not a moment of license and excess in which political and social hierarchies are inverted so as to make real the utopian longings of the populace. On the contrary, the Day of Renunciation is normative rather than transgressive. It is a ritual that is intrinsic to Allmuseri life and, as such, constitutes a heterotopia. Heterotopias play a preponderant role in the formation of social identity even though the citizens are unaware of them. The Day of Renunciation is never questioned, yet it is a ritual all Allmuseri tribesmen are expected to participate in and is thus an instrument of discipline. Furthermore, the Day of Renunciation seems to play simultaneously the two distinct roles Foucault ascribes to heterotopias. The first role of heterotopias, Foucault argues, is to create "a space of illusion that denounces all real space, all real emplacements within which human life is partitioned, as being even more illusory" (184). Whether deliberately or not, the Day of Renunciation, with its demands for penance and charity, implies a lack of fairness and equality in the seemingly ideal world of the Allmuseri. The Day of Renunciation can also be perceived as a heterotopia of compensation: i.e. a heterotopia whose role is to create "a different space, a different real space as perfect, as meticulous, as well-arranged as ours is disorganized, badly arranged, and muddled" (184). The Day of Renunciation, like any other festival, aims to promote social harmony and sends back both to the community and outsiders a perfected version of that community, a tale of equality and generosity which the destitute crew of the *Republic*, including Calhoun, has eagerly bought into.

The successful Allmuseri coup has introduced a racial dimension into Calhoun's conundrum: as a member of the crew, he has participated in the oppression of the Allmuseri captives; as an individual of African extraction, he belongs to the group that is being oppressed on the basis of his African

---

48   In *Rabelais and His World*, Mikhail Bakhtin writes: "As opposed to the official feast, one might say that the carnival celebrated temporary liberation from the prevailing truth of the established order; it marked the suspension of all hierarchical rank, privileges, norms, and prohibitions. Carnival was the true feast of time, the feast of becoming, change and renewal. It was hostile to all that was immortalized and completed"; *Rabelais and His World*, tr. Hélène Iswolsky (Bloomington: Indiana UP, 1984): 10.

identity—a liminal state that Calhoun can no longer ignore, for, while he has never played the race card, he has never been able to set aside his racial identity, either. While in New Orleans, Calhoun would neither be "a credit to the Race" nor "strive, like the Creoles, for respectability" (9). Once employed on the *Republic*, and in virtue of the de rigueur color-blindness among the crew, his racial heritage recedes into the background, but never completely disappears. The minute he steps off the deck and ventures out near the coastal trading post of Bangalang in West Africa, he is reminded of his racial identity by Squibb, who warns him about making himself too conspicuous upon the arrival of a coffle in the town square:

> Better yuh keep your noodle down, Illinois [...] Or yuh'll be sold too. Stolen right off the ship [...] and pressed into a gang. It's happened before. [...] These blokes don't know you're a sailor. And they don't care.
> *Middle Passage* 60

On the journey back from Africa, Calhoun somehow becomes a food provider and a surrogate father to Baleka, a child captive, arguably because her mother, Mama, wants it that way, "having decided her child's survival might depend on staying close to the one crew member who look[s] most African" (79). The extent to which Calhoun willingly consents to play this awkward role of caring for two captives who will be sold into slavery at the end of the journey is unclear, but it brings forth the issue of racial solidarity and identity.

Aboard the *Republic*, the Allmuseri captives see Calhoun's blackness as reassuring, and this is why Mama has selected him to become Baleka's caretaker. As for the Allmuseri leader Ngonyama, his initial motives are rather twisted: he befriends Calhoun because he cannot tell white crew members apart, but in his mind Calhoun remains (in an amusing adaptation of a Lévi-Straussian binary) a "Cooked" barbarian, as opposed to the "Raw Barbarians" (75) making up the rest of the crew. Furthermore, Ngonyama only teaches Calhoun the culture and the rudiments of the Allmuseri language for the purpose of learning, in exchange, basic English and navigational skills, which may prove useful for steering the ship back to Africa. Yet mutual friendship is to develop between Ngonyama and Calhoun, and when the latter feels threatened in a roomful of victorious, bloodthirsty Allmuseri insurgents, Ngonyama invokes racial kinship in order to reassure him: "'No one will hurt you here, Rutherford. These men are your brothers'" (131).

Diamelo, who now assumes control of the ship, is less friendly and, as established earlier, much more fastidious about racial identity. In Diamelo's mouth, the expression "Cooked Barbarian" (153) becomes more accusatory: of course, his mistrust of Calhoun is legitimate, to the extent that Calhoun, as a crewmate, is complicit in all the cruelty inflicted on the cargo; but Diamelo's resentment of Calhoun has deeper roots. Calhoun, it turns out, is "a shade or two lighter than [Diamelo's] own" (135), and even if Diamelo spares Calhoun's life on account of his African ancestry, Calhoun is simply not African enough. In this light, Diamelo may be seen as a forerunner of "the late sixties' Black Power movement and contemporary beliefs in Afrocentrism."[49]

By contrast, Calhoun does not seem to be obsessed with the issue of race. He mocks the haughty Creoles early in the story and later describes his former master, Peleg Chandler, as "a fair, sympathetic, and well-meaning man, as whites go" (111), but this is merely a flippant remark meant to entertain his shipmate Squibb. In fact, his initial identification with the Allmuseri is not formulated in terms of race, but in terms of culture: "As I live, they so shamed me I wanted their ageless culture to be my own" (78). It is in the aftermath of the insurrection, and upon learning from Falcon that the New Orleans mobster Philippe "Papa" Zeringue is one of the three owners of the *Republic*, that Calhoun becomes race-conscious: "But how could he [Papa Zeringue] do this, I wondered? Buy and sell slaves when he himself was black? Was this not the greatest betrayal of all?" (150). Calhoun will later qualify his judgment when he reflects on Papa Zeringue's complicated relationship with race. While Zeringue sells black men and women on the international market, he also makes sure that, once he has acquired a business on the local market in New Orleans, it never goes back into the hands of white men. In fact, many consider Zeringue "a patron of the race, a man who len[ds] money to other blacks, and sometimes back[s] stage plays written by Negro playwrights in New Orleans" (198). Thus, Zeringue has computed the race factor into his activities, not because he wants to play the "Race Man" (198) and atone for his slave-trading activities but, rather, because his belonging to the "colored" community is part of

---

49   Jonathan Little, *Charles Johnson's Spiritual Imagination* (Columbia: U of Missouri P, 1997): 148. Little takes the analysis further, interpreting the Diamelo character as Johnson's vehicle to satirize the essentialist views of the Black Nationalist leaders of the 1960s. Little also establishes a parallel between Diamelo and Falcon, but he steers his analysis toward what could be described as "martyromania": i.e. the desire to be considered a martyr. According to Little, Johnson "exposes Diamelo as paradoxically dependent on his oppressor's victimization of him. Diamelo suffers a loss when Falcon commits suicide since he depends on Falcon's existence for his identity. Diamelo [...] fixates on his victimization and is destroyed by it. Diamelo's position of victimology is dramatized as unstable in the depiction of his death—since his actions destroy all those in his path, including himself" (148). Thus, racial isolationism is self-defeating and detrimental to the nation at large.

his identity. Calhoun has come to this new understanding after his encounter with the Allmuseri god, which has shown him that he cannot abstract his racial heritage from his identity.

The Allmuseri god, which Falcon had captured for profit and fame, is caged in the hold of the *Republic,* and although Calhoun describes it as a "dangerous, shape-shifting god" (167), it is a rather peaceful creature that has the power not only to create counter-histories but also to allow its subjects to contemplate their own existence from a detached position. It is both a journey into one's ancestry and a conduit to self-discovery. Upon meeting Calhoun, the Allmuseri god assumes the shape of his father and shows Calhoun that the father he has resented from early childhood for running away was in fact "quickly captured by padderolls and quietly put to death" (170). Through his experience with the Allmuseri god, Calhoun frees himself from the deep-rooted prejudices he had developed against his absent father; and, given that his initial withdrawal into himself stemmed from that childhood trauma, Calhoun is to reconsider his antisocial stance and realize that he is ineluctably connected to both his father and a much larger community:

> A thousand soft undervoices that jumped my jangling senses from his last, weakly syllabled wind to a mosaic of voices within voices, each one immanent in the other, none his but all strangely his, the result being that as the loathsome creature, this deity from the dim beginnings of the black past, folded my father back into the broader, shifting field [...] his breathing blurred in a dissolution of sounds and I could only feel that *identity was imagined.* I had to listen harder to isolate him from the *We* that swelled each particle and pore of him, as if *the (black) self was the greatest of all fictions*; and then I could not find him at all. He seemed everywhere, his presence, and that of countless others, in me as well as the chamber, which had subtly changed. Suddenly *I knew the god's name: Rutherford.*
>
> *Middle Passage* 171 (emphases added)

The end of the passage above suggests that the Allmuseri god is a facilitator of introspection and self-realization. Yet the divine revelation bestowed on Calhoun is disconcerting, for it leaves him with a split interpretation of his existence: the association of the deity with "the dim beginnings of the black past" points to blackness as a key component of Calhoun's personality. But the voice of his father is diluted in a "mosaic of voices within voices," as if to emphasize that identity cannot be reduced to the single criterion of race. In fact, Calhoun concludes not only that identity is artificial and constructed but also that "the (black) self [was] the greatest of all fictions." Thus, Calhoun learns from the

Allmuseri god what the reader learns from Johnson himself: assuming one's black heritage does not necessitate embracing identity politics.

Johnson's position regarding race consciousness may seem paradoxical. On the one hand, he has been adamant about distinguishing himself from a line of African-American writers, running from Richard Wright to Toni Morrison, who have made themselves the exponents of the African-American experience. From Johnson's viewpoint, "The whole notion of being a spokesman—being *the* black writer—is ludicrous."[50] Johnson also criticizes publishers for assuming that any story by a black author necessarily "captur[es] the experience of millions of people."[51] On the other hand, Johnson shows racial partiality when he uses his own clout to promote other black writers whose lack of exposure on the literary scene he deplores. What accounts for this paradox is that Johnson's simultaneous rejection of so-called "protest" literature and his promotion of African-American writers are not mutually opposed in the sense that the latter have seen the reception and the scope of their work limited by the race label.

William Gleason best delineates Johnson's position when he calls the latter the "inheritor"[52] of a group of African-American thinkers and writers whom Ross Posnock, in *Color and Culture* (1998), defines as "antirace race men and women"[53]—that is, Gleason explains, "figures [...] who do not believe in essential racial identities (thus they are 'antirace') and [...] nonetheless act in what they perceive as the best interests of the race, instead of sitting idly by."[54] In *Middle Passage*, Papa Zeringue is, of course, a caricature of the "antirace race man." More relevant to the present argument, however, is the presence, in Posnock's pantheon of antirace race figures, along with W.E.B. Du Bois and Alain Locke, of Ralph Ellison, whose formative influence on Johnson is proverbial, as William Nash reminds us:

> One may say that Johnson is Ellison's spiritual heir and that the circularity of his aesthetic development and his literary career are of a piece with his return to his forebear's lessons.[55]

50   Johnson, quoted in Peter Monaghan, "Winner of National Book Award Won't Be a 'Voice of Black America' (1991)," in *Passing the Three Gates: Interviews with Charles Johnson*, ed. Jim McWilliams (Seattle: U of Washington P, 2005): 49.

51   Johnson, quoted in Monaghan, "Winner of National Book Award Won't Be a 'Voice of Black America' (1991)," 49.

52   William Gleason, "'Go There': The Critical Pragmatism of Charles Johnson," in *Charles Johnson: The Novelist as Philosopher*, ed. Marc C. Conner & William R. Nash (Jackson: UP of Mississippi, 2007): 87.

53   Ross Posnock, *Color and Culture: Black Writers and the Making of the Modern Intellectual* (Cambridge MA: Harvard UP, 1998): 8.

54   William Gleason, "'Go There': The Critical Pragmatism of Charles Johnson," 85.

55   William R. Nash, *Charles Johnson's Fiction* (Urbana–Champaign: U of Illinois P, 2002): 27.

Johnson, in a 2002 article for the *New Crisis*, reports that Ellison, when asked by a journalist if he wrote from the "Black experience," replied: "My God, you write out of your imagination, not your skin!"[56] Ellison's retort is much more than a celebration of art for art's sake: it is a steadfast refusal to indulge in communalism—a core tenet of Ellisonian thought that Johnson has made his own. Just like Ellison, Johnson has refused to confine his artistic creativity to the limits of the so-called "Black aesthetic." In that regard, *Middle Passage* is a good example of a novel that reaches beyond its racial boundaries, re-inventing as it does the slave narrative while pondering such issues as patriotism, ideology, and citizenship. Johnson is not only critical of race; he also believes that race is "an illusion [...] a lived-illusion, a delusion that causes enormous suffering."[57] As Marc Conner and William Nash argue, Johnson sees "the bankrupt doctrine of separatism, identity politics, and racialism" as "crippling real social growth in America."[58]

Johnson, in an essay denouncing the persistence of "the old black American narrative of persuasive victimization,"[59] warns about the dangers of "any story or idea or interpretation" that loses its relevance and soon crystallizes into an ideology. And, he continues,

> Think of this in light of novelist Ralph Ellison's brilliant notion of "invisibility," where—in his classic *Invisible Man*—the characters encountered by his nameless protagonist all impose their ideologies (explanations and ideas) on the chaos of experience, on the mysterious, untamed life that forever churns beneath widely accepted interpretations and explanations of "history" and "culture," which in our social world, for Ellison, are the *seen*.
> "The End of the Black American Narrative" 67

Johnson believes in character "evolution and change"[60] as much as he believes in social and political evolution and change. And it is Ellison, again, who

---

56   Charles Johnson, "Ralph Ellison: Novel Genius," *The New Crisis* (March–April 2002): 18.

57   Quoted in Amritjit Singh, "Afterword: Charles Johnson's Quest for a New African-American Narrative and His Literary Genealogy," in *Charles Johnson: Embracing the World*, ed. Nibir K. Ghosh & E. Ethelbert Miller (New Delhi: Authorpress, 2011): 282.

58   Marc C. Conner & William R. Nash, "Introduction" to *Charles Johnson: The Novelist as Philosopher*, ed. Conner & Nash (Jackson: UP of Mississippi, 2007): xviii.

59   Charles Johnson, "The End of the Black American Narrative," in *Charles Johnson: Embracing the World*, ed. Nibir K. Ghosh & E. Ethelbert Miller (New Delhi: Authorpress, 2011): 66.

60   Jonathan Little, "An Interview with Charles Johnson (1993)," in *Passing the Three Gates: Interviews with Charles Johnson*, ed. Jim McWilliams (Seattle: U of Washington P, 2005): 109.

provides Johnson with the link between artistic and civic responsibility when he argues that, "by a trick of fate (and our racial problems notwithstanding), the human imagination is integrative—and the same is true of the centrifugal force that inspirits the democratic process."[61] With the key notion of integration, Ellison turns his claim to all literary traditions beyond the realm of the black experience into both a legitimate right and a democratic endeavor. In the same manner, the literary imagination cannot be balkanized by race, class, gender, and other limiting categories; democracy cannot be turned into a monolith. Democracy is a work in progress; it does not fall into place *ex nihilo*; it is built up of many ideas and negotiations, and its coherence is achieved through constant adjustments. Johnson's *Middle Passage* can be read as an exploration of these Ellisonian issues. Rutherford Calhoun, after having been confronted with a variety of political creeds aboard the *Republic*, prepares to redefine his relationship to society by designing his own brand of political and civic responsibility, which he bases on active participative citizenship despite the limitations imposed on him by a country founded on racial hierarchy.

3   Patriotism from Calhoun to the Invisible Man

I love America more than any other country in this world, and, exactly for this reason, I insist on the right to criticize her perpetually.[62]

∵

Calhoun is a liminal character caught among three spheres of influence. Whichever sphere he chooses, he must relinquish part of his identity and masquerade as someone he is not: either a stool pigeon for a psychopathic slave-trading captain, or the accomplice of fellow crewmen eager to murder the captain and reap the benefits of the slave trade, or a brother-in-arms to a group of bigoted pan-Africanists *avant la lettre*. The lesson that Calhoun has learned from all these experiences aboard the *Republic* is that, in the long run, evading all commitments and living on the margins of society is not a viable solution. And thus, Calhoun will renounce the life of an antisocial cynic to

---

61   Ralph Ellison, "Preface," in Ellison, *Invisible Man* (1952; New York: Modern Library, 1994): xx.

62   James Baldwin, "Autobiographical Notes" (*Notes of a Native Son*, 1955), in James Baldwin, *Collected Essays*, ed. Toni Morrison (New York: Library of America, 1998): 9.

become a responsible individual eager to play an active role in society. His decision to marry the sententious Isadora seems conformist, and his newfound restrained tongue makes the reader long for the nonchalance and glibness of the defiant reprobate who opens the story. Yet Calhoun's decision to become a bona fide American citizen—not only a law-abiding citizen, but also a citizen protected by the law and duly involved in democratic processes and decision-making—can be compared to the equally surprising decision by the nameless protagonist of Ralph Ellison's *Invisible Man* to come out of the cellar where he has been hiding and face his destiny as an American citizen.[63]

Both Calhoun and the Invisible Man are in-between individuals who have experienced racial discrimination and social alienation in the United States, and both have gone through a phase of either rejection or subversion of the social and political institutions governing their life. In the end, however, both have chosen to embrace these institutions, the true meaning of which they hope to restore. As such, Calhoun and the Invisible Man are rebels in the sense Albert Camus gives this term in *The Rebel*. As mentioned earlier in this chapter, rebellion, in the Camusian sense, stems from absurdity, and the rebel, Camus argues, is "a man who says no, but whose refusal does not imply a renunciation."[64] If Calhoun and the Invisible Man reject authority when it deprives them of their rights, they return to the world that spawned them with the prospect of reform for the benefit of the commonweal. The rebel, according to Camus, "demands respect for himself [...] but only in so far as he identifies himself with a natural community" (16) which is, for Calhoun and the Invisible Man, the American

---

63   Jonathan Little also bases his reading of Johnson's *Middle Passage* on a comparison with
      Ellison's *Invisible Man*. Both analyses overlap on a few specific points. For instance, both
      discuss the "responsibilities of citizenship" (*Charles Johnson's Spiritual Imagination*, 157)
      and the challenge that living in America represents for both protagonists. However, while
      my analysis endeavours to demonstrate that both protagonists, in their own way, have
      made precisely the same choice about personal commitment and political action, Little
      warns, early in his analysis, that "Johnson's novel is markedly different from Ellison's in its
      conclusions about self and society" (136). Also, Little attributes Calhoun's sense of indebt-
      edness to his nation to some sort of Buddhist epiphany. This is a critical angle that my
      analysis deliberately leaves aside, preferring to focus on individual free will rather than
      spiritually induced initiative. Finally, Little argues that both novels "construct the philo-
      sophical foundations that support the politics of integrationism: a system that recognizes
      King's 'network of mutuality' and interracial cooperation" (158). While the conclusions of
      my analysis are congruent with the above argument, I also suggest that both protagonists,
      in their eagerness to see the founding principles of the nation restored to their rightful
      place, have placed their hopes in a society that is beyond the process of integration and
      based on universal principles.

64   Albert Camus, *The Rebel: An Essay on Man in Revolt*, 11. Further page references are in the
      main text.

people. Camus's famous line, "*I* rebel, therefore *we* are" (104; emphasis added), underscores this ontological articulation between the individual and the community: the rebel acts on his own but his action works as a coagulant for the whole community. The struggle against oppression and injustice requires solidarity and a set of values on which to lean. There is liberty neither in the mayhem of revolutions nor in the utopias the latter vow to establish. This is why Calhoun and the Invisible Man can conceive of freedom only within the limits of the legal system that binds the nation together. In other words, Calhoun and the Invisible Man have decided to re-invent themselves, but they will not do so through rebellion and destruction. On the contrary, they intend to do so from within the system, which already provides them with the tools for such a transformation. Thus, instead of denouncing the national institutions as the source of their misery, they prefer to see them as the remedy for their alienation; and they do so because they believe in the American rhetoric of a unified whole that the national motto, *E Pluribus Unum*, encapsulates. Many may dismiss the endeavor as credulous or even conservative, yet it would be misguided to claim that Calhoun and the Invisible Man ignore their nation's bigotry and history of abuses. In fact, it is their confrontation with discrimination and deleterious ideologies that has convinced them to exercise their citizenship and strive to uphold the values that American institutions purport to promote.[65]

Both *Middle Passage* and *Invisible Man* are bildungsromane in which a young African-American man is confronted with several models of politics that he eventually rejects because they do not meet his expectations. While Rutherford Calhoun and the Invisible Man respond to their ordeals in similar fashion, they do so after markedly different experiences. From the beginning, Calhoun has dismissed any possible way of living that a white-dominated society affords him and it is only after stowing-away on the *Republic* that he is compelled to become involved in the various political ventures that encourage him to find his own path. By contrast, the Invisible Man starts as a gullible neophyte who goes from one disillusion to the next—from the self-serving gradualism of Dr.

---

65   Ralph Ellison had an unshakable faith in the institutions and foundational texts (Declaration of Independence, Constitution, and Bill of Rights) of the United States. In "Perspective of Literature," for instance, Ellison expressed his fervent belief in the Constitution thus: "I look upon the Constitution as the still-vital covenant by which Americans of diverse backgrounds, religions, races, and interests are bound. They are bound by the principles with which it inspirits us no less than by the legal apparatus that identifies us as a single American people. The Constitution is a script by which we seek to act out the drama of democracy and the stage upon which we enact our roles"; Ellison, "Perspective of Literature" (1976), in *The Collected Essays of Ralph Ellison: Revised and Updated*, ed. John F. Callahan (New York: Random House, 2003): 777.

Bledsoe at the black college, to the Machiavellian opportunism of the Brother-hood, the bellicose separatism of Ras the Exhorter, and the falsely empowering ubiquity of Rinehart. It is after his fall down a manhole while escaping two policemen during a riot in Harlem that the Invisible Man starts reflecting on the events of his life and reaches the conclusion that he must emerge from his underground lair and confront his destiny.[66]

The Invisible Man decides to act rather than be acted upon: "I believe in nothing, if not in action,"[67] he declares, after realizing that his urban guerril-la tactics—stealing electricity from the greedy Monopolated Light & Power company—cannot be considered genuine civil disobedience, as they serve no greater cause, only his own. The Invisible Man is not Henry David Thoreau, who famously refused to pay his taxes as a form of protest against slavery and the Mexican–American war. But Thoreau is not the Invisible Man, either, for Thoreau risked neither imprisonment nor lynching for confronting the author-ities. Indeed, being black in the United States in the 1930s is no less dangerous than it was a century earlier at the time of Calhoun, and while Calhoun, at the beginning of *Middle Passage*, conceals his exclusion from American society behind a mask of cynicism and a self-deluding sense of freedom, the Invisible Man conceals his fears of coming out of his hiding place behind tergiversa-tions. Calling his "state of hibernation" a "covert preparation for a more overt action" (13), for instance, is sheer bravado even as it bespeaks a real desire to play an active role in the development of his nation.

Before engaging in political action, however, the Invisible Man endeavors to drop the hyphenated part of his identity and reclaim his birthright—his

---

66 The evolution of the Invisible Man from the personal to the national, his to-ing and fro-ing between his American and African-American identities, as well as his meditation on the frailty of the republic, echo Calhoun's own existential ruminations and the probing of national values in *Middle Passage*. Gary Storhoff's analysis of the Calhoun character bears some resemblance to the present analysis of the Invisible Man character. According to Storhoff, Calhoun is "literally the American self-made man, who creates, then revises, himself as he goes along"; Storhoff, *Understanding Charles Johnson* (Columbia: U of South Carolina P, 2004): 158. And like his nation, Calhoun "is constantly engaged in self-making" (159). Storhoff also argues that in *Middle Passage* "Johnson links his theme of person-al identity to the question of America's national identity: how is it imagined with the corporate cooperation of its citizens, then constantly revised communally through time" (148). And, finally, Storhoff notes that *Middle Passage* is very much about democracy—its fickleness and fallibility: "At no point is America ever finished, and it is a citizen's duty 'at any cost' to preserve this fragile thing—disorderly, 'flying apart,' but coming together again with its citizens' concerted efforts. American history is not simply made but remade again and again" (152).

67 Ralph Ellison, *Invisible Man* (1952; New York: Modern Library, 1994): 13. Further page refer-ences are in the main text.

full-fledged American identity. He does so rather clumsily at first, claiming that he is "kin to Ford, Edison and Franklin" (7) on account of his ingenuity (tapping his own electricity from a power line). Echoing Calhoun's definition of the Allmuseri in terms not of race but of culture, the Invisible Man defines Americans in terms not of race, but of their capacity for inventiveness and creativity: i.e. their capacity to transform the world. But the race issue cannot be wiped out at the stroke of a pen, and the Invisible Man addresses it again at the end of the prologue. While admitting that his invisibility results not only from ostracism by white people but also from his own hostility toward them, the Invisible Man argues that responsibility "rests upon recognition, and [that] recognition is a form of agreement" (14). The mutual respect and, by extension, basic equal rights that the Invisible Man invokes are, of course, *sine quibus non* for democracy, and when he taunts the reader by suggesting that he should have used his knife on the white man he mugged with a view to "protect[ing] the higher interest of society" (14), he means that his and his victim's destiny are inextricably linked. This argument, although far-fetched, is rational insofar as killing a man who will not "see" him helps curtail a pernicious social ill and thus enhances national cohesion.

Reflecting on Ralph Ellison's view that the invisibility of African Americans compelled them to affirm their existence and manifest their "American democratic individualism," Lucas Morel argues that "blacks could not wait for whites to 'see' or acknowledge them" and that, "due to racism's hold on their moral perception, visibility was each individual's duty"[68]—a duty the Invisible Man carries out with much zeal when confronted with the contumelious white man of the prologue. However, the Invisible Man's later desire for cooperation across the color line, as well as his eagerness to play his role as a committed citizen, is much more akin to the views of Ellison, for whom "the politics of the American regime, despite the segregation he experienced, left sufficient room for aspiring Negro individuals to make their mark."[69] The character of the Invisible Man, however, comes across as more Tocquevillean than that of his creator, as the individual freedom the Invisible Man embodies is not an end in itself but a step toward collective freedom. His decision to come out of his cellar may be interpreted as a commentary on the dangers of what Alexis de Tocqueville called egoism as opposed to "self-interest properly understood."[70]

68   Lucas E. Morel, "Ralph Ellison's American Democratic Individualism," in *Ralph Ellison and the Raft of Hope: A Political Companion to* Invisible Man, ed. Lucas E. Morel (Lexington: UP of Kentucky, 2004): 59.

69   Morel, "Ralph Ellison's American Democratic Individualism," 60.

70   In *Democracy in America* (1835), Alexis de Tocqueville distinguishes between "self-interest properly understood" and egoism. Tocqueville defines the latter as "a passionate and ex-

While individual freedom is a key feature of democracy, too much individual freedom ends up undermining democracy for democracy requires a concerted effort and a sizeable amount of selflessness. The Invisible Man's endeavor to think of his own freedom as inseparable from national freedom accounts for his choice of a collective first-person plural in the line that follows: "Some day that kind of foolishness will cause us tragic trouble" (14).

And this idea that the nation as a whole is threatened by racial discord is echoed once again in the epilogue when the Invisible Man, referring to those who have violated the founding principle of national harmony, argues that "what they're doing is making the old eagle rock dangerously" (576).[71] The "old eagle" reference to the United States bespeaks affection and perhaps familiarity,

---

aggerated love of self that impels man to relate everything solely to himself and to prefer himself to everything else"; *Democracy in America*, tr. Arthur Goldhammer (1835; New York: Library of America, 2004): 585. In contrast, Tocqueville defines the former as an attitude whereby a citizen relinquishes a little bit of his/her individual freedom for the good of the whole community. Altruism is an imperative of democracy: "When the bonds among men cease to be solid and permanent, it is impossible to get large numbers of them to act in common without persuading each person whose cooperation is required that self-interest obliges him to join his efforts voluntarily to those of all the others" (600). Tocqueville argues that the doctrine of self-interest properly understood is "universally accepted by today's Americans" (611) who "will obligingly demonstrate how enlightened love of themselves regularly leads them to help one another out and makes them ready and willing to sacrifice a portion of their time and wealth for the good of the state" (611). Tocqueville raises doubts about the veracity of this claim, but he acknowledges the virtues of the doctrine of self-interest: "properly understood [it] may prevent a few men from climbing high above the ordinary level of humanity, but a great many others who used to fall below that level will rise to it and remain there. Consider a few individuals and the doctrine brings them down. Think of the species and the doctrine raises [the level] up" (612). The Invisible Man shares both Tocqueville's skepticism about, and confidence in, the doctrine of self-interest. Securing the rights of the individual without undermining collective freedom is the challenge Ellison takes on in *Invisible Man*.

71   In reference to the much debated "grandfather's principle," which haunts the conscience of the Invisible Man throughout the story, the present argument echoes that of James Seaton, who admits that the most likely candidate for this principle is "the assertion in the Declaration of Independence that 'all men are created equal'"; "Affirming the Principle," in *Ralph Ellison and the Raft of Hope: A Political Companion to "Invisible Man,"* ed. Lucas E. Morel (Lexington: UP of Kentucky, 2004): 25. However, reducing all references to the principle in the epilogue, Seaton continues, "has the effect of turning the 'equality' referred to repeatedly into a doctrine rather than a principle" (25). According to Seaton, "Ellison's purposefully vague 'principle' is broader than any doctrine" (25), and the "equality" Ellison refers to is "the equality asserted by the Declaration of Independence, but [...] also that equality as embodied in the Constitution and its amendments" (26). Following up on Seaton's point, the present argument shows that beyond the polysemy of the term "equality," the "principle" entails a spate of attitudes that falls under the wider notion of political and civic responsibility.

but, just as with Calhoun in *Middle Passage*, the national "we" is always challenged by a more communal and restrictive African-American "we" as if race
were, first, an issue; and, secondly, one that could not be transcended. In fact,
the epilogue starts again with ratiocinations about the racial divide and how
African Americans are compelled to "wear the mask"[72] in a white-dominated
society: "I was never more hated than when I tried to be honest" (572). In an
attempt to transcend his alienation, the Invisible Man is going to try to resolve
this tension between his African-American identity and his national identity.

The national "we" of the prologue is not meant to erase or ignore differences, and in the epilogue the Invisible Man places racial diversity at the heart
of the national project. He first brings blacks and whites together by rethinking
the national motto, *E Pluribus Unum*, in the following terms: "Our fate is to become one, and yet many—This is not prophecy but description" (577). In this
perspective, the social contract envisioned by the Invisible Man posits racial
harmony, but not color-blindness—a position that echoes Ellison's own:

> the true subject of democracy is [...] the extension of the democratic pro-
> cess in the direction of perfecting itself. The most obvious test and clue
> to that perfection is the *inclusion*, not *assimilation*, of the black man.[73]

The Invisible Man sees the future of the United States as a mosaic rather than
a melting pot. Coincidentally, this concept of mosaic echoes the "mosaic of
voices" in which the Allmuseri god has enveloped Calhoun, leading the latter
to realize that identity cannot be reduced to race and that, in fact, it transcends
race. While widely accepted today as the model of reference for multi-ethnic
societies, the mosaic model was not well known in the United States of the
early 1950s when Ellison wrote *Invisible Man*, let alone in the 1930s when the
story takes place. The Invisible Man's call for more acceptance and justice is
nothing new, but his approach to achieving a better society is more elaborate
than his emotional tone suggests.

Although the Invisible Man lives at a time when negrophobia and lynching are rife, and although he has repeatedly witnessed and undergone racial
discrimination, he never has recourse to race as a catalyst for action, because
he sees the political freedom of both his community and his nation as one.

---

72 Laurence Dunbar, "We Wear the Mask" (1896), in *The Collected Poetry of Paul Laurence
    Dunbar*, ed. & intro. Joanne M. Braxton (Charlottesville: UP of Virginia, 1993): 71.
73 Ralph Ellison, "What America Would Be Like Without Blacks" (1970), in *The Collected
    Essays of Ralph Ellison: Revised and Updated*, ed. John F. Callahan (New York: Random
    House, 2003): 586. (Emphases added).

This may be explained by the fact that the Invisible Man is a pure product of American culture and that he has internalized core American values regardless of racial discrimination. Thus, the traumatizing episode of the "Battle Royal" in which the Invisible Man earns a scholarship for college by winning a grotesque blindfolded boxing match against other African-American competitors for the entertainment of rich white benefactors is one example of how American ideology may both humiliate and socialize a young man. Indeed, the idea of competing for self-improvement is highly valued in the United States, and the Invisible Man's conviction that he will be rewarded for his efforts goes unabated in spite of repeated setbacks as a student at the black college, a worker at the Liberty Paint plant, and a spokesperson for the Brotherhood. The Invisible Man acknowledges as much in the epilogue when he confesses that, like most other Americans,

> I started out with my share of optimism. I believed in hard work and progress and action, but now, after first being "for" society and then "against" it, I assign myself no rank or any limit, and such an attitude is very much against the trend of the times. But my world has become one of infinite possibilities. What a phrase—still it's a good phrase and a good view of life, and a man shouldn't accept any other; that much I've learned underground.
>
> *Invisible Man* 576

The above argument verges on the tautological, as the Invisible Man dismisses one set of values to replace it with a similar one. He claims that he no longer believes in hard work, progress, and action, but his newfound creed of individual freedom and responsibility entails precisely those values. His attitude, then, is still very keen and highly optimistic and proactive, and it is still strongly anchored in the American value system. What has changed, however, is that he intends to live his life on his own terms rather than under the yoke of an oppressive society. Significantly, this statement follows a bout of self-criticism in which the Invisible Man holds himself partly responsible for his alienation— which he calls "sickness"—and resolves to take action in the face of adversity: "But live you must, and you can either make passive love to your sickness or burn it out and go on to the next conflicting phase" (576). In other words, as the adage goes, "God helps those who help themselves."

The Invisible Man's perception that life is a series of "conflicting phases" is later refined in the notion that social harmony is best achieved through a certain amount of disharmony: "Now I know men are different and that all life is divided and that only in division is there true health" (576). This apparent paradox is more than a response to those intent on "putting the world in a strait jacket" (576); it echoes the fourth thesis of Immanuel Kant's essay on universal history:

> The means which nature employs to bring about the development of innate capacities is that of antagonism within society, in so far as this antagonism becomes in the long run the cause of a law-governed social order. By antagonism, I mean in this context the unsocial sociability of men, that is, their tendency to come together in society, coupled, however, with a continual resistance which constantly threatens to break this society up.[74]

Kant is here referring to the dual nature of each and every individual to both embrace and reject life in society, and although his theory of "unsocial sociability" has little to do with the racial strife that has typified American society since its inception, it is reminiscent of Calhoun's difficulties in determining his position and role in the social order. Calhoun rejects society as a small-time criminal in New Orleans; he resists three variously unsuitable models of society aboard the *Republic*; and he defines his own values and chooses the type of citizen he will be once back in the United States. More strikingly, Kant's theory of "unsocial sociability" overlaps on several counts with the views of the Invisible Man. For instance, Kant argues that it is that very tendency to resist socialization that "awakens all man's powers and induces him to overcome his tendency to laziness"[75] (45)—a notion not far removed from the Invisible Man's recurrent claim that action is crucial. Kant furthers his demonstration by arguing that "without these asocial qualities [...] man would live an Arcadian, pastoral existence of perfect concord" (45), but he warns that, in such a world,

> all human talents would remain hidden forever in a dormant state, and men, as good-natured as the sheep they tended, would scarcely render their existence more valuable than that of their animals.
>
> "An Idea for a Universal History with a Cosmopolitan Purpose" 45

Kant's caution about the danger of falling into a "dormant state" is similar to that of the Invisible Man, who has realized that his so-called "state of hibernation" is counterproductive, as it thwarts any effort toward improving

---

74   Immanuel Kant, "An Idea for a Universal History with a Cosmopolitan Purpose" (1784), in *Kant's Political Writings*, ed. H.S. Reiss (Cambridge: Cambridge UP, 1970): 44–45.

75   Kant, "An Idea for a Universal History with a Cosmopolitan Purpose," 45.

society. As for Kant's use of the sheep metaphor, it is reminiscent of the Invisible Man's remark about a recent tendency to "make men conform to a pattern" (576): i.e. to ignore differences and standardize citizens so that they follow the rule of a dominant group: "Let man keep his many parts," the Invisible Man advises, "and you'll have no tyrant states" (577).[76]

The point of divergence between the abstract theories of Kant and the concrete experiences of both Calhoun and the Invisible Man occurs when one considers the evolution of mankind. According to Kant, the asocial qualities of man will facilitate his transition from barbarism to culture. "All man's talents," Kant argues,

> are now gradually developed, his taste cultivated, and by a continued process of enlightenment, a beginning is made towards establishing a way of thinking which can with time transform the primitive natural capacity for moral discrimination into definite practical principles; and thus a pathologically enforced social union is transformed into a moral whole.
>
> "An Idea for a Universal History with a Cosmopolitan Purpose" 45

Kant's insistence on the establishment of moral principles for the good working of a society is particularly relevant, as it is precisely on the lack of principles that the Invisible Man blames the failure of the society he lives in. Indeed, the whole argument of the Invisible Man is based on the premise that what he calls "the principle"—i.e. the founding principles of the nation—has been violated.

The Invisible Man is compelled to address this issue of founding principles through the prism of race, for he can never really leave race out of any reflection on what it means to be of African extraction in the United States. In *Middle Passage*, Calhoun endeavors to live as if race had no impact on his life and he manages to do so as a member of the crew on the *Republic*, away

---

76   Linda Selzer structures her analysis of Johnson's *Middle Passage* around a new form of cosmopolitanism, which, she claims, "attempts to rearticulate older conceptions of world citizenship and human rights [...] in ways that will make them effective tools for advancing human rights in late modernity"; Linda F. Selzer, *Charles Johnson in Context* (Amherst: U of Massachusetts P, 2009): 167. Selzer invokes a "new interest in universals" that is nonetheless "tempered by a respect for cultural, local, and ethnic specificity," and makes Johnson's position on race match these theories. She then offers a range of cosmopolitanisms (e.g., predatory, nonproprietary, and consumerist) that is far wider than the one referred to in the present study. However, her expansion, in line with the theories of Kwame Anthony Appiah, of "the conceptual borders of cosmopolitan thought by articulating a 'situated,' 'patriotic,' or 'rooted' cosmopolitanism" (6) leads her to conclusions very similar to those reached herein.

from the realities of his country. However, his encounter with the Allmuseri god will remind him that he cannot ignore his racial heritage, and it is with this knowledge in mind that he prepares himself for his new life on land. Conversely, the Invisible Man has never really thought of his identity as other than African-American, even following his initial experience with the political organization of the Brotherhood, as a spokesperson for their cause, which gave him the illusion that some people could see beyond the color of his skin. He is to be proven wrong, however, and will find himself compelled to play the race card (Tod Clifton's funeral) and face the brutal consequences of racism (the race riot in Harlem). By the end of the novel, the Invisible Man is entangled in the politics of race, with Sybil, a white woman from whom he hoped to gather information about the Brotherhood. But the plan misfires, as Sybil is interested exclusively in acting out her fantasy of being raped by a "big black bruiser" (522). In the epilogue, however, the Invisible Man has abandoned any leaning toward factionalism—his reflection on "the principle on which the country was built" (574) posits racial harmony as indispensable to the future of the nation.

It is through his grandfather's deathbed admonition to undermine whites, to "agree 'em to death and destruction" (576), that the Invisible Man tackles the issue of "the principle":

> hell, he must have meant the principle, that we were to affirm the principle on which the country was built and not the men, or at least not the men who did the violence.
>
> *Invisible Man* 574

Struggling to justify his grandfather's legacy, the Invisible Man surmises that his grandfather would be subservient to his white oppressors "because he knew that the principle was greater than the men, greater than the numbers and the vicious power and all the methods used to corrupt its name" (574). The Invisible Man's dissociation of "the principle" from what people have made of it helps make sense of Calhoun's disingenuous question: "What Negro, in his heart (if he's not a hypocrite), is not [a patriot]?" (179). This is unsettling because one is likely to have formed precisely the opposite view, whereby an African-American individual in the United States in the 1830s would be fully justified, "if he's not a hypocrite," to harbor unpatriotic feelings about his country. Calhoun is well aware of "the endless round of social obstacles and challenges and trials colored men faced every blessed day of their lives" (179), and he remembers "home" as "a battlefield," a boiling cauldron [that] created white rascals like Ebenezer Falcon, black ones like Zeringue, uppity Creoles, hundreds of slave lords, [and] bondmen crippled and caricatured by the disfiguring hand of servitude.

Middle Passage 179

Yet he concurs with Isadora's opinion that there are small "triumphs," and even though he does not elaborate, his devotion to "this weird, upside-down caricature of a country called America" (179) is unquestionable. While Calhoun leaves his feelings unexplored and unexplained, the Invisible Man makes "the principle on which the country was built" the linchpin of his argument and thereby provides elements of analysis with which to interpret Calhoun's decision to go back to New Orleans, marry Isadora, and face his American destiny.

Establishing a clear split along racial lines and thus dropping the national "we" of the prologue, the Invisible Man reverts to a communal "we" in the epilogue and ascribes a special role to Americans of African descent:

Did he [the grandfather] mean to affirm the principle, which they themselves [the whites] had dreamed into being out of the chaos and darkness of the feudal past, and which they had violated and compromised to the point of absurdity even in their own corrupt minds?

Invisible Man 574

The Invisible Man does not merely lambast whites for their failure to live up to their ideals; he also places on the shoulders of blacks a national responsibility:

Or did he [the grandfather] mean that we had to take the responsibility for all of it, for the men as well as the principle, because we were the heirs who must use the principle because no other fitted our needs? Not for the power or for vindication, but because we, with the given circumstance of our origin, could only thus find transcendence.

Invisible Man 574

The notion that the African-American community—primarily because of the crime of slavery—is the natural inheritor of the founding principle whereby "All men are created equal" gives that community a particular aura which makes any leaning toward retaliation pointless. In fact, the situation in which the Invisible Man envisions the black community is beyond even Hegelian dialectic, since this is a situation in which the black community need not discover itself through confrontation with another:

Was it that we of all, we, most of all, had to affirm the principle, the plan
in whose name we had been brutalized and sacrificed—not because we
would always be weak nor because we were afraid or opportunistic, but
because we were older than they, in the sense of what it took to live in
the world with others and because they had exhausted in us, some—not
much, but some—of the human greed and smallness, yes, and the fear
and superstition that had kept them running.

Invisible Man 574

The words of the Invisible Man allow two possible interpretations. On the
one hand, these words are imbued with references to the myth of the Exodus, which from slavery to the Jim Crow era and beyond has helped African
Americans cope with the hardships of life, dream of freedom, and fantasize
about a return to their roots. The rhetoric of martyrdom (being "brutalized and
sacrificed"), antiquity (being older than whites), and experience (being forced
to coexist with other peoples—whites especially) is a clear reference to the
persecution of the Jews in Egypt and their triumphant return, under the guidance of Moses, to the Promised Land as a divinely elected people (a people
driven neither by "human greed and smallness" nor by "fear and superstition").
On the other hand, the words of the Invisible Man echo the words of Jean-
Paul Sartre in "Black Orpheus," a text Sartre wrote as a foreword to Léopold
Sédar Senghor's manifesto of Négritude, *Anthologie de la nouvelle poésie nègre
et malgache de langue française* (1948). In "Black Orpheus," Sartre establishes
a correspondence between suffering and responsibility, ascribing a Christ-like
consciousness to individuals of African descent:

To the absurd utilitarian agitation of the white man, the black man opposes the authenticity gained from his suffering; the black race is a chosen race because it has had the horrible privilege of touching the depths
of unhappiness. And even though these poems are anti-Christian from
beginning to end, one might call negritude a kind of Passion: the black
man who is conscious of himself sees himself as the man who has taken
the whole of human suffering upon himself and who suffers for all, even
for the white man.[77]

But one does not lead by suffering alone, and a bit later Sartre endows black
people with a mission to liberate all oppressed peoples across the world:

---

77   Jean-Paul Sartre, "Black Orpheus" ("Orphée Noire," 1948), tr. John MacCombie, *Massachu-
      setts Review* 6.1 (Autumn 1964–Winter 1965): 42–42.

> Previously, the Black man claimed his place in the sun in the name of ethnic qualities; now, he establishes his right to life on his mission; and this mission, like the proletariat's, comes to him from his historic position: because he has suffered from capitalistic exploitation more than all the others, he has acquired a sense of revolt and a love of liberty more than all the others. And because he is the most oppressed, he necessarily pursues the liberation of all, when he works for his own deliverance [...].
>
> "Black Orpheus" 47

Ellison did not share Sartre's communist sympathies, and he would not endorse the idea of the proletariat establishing a new world order, but he would not reject the idea that the black individual is destined to play the role of the prophet for others. This vision of self-emancipation as a catalyst for universal emancipation fits the scenario the Invisible Man has in mind for the United States—the achievement of individual freedom leads to political freedom for all. This view of blacks as the chosen people borders on black nationalism and supplements the Invisible Man's condemnation of "conformity" (577): i.e. the standardization of American society by white values and rules. But it also conflicts with the enduring myth of American exceptionalism—the belief that the United States is predestined to be a model nation that the rest of the world should emulate. In other words, the Invisible Man finds himself caught between black and American forms of exceptionalism, and he chooses neither one nor the other.

Falling into the manhole and living underground has made the Invisible Man realize that he has been kept outside reality—reality as devised by a white majority eager to keep the black minority at bay. The Invisible Man's self-imposed withdrawal is a variant of the Du Boisean veil, since a liability has been turned into a blessing once it has made African Americans more lucid, knowledgeable, and stronger in their efforts to confront racism. As the Invisible Man points out, "I'm invisible, not blind" (576). However, the metaphor of the veil presents race relations in a dialectical framework that the Invisible Man, eager to dodge the trap of ethnic clannishness, endeavors to transcend. W.E.B. Du Bois himself, through his theory of double-consciousness, implies that diversity and cultural cross-pollination benefit all Americans:

> The American Negro [...] does not wish to Africanize America, for America has too much to teach the world and Africa. He wouldn't bleach his Negro blood in a flood of white Americanism, for he knows that Negro blood has a message for the world. He simply wishes to make it possible for a man to be both a Negro and an American without being cursed and

spit upon by his fellows, without having the doors of opportunity closed roughly in his face.[78]

Du Bois's insistence that the "American Negro" should preserve his racial identity while being fully accepted as a citizen of the United States finds an echo in the words of the Invisible Man, but the latter pushes the theory toward a more practical application. Obviously, the postwar years of Ellison's career held more promise for African Americans than the early years of the century when Du Bois was developing his seminal reflection on what he called the "problem of the color line."[79] Hence, Ellison has his protagonist insist on the importance of playing his role as a citizen in US society, and the Invisible Man's strategy for achieving such a goal is to rely on "the principle" on which America was built, because this principle (universal equality) already guarantees to all citizens full and unconditional participation in the life of the nation. This is why the Invisible Man reverts to a national "we" toward the end of the epilogue, and this "we" does not suppose a passive, wait-and-see attitude but, rather, a wilful and self-assertive participation in the democratic debate on the national level. By the end of the epilogue, the Invisible Man summarizes what he went through and urges his white fellow citizens to cooperate across the color line, as this will eventually benefit the whole nation:

> So it is that now I denounce and defend, or feel prepared to defend. I condemn and affirm, say no and say yes, say yes and say no. I denounce because though implicated and partially responsible, I have been hurt to the point of abysmal pain, hurt to the point of invisibility. And I defend

---

78   William Edward Burghardt Du Bois, "The Souls of Black Folk" (1903), in Du Bois, *Writings: The Suppression of the African Slave-Trade / The Souls of Black Folk / Dusk of Dawn / Essays and Articles*, ed. Nathan Huggins (New York: Library of America, 1987): 365.

79   The civil rights movement did not start out unexpectedly with school desegregation (1954) and the Montgomery Bus Boycott (1955), and a few major steps were taken before 1952 when Ellison's *Invisible Man* came out. For instance, the National Association for the Advancement of Colored People (NAACP) was founded in 1909 with the help of W.E.B. Du Bois as a response to such setbacks as *Plessy v. Ferguson* (1896). The Harlem Renaissance of the 1920s helped nurture a black cultural identity while putting black arts and culture in the national spotlight. In 1941, President Franklin D. Roosevelt, pressured by the National Negro Congress president A. Philip Randolph, signed Executive Order 8802, which prohibited racial discrimination in the federal government and war industry. In 1946, President Harry S. Truman established, with limited success, the Committee on Civil Rights and, in 1948, desegregated the armed forces with Executive Order 9981. The previous year, Jackie Robinson had become the first black professional baseball player in the major leagues, and in 1950 the United Nations diplomat Ralph Bunche was the first individual of African extraction to be awarded the Nobel Peace Prize.

because in spite of all I find that I love. [...] I sell you no phony forgive-
ness, I'm a desperate man—but too much of your life will be lost, its
meaning lost, unless you approach it as much through love as through
hate. So I approach it through division. So I denounce and I defend and
I hate and I love.

Invisible Man 579

The loquacious Calhoun in *Middle Passage* is not so eloquent about his desire
to play his part as a citizen, and yet his professed patriotism can only be of the
same kind. Tellingly, Calhoun discovers his patriotic feelings after Falcon—a
bird of prey and a lesser version of the "old eagle"—is dead, as if the ruthlessness of Falcon, and by association that of the nation he embodies, had been
hiding the true nature and potential of the young republic. Calhoun's sexual im-
potence at the end of *Middle Passage* suggests that it will take time to get rid of
the corruption and restore the respectability of the republic. However, the fact
that Calhoun is rescued by a ship named the *Juno*—the Roman goddess of marriage, vital energy, and fertility, and the sovereignty of the people—augurs well.

In "What Does It Mean to Be an American," Sarah Song argues that the nation's "history of racial and ethnic exclusions has undercut the universalist
stance" implicit in the motto *E Pluribus Unum*.[80] Indeed, both Calhoun and the
Invisible Man, a century apart, experience *de facto* and *de jure* discrimination,
and yet they still want to believe in the universalist values their nation stands
for. Song, extending her description of Americans' attachment to their nation,
borrows Jürgen Habermas's notion of constitutional patriotism and writes:
"what binds citizens together is their common allegiance to the ideals embodied in a shared political culture."[81] The irony, of course, is that neither Calhoun
nor the Invisible Man is invited to partake in that political culture, and when
they decide, against the odds, to participate in national politics, they do so not
as representatives of their community but as full-fledged American citizens
and champions of American values and principles. Although constitutional
patriotism "de-ethnicizes citizenship by replacing cultural attachments, which
by definition are specific, by allegiance to institutions and symbols which are
potentially universalizable,"[82] it does not ignore the claims of minorities. Pauline Kleingeld describes what she calls civic patriotism[83]—a notion akin to

---

80   Sarah Song, "What Does It Mean to Be an American," *Daedalus* 138.2 (Spring 2009): 31.
81   Song, "What Does It Mean to Be an American," 32.
82   Cécile Laborde, "From Constitutional to Civic Patriotism," *British Journal of Political Sci-
      ence* 32.4 (October 2002): 596.
83   In "Kantian Patriotism" Pauline Kleingeld writes: "Civic patriotism is found in the tradi-
      tion of republicanism. The republican state (*res publica*, commonwealth) is regarded as

Song's definition of constitutional patriotism—as a system that welcomes criticism of "social and political practices" so long as such criticism "is intended to enhance the common political good by calling for reforms."[84] Kleingeld also invokes Habermas, citing his argument that civic patriotism "is compatible with ethnic and national pluralism, provided the ethnic and national traditions are not inimical to the ideals embodied in the political commonwealth."[85] This is the path that the Invisible Man has chosen to follow, and that Calhoun is bound to follow once he is back home.

The harsh criticism levelled at Ralph Ellison by some since the publication of *Invisible Man* may also be appreciated from this political angle. Ellison's creation of a character who fosters political cooperation and dialogue in the climate of racial discord of the 1950s was sure to incur the wrath of black intellectuals who pushed for the radicalization of the black movement across the nation; and such anger persisted unabated. At the dawn of the twenty-first century, in a rather scurrilous charge, Houston Baker wrote of Ellison's "philosophizing hibernation," arguing that Ellison "missed altogether the revolutionary possibilities of black life in America as they unfolded, even while his book was in page proofs."[86] Ellison's detractors seem to dislike the man and his work equally, and accuse him of being a sellout. Thus, in the opinion of Toni Morrison,

> the contemporary world of late twentieth century African Americans was largely inaccessible, or simply uninteresting to [Ellison] as a creator of fiction. For him, in essence, the eye, the gaze of the beholder remained white.[87]

For all their scrutinizing of African-American literary production, these keepers of the flame found fault with neither *Middle Passage* nor its author. Toni Morrison, whom Johnson had criticized for her concept of "empowerment

---

serving the common good of the citizens in the political sense. The citizens are regarded as free and equal (and, often, as male and propertied) individuals who are united in their pursuit of a common political good. Civic patriotism is the love of their shared political freedom and the institutions that sustain it"; Kleingeld, "Kantian Patriotism," *Philosophy and Public Affairs* 29.4 (Autumn 2000): 317. (Italics in the original).

84   Kleingeld, "Kantian Patriotism," 318.
85   "Kantian Patriotism," 318.
86   Houston A. Baker, Jr., "Failed Prophet and Falling Stock: Why Ralph Ellison Was Never Avant-Garde," *Stanford Humanities Review* 7.1 (Summer 1999): 8, 5.
87   Toni Morrison, letter to Arnold Rampersad, quoted in Rampersad, *Ralph Ellison: A Biography* (New York: Alfred A. Knopf, 2007): 575.

through literature"[88] and whose acclaimed *Beloved* he deemed a "middlebrow book,"[89] has never criticized *Middle Passage*. Arnold Rampersad, somewhat derisively, notes that Charles Johnson's acceptance speech on the occasion of the 1990 National Book Award for *Middle Passage* "seems to be one long tribute to Ralph."[90] And Houston Baker, so prompt to denounce black intellectuals who have lost their radical edge, mentions Johnson along with Julia Cooper, Carter G. Woodson, and Ida Wells-Barnett as "fellow travelers"[91] with W.E.B. Du Bois.

One may dismiss Calhoun's impassioned patriotic spiel as provocative, ironic, or simply circumstantial: any shipwreck survivor would yearn for home. But Calhoun knows that, in spite of Isadora's positive outlook, the life journey he is about to embark on is not going to be a pleasure-cruise. In terms of civic rights, he and Isadora will live on the margins of American society, and while such a status may have been enough for Calhoun when he measured his sense of freedom with respect to his independence and social invisibility, it will not agree with the ordinary life he is about to lead. Calhoun has renounced his individual liberty, for he knows that individual liberty, a founding principle of American democracy, becomes a myth as soon as the rule of law is not the same for all. His sudden patriotic enthusiasm is not merely an emotional response to a dire situation but a rational endeavor to replace individual freedom with political freedom. On the slave ship *Republic*, Calhoun was exposed to three faulty political systems based on the repression, elimination, or subjugation of others. Calhoun was offered invitations to join each of them, but always to the detriment of the two others. The life of a second-class citizen awaiting him back home is not much more enviable, and yet he chooses that life on the premise that the national rhetoric of *equality for all* has the potential to transcend such Manichean systems. Calhoun, like the Invisible Man, is not a revolutionary eager to overthrow those who hold power. Instead, he is pursuing the seemingly rash idea that the principles on which his nation was based can be enforced and respected. Whether the Calhouns and the Invisible Men of today's America have lost or won their battle remains a moot point. However, the fact that Ellison's critics failed to notice that Johnson's protagonist is, in terms of political

---

88   Charles Johnson, in Jonathan Little, "An Interview with Charles Johnson (1993)," 108, and in Sarah Robbins, "Gendering the History of the Antislavery Narrative: Juxtaposing *Uncle Tom's Cabin* and *Benito Cereno, Beloved* and *Middle Passage,*" *American Quarterly* 49.3 (September 1997): 532.

89   Charles Johnson, in Little, "An Interview with Charles Johnson (1993)," 106.

90   Arnold Rampersad, *Ralph Ellison: A Biography*, 574.

91   Houston A. Baker, Jr., *Betrayal: How Black Intellectuals Have Abandoned the Ideals of the Civil Rights Era* (New York: Columbia UP, 2010): 79.

orientation, patterned after Ellison's suggests that politics and race relations in the United States have evolved. "Who knows but that, on the lower frequencies," as the Invisible Man says in the final line of Ellison's novel, Calhoun is not speaking for all Americans?[92]

4   From Slave Trade Politics to a World Beyond

In Johnson's *Middle Passage*, the tragedy of the transatlantic slave trade becomes a backdrop for a reflection on such contemporary issues as identity politics, political ideologies, and patriotism. Although the tragicomic tone and adventure format of the narrative tend to make the sordidness of the slave trade recede into the background, Johnson successfully establishes a continuum between the slave trade era and our present world. The problems of inequality we face today were not born with the slave trade, but the slave trade exacerbated them. In addition to its paroxysms of cruelty and suffering, the slave trade was a global arena where intense commercial activities, massive financial investments, complex political and diplomatic maneuvers, and fierce ideological debates were taking place. In Europe, Africa, and America, the slave trade invaded every sector of the economy, every social class, and every area of life. Not surprisingly, some writers and philosophers of the Enlightenment began to imagine alternatives to the moral darkness, corruption, and extravagance into which their nations had cast themselves and those they exploited.[93]

---

92   The quotation in its full form reads: "Who knows but that, on the lower frequencies, I speak for you?" (579).

93   From the incoherence of John Locke, an investor and shareholder in the Royal African Company who thought that slavery "is so vile and miserable" that no Englishman "should plead for't"—Locke, *Two Treatises of Government*, ed. Peter Laslett (1689; Cambridge: Cambridge UP, 1988): 141 (Second Treatise)—to the contrast, in Diderot and D'Alembert's *Encyclopédie*, between the casuistry of the entry for the term *Nègre* and the wholesale condemnation, further on, of the slave trade as a "negotiation that violates all religion, morals, natural law, and human rights"—Louis, chevalier de Jaucourt, "Slave trade," in *The Encyclopedia of Diderot & d'Alembert Collaborative Translation Project*, tr. Stephanie Noble (Ann Arbor: University of Michigan Library, 2007); tr. of "Traite des nègres," *Encyclopédie ou Dictionnaire raisonné des sciences, des arts et des métiers*, vol. 16 (Paris, 1765): online (accessed 21 March 2018)—thinkers of the Enlightenment frequently contradicted each other and themselves on issues of race, the slave trade, and slavery. Emmanuel Chukwudi Eze, in his introduction to *Race and the Enlightenment* (1997), points out that "Enlightenment philosophy was instrumental in codifying and institutionalizing both the scientific and popular European perceptions of the human race"; Eze, "Introduction" to *Race and the Enlightenment: A Reader*, ed. Emmanuel Chukwudi Eze (1997; Oxford & Malden MA: Blackwell, 2005): 5. Conversely, this same "Enlightenment philosophy"

The fascination the crew of the *Republic* develops for the Allmuseri, as well as Calhoun's decision to embrace, against all odds, the democratic principles of his budding nation are part of this longing for a better world. Barry Unsworth's *Sacred Hunger* (1992), which is discussed in the next chapter, features a world of perfect racial and social equality. When the cargo and the crew of a slaver maroon themselves on the Atlantic coastline of Florida, they come together in order to survive in the wilderness, and they establish a settlement based on absolute personal and political freedom. The settlement—the brainchild of a utopian aristocrat—soon comes apart not because of race but because of a lack of political leadership and governing institutions, and an excess of personal ambition and greed. *Sacred Hunger* is the opportunity to go beyond the politics of the slave trade into the heart of community, for, although the individuals who compose the settlement come with completely different social and cultural backgrounds, they have no choice but to start from scratch, pull together, and agree on a set of basic rules to save themselves from perishing. They thus form, in spite of themselves, a primitive community—an experiment that allows us to dissect the notion of community and thereby dispel a number of misconceptions about what it means to live together.

---

promoted the ideal of the natural rights of man, which became a core argument for the abolition of the slave trade and, later, slavery.

CHAPTER 3

Community as Utopia: Barry Unsworth's *Sacred Hunger*

"White man, black man, all free man, all bradder, live tagedder dis place, all same boat."
"Same boat? [...] Dat de slaveboat you talkin' bout?"[1]

∴

Barry Unsworth's *Sacred Hunger* (1992) takes the reader from the bustling slave-trading port of Liverpool in 1752 to a small settlement hidden in the marshes of coastal Florida twelve years later. The settlement is a veritable experiment in social anthropology, as it harbors a small racially mixed community composed of the crew and captives of the slave ship *Liverpool Merchant*. Together, the sailors and their cargo have rebelled against and murdered the captain, Saul Thurso. The story of this settlement, which closes *Sacred Hunger*, is a unique opportunity to examine the making, development, and demise of a community born of the most unlikely collaboration.

In order to illuminate the complex system of human interactions that rule a community, this chapter sets out to untangle the roots of the settlement's failure. The first section focusses on the birth of the settlement, with particular emphasis on its founder, Delblanc, who, putting his radical theories of social justice to the test, will save his fellow survivors from both their hostile environment and themselves. This part goes on to measure Delblanc's political theories against those of such prominent social-contract theorists as Thomas Hobbes, John Locke, and Jean-Jacques Rousseau. While Rousseau's ideas about the perfectibility of man and the crucial role citizens play in enacting the "general will" are closest to those of Delblanc, Delblanc's community stands apart from any other political model of its time, especially as its institutions are minimized. This weak political structure, which stems from Delblanc's distrust of authority, will eventually impair the efficiency of the community.

The vulnerability of the community is at the heart of the second section of this chapter, which demonstrates how discontented members of the

---

1 Barry Unsworth, *Sacred Hunger*, 578. Further page references are in the main text.

community undermine its organization and values. By contrasting Delblanc's vision of a world that is not defined by money, property, or class and a world of free enterprise in which individuals compete for wealth and dominance— a theme that connects the slave trade to Unsworth's own engagement with the neoliberal ideology of the Thatcher years—*Sacred Hunger* suggests that private and collective interests often conflict, thus hindering the flowering of community.

The following section traces the genealogy of modernity in order to understand the ideological and political branchings linking the slave trade and the globalized, free-market world we live in. Starting from the early stages of the industrial revolution, signified in *Sacred Hunger* by the tragic downfall of William Kemp, the hapless underwriter and shipowner of the *Liverpool Merchant*, and the rise to prominence of his son, the banking and sugar industry magnate Erasmus Kemp, and moving on through time and space, from plantation slavery to wage slavery, and between Europe, America, and the colonized world, this part exposes the inconsistency between the Enlightenment's promotion of democratic principles and its incapacity, or perhaps reluctance, to apply these principles on a universal scale. Early responses to the blatant injustices of the so-called Age of Reason took the form of utopian writings and experiments. Soon, new political theories emerged, offering alternatives that often proved unreliable because they were entangled in the same ideological framework that organized the social and cultural beliefs and practices they meant to reform. This meandering through the philosophical and political foundations of modernity suggests that the possibility of change can only be envisaged through a return to basic human interaction, even before philosophical and political values shape the way we relate to our life in the community.

The fundamental nature of community, as the recent theories of such thinkers as Roberto Esposito and Jean-Luc Nancy show, entails more than pertinent political choices and a grand pledge of collective solidarity. Building on Nancy's contention that "there is no common being, but [...] being *in* common,"[2] Esposito argues that a community is not a "wider subjectivity"[3] within which each individual forges his/her identity in opposition to an outsider. Focussing on the Latin root *munus* (debt, gift, duty) of *communitas*, Esposito demonstrates that the essence of a community inheres in alterity, for "what predominates in the *munus*," he argues, is "reciprocity or 'mutuality' [...] of giving that assigns

---

2   Jean-Luc Nancy, "Of Being-in-Common," in Nancy, *Community at Loose Ends*, ed. Miami Theory Collective (Minneapolis: U of Minnesota P, 1991): 4.
3   Roberto Esposito, *Communitas: The Origin and Destiny of Community*, tr. Timothy Campbell (*Communitas: origine e destino della comunità*, 1998; Stanford CA: Stanford UP, 2009): 2.

the one to the other in an obligation."[4] This necessary openness to the other and its attendant relinquishment of the self, this chapter concludes, is bound to incite some community members to "immunize" themselves against the rest of the community, thus prefiguring the downfall thereof.

1   Birth and Organization of the Settlement

One would expect the captain's death on the *Liverpool Merchant* to be followed by a bloodbath, but the antagonism between the white crew and the black captives is circumstantial only—both groups were brought aboard the slave ship to fulfill their respective roles of oppressor and oppressed. Influenced both by the humanity of the surgeon, freethinker, and evolutionist Matthew Paris and by the spectacle of their respective suffering at the hands of Captain Thurso, crew and captives have found frequent opportunities to express mutual sympathy and to demonstrate mutual solidarity. But other determining events, which occurred in the wake of the insurrection, have helped lay the foundations of the community.

Some of these events are quite fortuitous. For instance, the captain's decision to throw ailing captives overboard in order to claim insurance money spurs Paris to interfere and spark the uprising.[5] Another determining event

---

4   Esposito, *Communitas*, 5.
5   Captain Thurso's jettisoning of the sick in order to collect an insurance payment is a direct evocation of the infamous *Zong* massacre. In November 1781, the captain of the slave ship *Zong*, Luke Collingwood, decided to throw 142 sick captives overboard when he realized that insurers would not compensate him for their natural death. The case was taken to court and Collingwood invoked a shortage of water to justify his decision. The case became a *cause célèbre*; it boosted the abolitionist movement, and the English artist J.M.W. Turner, after reading of it in Thomas Clarkson's *The History and Abolition of the Slave Trade* (1808), immortalized it in *The Slave Ship* (1840). Recently, the story of the *Zong* was the topic of Fred D'Aguiar's *Feeding the Ghosts* (1997) and M. NourbeSe Philip's *Zong!* (2008). It lies also at the heart of Ian Baucom's *Specters of the Atlantic*, which explores the rise of finance capitalism in eighteenth-century England. According to Baucom, the *Zong* trials "constitute an event in the history of capital not because they treat slaves as commodities but because they treat slaves as commodities that have become the subject of insurance, treat them [...] not as objects to be exchanged but as the 'empty bearers' of an abstract, theoretical, but entirely real quantum of value, treat them as little more than promissory notes, bills-of-exchange, or some other markers of a 'specie value,' treat them as suppositional entities whose value is tied not to their continued, embodied, material existence but to their speculative, recoverable loss value. The *Zong* trials constitute an event not because they further subject the world to the principle of exchange but because they subject it to the hegemony of that which superordinates exchange: the general equivalents of finance capital"; Baucom, *Specters of the Atlantic: Finance Capital, Slavery and the Philosophy of History* (Durham NC: Duke UP, 2005): 139.

is the secret expedition of the first mate, Barton, and the boatswain, Haines, to the ship, de-masted and beached a few miles away from the group's initial encampment, to retrieve two bags of gold-dust that the captain had taken with him. Only Barton returns, with two empty bags and the story of how Haines was caught and scalped by Indians—a blood-curdling story that, in these early times of chaos and death, will persuade all of them to stick together for survival. As decisive as these events may be, so, too, is the capacity of some members to channel the energies of others toward developing an esprit de corps.

Paris, the central character in the novel, is a respected individual in the settlement: in addition to triggering the insurrection, he provides medical care to all, black and white, both during and in the aftermath of the Middle Passage. But, for all his charisma and empathy, Paris is unable to take a prescient view of the future of the community. It is another figure, Delblanc, who will be the architect of the settlement. Paris first meets Delblanc at a slave factory on the coast of West Africa. Initially distrustful of Delblanc's aristocratic lineage, Paris soon befriends the "reckless" but "generous-hearted man [...] accountable to no one and free to follow the promptings of his nature" (334). Delblanc is an unbridled version of Paris: he sneers at the hypocrisy of the Church, the ignominy of the private company running the factory, and the worship of money and profit—that "sacred hunger" (328) at the root of the transatlantic slave trade, in which both he and Paris, their enlightened views notwithstanding, are complicit. Both men typify the Age of Reason, but their life circumstances have prompted them to respond very differently to the world they inhabit.

Paris has accepted his uncle William Kemp's offer to be the surgeon on his ship, the *Liverpool Merchant*, in the vain hope of evading his traumatic past: he was once pilloried and then imprisoned for his evolutionary beliefs, which led to his wife's miscarriage and her premature death. Delblanc, by contrast, sees his passage from Africa to the New World as an opportunity: he is free of the slave factory, its chicaneries, and its corrupt governor. Furthermore, Delblanc is unburdened by his past, and eager to promote his views:

> He had espoused theories of liberty and equality, as many do who feel they have made no mark on the world; but these had been diluted in society at large and by his own diffidence.
>
> *Sacred Hunger* 373

However, Delblanc's boarding of the *Liverpool Merchant* is going to be a catalyst, for he finds in the slave ship "a world reduced, concentrated, the perfect model of a tyranny" (373), against which he can deploy, as Paris writes in his journal, "his arguments in defence of untrammelled liberty and the natural goodness of the heart" (334). Borrowing Locke's argument on innate knowledge,[6] Delblanc tries to convince the skeptical Paris that people can be changed: "If ideas are not innate [...] they cannot be so deeply lodged as to be beyond uprooting, [and] [i]t is only a question of supplanting one set of associations with another" (374). Man, Delblanc concludes, "can live free and not seek to limit the freedom of others so long as no one seeks to limit his" (374). Undeterred by Paris's skepticism, Delblanc then turns to the illiterate but deferential crew, and tries to make converts by addressing, for instance, the simple-minded Calley thus: "By nature we are equal. [...] Does it not therefore follow that government must always depend on the consent of the governed?" (375). Whether such arguments have any impact on the crew and whether Delblanc means to foment a rebellion is debatable, but Delblanc's enthusiasm and convictions eventually help the community survive and grow.

Delblanc's settlement is organized around egalitarian principles of political consensus and shared economic resources. All the huts in the compound are built on the same model and enclosed in a stockade: property is reduced to the minimum and social hierarchies erased. Furthermore, as female survivors are much fewer than male survivors, the community is polyandrous—a rule some men are not easily reconciled to. As for children, they belong to everyone, which may be a way of dissuading either tribal resurgence or paternity claims and conflict between men sharing a woman. Delblanc also institutes the use of the "beck-man," a stick that gives its holder the right to talk during palavers. With Paris, the community even has a competent doctor; and Jimmy, the former ship "linguister," becomes a schoolteacher particularly keen on fostering not only civic responsibility but also collective memory, for the creation of a communal mythology will prove essential to strengthening the sense of unity among the members of this fragile community.

After Hughes, the community's solitary tree-climber, spots a canoe with three Indian prisoners guarded by four men—two blacks and two whites—Delblanc convinces Paris and the rest of the settlement to organize a raid in order to liberate the Indians, who, there is no doubt in the minds of most community members, have been captured to be sold into slavery. The decision to go after the captors is resolved during the first communal debate of the settlement—a moment no one forgets:

---

6   Locke's argument that the term 'idea' "stands for whatsoever is the Object of the Understanding, when a man thinks"—*An Essay Concerning Human Understanding*, ed. Peter H. Nidditch (1689; Oxford: Oxford UP, 1979), Book II, 47—implies that individuals get their ideas from experience and that, in consequence, their ideas will change if their experience is different. Hence Delblanc's belief that "any people, any nation or group, [can] change their condition immediately and radically by changing their habits of mind" (*Sacred Hunger*, 374).

> Everyone who had been present—and that was all of the fugitives, men and women, black and white, who had survived the voyage and the landing and the hardships of the first week—knew that the actions stemming from this debate had saved the settlement.
>
> *Sacred Hunger* 514

For most individuals in the settlement, the necessity of punishing slave traders is plain, and a vital security issue: what if they come back for us some day? And so a posse is organized to track them down. As the posse draws nearer, a group of six men, racially balanced, is selected for the final assault. After the successful operation, the Indians are taken to the settlement, still roped, and finally liberated in front of everybody during an official ceremony. The dramatization and solemnity of the Indians' liberation does more than enhance the unity of the community: three days later, an Indian delegation visits the settlement, offers gifts, and implicitly accepts the presence of the newcomers on their land. They also show the settlers how to make flour from the local koonti plant, which will become their staple food, guaranteeing their survival in this inhospitable environment.

Another milestone in the growth of the settlement is the execution of Wilson, a member of the community who broke the established rule of polyandry by killing the black man with whom he shared a woman. Wilson's execution is not only public, it is also carried out, at Delblanc's instigation, by everybody, so as to show "the black people that their lives were valuable to the white people" (548). To the children, the execution of Wilson is presented as justice: "It was justice, it was all the people showing how much they hated this crime. Killing was justice when everybody joined in" (548). But the reader knows more than the children do, and this justified violence has a deeper origin. Indeed, Wilson was among those who would not go after the slave traders to free the Indians and thus, after the murder of his woman's other partner, he becomes the ideal victim, the bad apple or, as René Girard puts it in *Violence and the Sacred*, "the single 'polluted' enemy who is contaminating the rest."[7] This search for a scapegoat, according to Girard, typifies "[a]ny community that has fallen prey to violence or has been stricken by some overwhelming catastrophe."[8] Wilson is slaughtered and left rotting in his ropes for two days for everyone to see. This spectacular shedding of blood has the effect of appeasing other community members' thirst for violence: it works as a stabilizer for the community. And in

---

7　René Girard, *Violence and the Sacred*, tr. Patrick Gregory (*La violence et le sacré*, 1972; Baltimore MD: Johns Hopkins UP, 1979): 67.

8　Girard, *Violence and the Sacred*, 65.

this particular case, as Delblanc's remark above makes clear, it is a significant step toward taking race out of the equation and strengthening group cohesion. This is also why the memory of Wilson, paradoxically, is respected. As the narrator notes, Wilson, the murderer who was sacrificed, and Haines, the betrayer who was scalped alive, are "the martyrs and the founding fathers of the community" (541).

Relative harmony reigns in the settlement: children are born out of polyandrous households, blacks and whites form ties of diverse kinds, and the law, administered in the form of a strictly organized council, successfully arbitrates disputes. Delblanc's dream of a republic, where people live "free and equal in a state of nature" (541), is taking shape. Aside from its rudimentary court of justice where everyone can judge and be judged, the settlement is a stateless society with neither legislative nor executive institutions, let alone an elected leader. A few charismatic individuals may hold sway over some of their peers, but it remains a non-hierarchical society, where money and private ownership have been banished. There is no explicit rule of the redistribution of wealth, either, but everyone, through all kinds of bartering, seems to have found his or her place in society. And although Delblanc dies long before he can fully appreciate the fruits of his efforts, community members seem happy with their lot.

Delblanc's belief that, "if constraint and coercion can once be removed, [men] will be happy, and if they are happy they will also be good" (617) reflects some contemporary ideas, including those of the sentimentalist Francis Hutcheson, who defined moral sense as "the general calm desire of the happiness of others."[9] However, a more revealing way of probing the workings of Delblanc's "infant republic" (516) is to compare it to those envisaged in the social-contract theories of Hobbes, Locke, and Rousseau. Central to the work of these three is the concept of the state of nature, which considers mankind before the establishment of society, and their endeavor to understand how governments are born. Whether these prominent contractualists believed that life in a state of nature was once a reality, or whether they simply used the concept as a working hypothesis, they all lived in nation-states with well-established laws and institutions; none of them ever experienced life in a state of nature.[10]

---

9   Francis Hutcheson, *An Essay On the Nature and Conduct of the Passions and Affections, with Illustrations on the Moral Sense*, ed. Aaron Garrett (1742; Indianapolis IN: Liberty Fund, 2002): 31–32.

10   Of these three prominent contractualists, only Locke seems to have considered the "state of nature" as more than a tool for analysis, as he imagines the New World as a place of sheer abundance where every individual may claim ownership over whichever piece of land they decide to cultivate for their own personal needs: "For supposing a Man, or Family, in the state they were at first peopling of the World by the Children of *Adam*, or *Noah*;

The same goes for Delblanc until the mutiny, and the beaching of the *Liverpool Merchant* appears to have created, *ex nihilo*, a situation where a small group of survivors find themselves in a state of nature, as it were. It is there, in the wilderness of coastal Florida, that Delblanc sees the opportunity "to test his theories, vindicate man's natural goodness in this dream of a community living without constraint of government or corruption or money" (536).

Life in the immediate aftermath of the mutiny is reminiscent of a Hobbesian state of nature—a state of war in which "every man is enemy to every man" and lives in "continual fear and danger of violent death."[11] In the state of nature, "the life of man [is] solitary, poor, nasty, brutish, and short";[12] thus, Hobbes concludes, men had better live under the authority of a sovereign who guarantees their protection and saves them from the state of nature, in which there is no liberty whatsoever. It may be argued that the laws limit subjects' freedom, but the subjects, Hobbes argues, have consented, by contract, to surrender their rights to the sovereign; thus, so long as the subjects are not in chains, they are free.[13] By claiming that the subjects are bound to the contract out of pragmatic self-interest, Hobbes implies that they are responsible for whatever befalls them, while also exculpating the sovereign of any abuse of power. Hobbes's claim that liberty—i.e. emancipation from the state of nature—is achieved by a contract is antipodal to Delblanc's vision of a community without a ruler or hierarchy of any sort.

Locke, in contrast to Hobbes, sees the state of nature as one of complete freedom, equality, and abundance, in which reasonable men are bound by mutual love. While Delblanc shares Locke's confidence in the capacity of men to live together in harmony, he does not share his advocacy of property rights. In the second of his *Two Treatises of Government* (1689), Locke states that "every

---

let him plant in some in-land, vacant places of *America*, we shall find that the *Possessions* he could make himself, upon the *measures* we have given, would not be very large, nor, even to this day, prejudice the rest of Mankind, or give them reason to complain, or think themselves injured by this Man's Incroachment, though the Race of Men have now spread themselves to all the corners of the World, and do infinitely exceed the small number [which] was at the beginning"; John Locke, *Two Treatises of Government*, ed. Peter Laslett (1689; Cambridge: Cambridge UP, 1988): 293 (Second Treatise). Locke's positive outlook on the wilderness, however, will not encourage European colonists to idealize Native Americans, whom they will expropriate, persecute, or, in the case of resistance, decimate.

11   Thomas Hobbes, *Leviathan*, ed. Edwin Curley (1651; Indianapolis IN: Hackett, 1994): 76.

12   Hobbes, *Leviathan*, 76.

13   For Hobbes, to be free under sovereign power means that one can act according to one's will without being physically hindered: "a free man is he that in those things which by his strength and wit he is able to do is not hindered to do what he has a will to" (*Leviathan*, 136).

Man has a Property in his own Person,"[14] and by mixing his labor with something from nature, he "makes it his Property."[15] Mindful that the munificence of nature is not infinite, and that the kind of appropriation of natural resources he envisions will lead to inequalities and strife among men, Locke adds the following caveat:

> As much as any one can make use of to any advantage of life before it spoils; so much he may by his labour fix a Property in. Whatever is beyond this, is more than his share, and belongs to others. Nothing was made by God for Man to spoil or destroy.
>
> *Two Treatises of Government* 290

Finally, Locke argues that there would be plenty for all, "had not the Invention of Money, and the tacit Agreement of Men to put a value on it, introduced (by Consent) larger Possessions, and a Right to them."[16]

Delblanc's anticlerical feelings[17] suggest that he would be less inclined than Locke to invoke any sort of divine ascendancy over men, but he no doubt agrees with Locke that men should use only what they need from nature and share the rest; and he agrees with Locke about the dangers of money, too, since he intends to ban money from his ideal community. The Lockean influence on Delblanc, however, remains limited because of the importance the philosopher places on the individual, which runs contrary to Delblanc's conception of a community that prioritizes collective over personal interests. Historically, the Lockean emphasis on the individual has been praised for playing a role in the constitutional development of the United States of America; but it has also been decried for fostering greed and thwarting commitment to the community. C.B. Macpherson calls this precedence of individual liberties over civic responsibilities "possessive individualism." Macpherson argues that it is at the core of liberalism in its crudest manifestation and that it should be reformed.[18] Locke could not have foreseen that his ideas of individuals as proprietors of

---

14   John Locke, *Two Treatises of Government*, 287.

15   Locke, *Two Treatises of Government*, 288.

16   *Two Treatises of Government*, 293.

17   Back at the factory in Africa, the black chaplain argues that Africans should worship the Christian god of the slave owners, since it is that very god who has "endowed us [Africans] with this respect for the powerful" (*Sacred Hunger*, 318). Delblanc politely but firmly rebuffs the chaplain: "Christ spoke to the wretched and powerless as one of them, did he not? I have always understood that the Christian religion was spread among slaves" (318).

18   Macpherson's opinion is uncompromising with regard to the type of liberalism that Locke's celebration of individual liberty has led to: "The repair that was needed was one that would bring back a sense of the moral worth of the individual, and combine it again with a sense of the moral value of community, which had been present in some measure

their own person, and of whatever they acquired through labor, would lead to excessive accumulation and destroy men's propensity to live together and share their resources. But other thinkers of the Enlightenment, such as Rousseau, were more perspicacious in sensing the dangers that private property represented for humanity.

Rousseau, whose *Discourse on the Origin and Basis of Inequality Among Men* (1754) came out more than six decades after Locke's *Two Treatises*, was more prescient than the latter in sensing the dangers that private property represented for humanity. Since the *Discourse* was written more than a year after the birth of the community in *Sacred Hunger*, Delblanc could not have read it; yet he would have concurred with Rousseau that the desire to dominate leads to the "destruction of equality" among men, which, in turn, leads to violence and chaos:

> the usurpations by the rich, the acts of brigandage by the poor, the unbridled passions of all, stifling natural pity and the still weak voice of justice, made man greedy, ambitious, and wicked.[19]

Emerging societies, Rousseau continues,

> gave way to the most horrible state of war; since the human race, vilified and desolated, was no longer able to retrace its steps or give up the unfortunate acquisitions it had made, and since it labored only toward its shame by abusing the faculty that honor is, it brought itself to the brink of its ruin.
>
> *Discourse on the Origin of Inequality* 55

And so laws were born,

> destroy[ing] natural liberty, establish[ing] forever the law of property and of inequality, chang[ing] adroit usurpation into an irrevocable right, and for the profit of a few ambitious men henceforth subjected the entire human race to labor, servitude and misery.
>
> *Discourse on the Origin of Inequality* 57

---

in the Puritan and Lockean theory"; Macpherson, *The Political Theory of Possessive Individualism: Hobbes to Locke* (1962; Oxford: Oxford UP, 2011): 2.

19   Jean-Jacques Rousseau, *Discourse on the Origin of Inequality*, tr. Donald A. Cress, intro. James Miller (1754; *Discours sur l'origine et les fondements de l'inégalité parmi les hommes*, Pléiade ed. 1965; Indianapolis IN: Hackett, 1992): 55. Further page references are in the main text.

Rousseau's scenario of the evolution of mankind is rather bleak, but it is not entirely pessimistic; for, while civil society has corrupted the natural goodness of mankind, the latter may nonetheless improve. Rousseau believes in the "perfectibility" (26) of mankind, and this is the one idea that Delblanc shares in full with him, since the latter's community is based on the premise that, given the right circumstances, people can change. What distinguishes Rousseau from Delblanc, however, is that Rousseau has never actually imagined a group of men harmoniously living together in the wild. He has never idealized primitive life, and his proverbial "noble savage" has never been more than a concept to assist in understanding this world. Rousseau does believe that man is social by nature, but the disposition of man to reason and sociability must be properly channeled to create a better world. In order to create such a world, Rousseau envisions a society in which individuals relinquish their rights to "the whole community" (15), which he calls the "sovereign" (16). In this system, the role of the government is to unite the people under the "general will" (18) and make laws for the "public good" (103). Such a system implies a direct and very active involvement of all community members. It also means that the "individual will" yields to the will of the "sovereign," and that freedom is achieved collectively through participation in the process that controls and regulates the community.

Freedom, in the Rousseauvian sense, does not mean a complete absence of control from external forces (e.g., the government). Rather, freedom is achieved by a set of rules that individuals have instituted for themselves. This is perhaps the sticking point between Rousseau's and Delblanc's concepts of freedom and community. For the former, freedom is civic freedom: the individual fulfills himself or herself through the social contract (which he or she helps create) and within the community. For the latter, freedom is freedom from political, social, and economic control. There is no social contract in Delblanc's community, because it is assumed to be an ideal environment from which all the wrongs of his mid-eighteenth-century world (greed, social disparities, political corruption, etc.) have been eradicated. Unlike Delblanc, Rousseau does not start with a blank slate; he stays in the realm of theory. Rousseau devises an ideal society in which he hopes to preserve man in his primitive state.[20]

---

20   Robert Derathé explains that Rousseau's "natural man" designates both a brute (i.e. a savage who lives in a state of nature) and a man who lives in society. This natural man is opposed to civil man, and civil man is either a bourgeois or a citizen. For Rousseau, the bourgeois is a superficial, conceited individual, who "can only live in the opinion of others"; Derathé, *Jean-Jacques Rousseau et la science politique de son temps* (Paris: Librairie Philosophique Vrin, 2000): 50. As for the citizen, he has also been "denatured" by social institutions, in that he does not live in a state of nature any longer; but he is less cor-

Such a man is characterized not only by his capacity for compassion and for-giveness but also by his inclination to share and be with others. Every society, Rousseau argues in *Émile* (1762), "must choose between making a man or a citizen," and the best "social institutions are those that best know how to denature man, to take his absolute existence from him in order to give him a relative one and transport the *I* into the common unity."[21] This surrendering of the *I* (the individual will) to the will of the community is what Delblanc, to some extent, has achieved; but his little world is very fragile, if only because it is not based on a social contract. In the microcosm of the settlement, common rule is tacit rather than agreed. Individual commitment to the group is voluntary rather than compulsory; and, in consequence, it is binding only in principle. The social contract requires from the constituents that they cede some of their rights to a sovereign, or a governing body; but Delblanc, because of his aversion to authority, has refused to establish a system in which the freedom of the individual is subordinated to that of the community. In his dogged pursuit of absolute freedom, Delblanc overlooks the simple fact that the freedom of the individual and of the group are inextricably interdependent, and that the latter can only be achieved to the detriment of the former. This delicate negotiation between individual and collective freedom will upset the precarious balance of the young community.

2   **The Fall of the Settlement**

The prologue to *Sacred Hunger* features Luther Sawdust, an old eccentric mulatto beggar, once a plantation slave, whom the New Orleans riverfront crowd has nicknamed the "Paradise Nigger" because he rambles on about a Liverpool ship, a white father, and "a childhood of wonders in a place of eternal sunshine, jungle hummocks, great flocks of white birds rising from flooded savannahs, [and] a settlement where white and black lived together in perfect accord" (1). The Paradise Nigger is none other than Kenka, the son Matthew Paris had with Tabakali, a Fulani woman who survived the Middle Passage and the chaos of the early days in Florida. Kenka was still a child when captured and sold into slavery by Erasmus Kemp (now the rightful owner of the *Liverpool Merchant*

---

rupt than the bourgeois, because virtuous laws and institutions have elevated him toward more noble sentiments. Thus, the man whom Rousseau wants for his ideal society (man in his primitive state) can be defined in opposition both to the brute and to the bourgeois.

21   Jean-Jacques Rousseau, *Émile, or On Education*, tr. Allan Bloom (*Émile, ou De l'éducation*, 1762; New York: Basic Books, 1979): 39, 40.

and its cargo), but Kenka hasn't forgotten the blissful years of his early childhood. Many adults in the settlement, black and white, must also have found contentment in a way of life that affords them unhoped-for respect and well-being. Paris is certainly one of them, as this new life, far from the opprobrium that ruined him, is a form of redemption. Other community members, however, do not feel better-off. Delblanc's egalitarian principles have become a hurdle for the more ambitious among them, and discontent with the status quo has been growing by the time Erasmus and a small contingent of redcoats storm the settlement.

After surviving the chaos of the early days, the settlement achieves self-sufficiency, but it does not thrive. Entrepreneurs within the community are growing frustrated, and some of them have already expanded their business beyond the confines of the surrounding marshes. The development of commercial activities beyond the settlement should augur well for the small community; but Paris is concerned about "the growth of trading partnerships and the increasing rivalry and secrecy of their operations" (533). Such men, including the successful traders Tongman and Kireku, break the tacit rule of equal property by building another hut for business outside the stockade. This quest for self-advancement leads to competition, marking the emergence of a free-trade spirit amidst a society based on the very eradication thereof. Historically, the system of a free-market economy has been perceived as either a conduit to individual freedom and self-realization or an impediment to cooperation and altruism. The mounting tension between merchants and egalitarians in the settlement reflects these opposite perceptions of a free-market economy, and a quarrel finally breaks out on the occasion of the so-called Iboti trial—the first big affair to shake the political foundations of the settlement.

The elements of the Iboti trial seem rather banal at first. Hambo, a man of the Shantee tribe, has accused Iboti, a simple-minded man from the Bulum tribe, of witchcraft. If proven guilty, Iboti will no doubt forfeit his right to see Arifa, the woman they share. But there is more than a simple sex case behind the legal action. In fact, Hambo has business dealings with two other Shantee tribesmen, Kireku and Danka. As for Danka, he has been trading with Tongman, a respected individual who is not a Shantee and who may be an obstacle to Shantee's influence in the settlement and commercial networks. Tongman is not only a fierce competitor but also a skillful orator, and, sensing that the Iboti case has something to do with business competition, he has decided to assume Iboti's defense. It is what the prosecution is suing for that poses a moral problem: should Hambo win his case, he will make Iboti his slave for three years, a practice no one except Paris objects to. The community is unaware that setting a legal precedent can pave the way for a custom. In the end, the charismatic Tongman proves Iboti innocent, and the prosecution is exposed for what it is: a Shantee conspiracy.

Two lessons can be learned from the Iboti trial. The first is that people in the settlement are split along tribal and racial lines, despite Delblanc's efforts during the building phase of the community to eliminate such differences. The Shantee tribesmen, in addition to forming a "phalanx of power" (568) at the trial in order to extend their influence, also begin "to claim their male children" (503), which runs counter to the custom of partible paternity in effect in the settlement. Arguably, the fading of collective consciousness is facilitated by the very political structure of the community—a headless polity. The second lesson to be learned from the Iboti trial is that greed lies behind this sordid affair of witchcraft. Confirming Rousseau's argument—that early man's frantic race to accumulate wealth led to conflict and the creation of special rights and privileges for the rich—the power-hungry individuals who try to set up Iboti find it perfectly reasonable to manipulate the law, so as to circumvent the principles of solidarity that have been governing life in the settlement, because such principles frustrate their efforts to improve their lot.

A few hours after Iboti's acquittal, Paris pays a visit to Kireku, the most successful of the Shantee merchants, who has not only developed "trade links [...] to the north [and] with the sea-going Indians who [carry] dried fish and heron plumes and freshwater pearls to the Spanish islands" (522), but has also made James Barton, formerly Thurso's first officer on the *Liverpool Merchant*, his lackey. Paris hopes that Kireku will reason with Hambo about the risks of normalizing servitude. Paris fears that "in the course of time, the people would come to believe that a term of servitude was fitting punishment" (568). And he is all the more concerned that Iboti was targeted because, in Kireku's words, "Iboti got brain of de bird, not got the wing" (577). What would happen to the settlement, Paris wonders,

> if it became accepted among them that a man's weakness or stupidity or simply his poverty was reason enough for that man to be made the possession of another and forced to do that other's bidding?
>
> *Sacred Hunger* 577

Paris deems Kireku "a man of sense and experience [who] would know that once a thing became customary it soon came to be regarded as lawful and was then extremely difficult to root out" (577). But Paris does not anticipate Kireku's highly rational but also scathing response.

First, Kireku invokes racial differences to tell Paris that he owes him nothing: "'Man born me I favour dat man, no madder what, but you no born me, you buckra white man come off slaveship'" (578). Paris tries rather clumsily to dismiss the race argument: "'White man, black man, all free man, all bradder, live tagedder dis place, all same boat'" (578). This unfortunate remark gives Kireku all the arguments he needs to set the record straight: "'Dat de slaveboat you talkin' bout? [...] Hear [Barton] laff, heh, heh? [...] Barton, he sabee when to laff'" (578). Kireku then shows the brand mark on his chest and comments:

> Barton do dis [...] Barton put hot iron, burn me. How ken he do dat? I tell
> you. It cause Barton strong pas' me dat time. Now Barton my man, fetch
> dis, carry dat. He no do it I kick him arse. Dat de same boat?
>
> *Sacred Hunger* 578

Two simple but significant ideas stem from Kireku's argument; both are a denial of Delblanc's theory that human beings, given the right conditions, can change and create a world of harmony and equality. The first idea is that a person can never recover from the traumas of the past: Kireku cannot, and will not, act as if the Middle Passage had never taken place, and the branding scars on his chest are a constant reminder of this. The other one is that, put simply, the wheel of fortune goes round and round: first mate Barton is now at Kireku's beck and call, and this role reversal is evidence that Kireku has turned the tables on Barton and, at least symbolically, on the system that had once turned him into a commodity.

Kireku rejects Paris's argument that God's hand brought them all there in order to give them "'de chance put ting altagedder right agin'" (579). In Kireku's opinion, Paris is the one who needs a second chance, because of his participation in the slave trade:

> I no panyar people from house put slavemark on dem, take for sell. You
> de one do dat. You tink one mind belong all us here, dat mind same-same
> you mind. Why you tink I belong you idea right-wrong? I tell you why, Pa-
> ree. It cause you tink you clever pas' me, you think you idea right-wrong
> strong pas' my idea.[22]
>
> *Sacred Hunger* 579

---

22   Rebecca Shumway defines and puts the term *panyar* in perspective: "A common term in the eighteenth-century literature regarding the Gold Coast, *to panyar* literally means to seize or capture. [...] In the days of the Portuguese monopoly on the coast (c.1470–1630), the term *penhóràr* would have been used by Portuguese observers to describe the local African practice whereby a creditor could temporarily detain a person or 'pawn' from a debtor's

Kireku's confrontational mindset reflects his understanding of human relationships, whether in the world of business, a court of law, or a heated discussion, as above. And Kireku makes clear that the peculiar experience of the
settlement does not set it apart from any other experience:

> You tink dis speshul place but it altageddar same adder place. Iboti, Cal-
> lee, Libbee, dese men slave, you no change dat never. Go look for Iboti
> now, where you find him? Find him Tongman field, workin' for Tongman.
>
> *Sacred Hunger* 579

In other words, the acquittal of Iboti did not really change Iboti's fate, which
seems to lend credence to Kireku's argument that some men are meant to be
dominated, while others are meant to dominate. This is a rather blunt opinion on the part of someone who, just a few years back, had been reduced to
the most abject level of humanity. But this is also how Kireku can justify his
support of free trade. Paris does not deny that some men are more gifted than
others and will inevitably rise to the top; but without solidarity, Paris tells
Kireku, powerful men will end up destroying one another and eventually the
whole community. This is Paris's last salvo; Kireku decries it with an argument
worthy of the trickle-down theory emanating from Milton Friedman and the
Chicago School and typifying the neoliberal policies espoused by the group of
economists advising Britain's Thatcher administration in the 1980s:

> Now I here I fight for place. Strong man get rich, him slave get rich. Strong
> man make everybody rich. Everybody dis place happy an' rich come from
> trade. Some man not free, nevermind, buggerit, trade free. Dis palaver
> finish now. Barton, take Paree show him way along.
>
> *Sacred Hunger* 581

The resonance between Kireku's rhetoric and the resurgence of laissez-faire
economic liberalism in the decade preceding the publication of *Sacred Hunger*

household as collateral for repayment of a debt. The practice of pawnship—common
throughout Atlantic Africa—was a carefully regulated institution through which a trader
handed over family members or other dependents to be held as a sort of collateral in
the advance of credit. [...] By the eighteenth century, however, European accounts of
commercial activity on the Gold Coast refer more commonly to *panyarring*, a practice
that bears some similarity to pawnship but involves far less security for the person held
as collateral. To *panyar* someone was to seize him or her as a form of human collateral,
the primary difference being that, unlike pawnship, *panyarring* was initiated by the self-
proclaimed 'creditors,' not arranged by the debtors"; Shumway, *The Fante and the Transatlantic Slave Trade* (Rochester NY: U of Rochester P, 2011): 59.

is not accidental: the privatization, deregulation, and promotion of trade un-hampered by the safeguards of the modern welfare state marked a return to the type of capitalism which, starting in the mid-eighteenth century, made possible the rapid exponential growth of the transatlantic slave trade.[23] In a 1992 interview, Unsworth set out explicit connections between the Thatcher years and the slave-trade era:

> As I wrote I began to see more strongly that there were inescapable anal-ogies. You couldn't really live through the '80s without feeling how crass and distasteful some of the economic doctrines were. The slave trade is a perfect model for that kind of total devotion to the profit motive without reckoning the human consequences.[24]

Once outside Kireku's hut, it is Barton's turn to lecture Paris. Parroting Kireku's argument, Barton tells Paris that he will neither "'stop men of talent from risin' up nor 'top cuddies like Iboti from sinkin'" (581). He "'will never stop ooman bein's tryin' to improve themselves,'" Barton goes on, for "'that is the way we go forrad'" (582). Barton's theory is that men, by nature, are greedy, and that such greed is salutary. Unbeknownst to Barton, his view has been a matter of fierce debate in England, especially after Bernard Mandeville theorized it in *The Fable of the Bees: or Private Vices, Publick Benefits* (1723). In "The Grum-bling Hive: or, Knaves Turn'd Honest" (1705), the poem at the foundation of the *Fable*, Mandeville describes a wicked but flourishing bee community. When Jove decides to make all the bees honest, they stop competing with one an-other, with disastrous results: the economy collapses, and society unravels. In the end, "many Thousand Bees were lost,"[25] and the surviving ones "flew into a

---

23   At the beginning of *Sacred Hunger*, William Kemp, who has invested all his money in the building of the *Liverpool Merchant*, deems the year 1752 "the most auspicious possible" (13), for "the wars are over" (13) and "The Royal African Company has lost its charter and the monopoly that went with it" (13). Now, Kemp concludes, entrepreneurs like himself can "trade to Africa without paying dues to those damned rogues in London" (13). Indeed, it is in 1752 that the Royal African Company of England, which had exercised the Crown monopoly over the triangular trade for the past eight decades, was dissolved and replaced by the Company of Merchants, on the governing committee of which the Corporation of Liverpool "secur[ed] a third of the seats" (Baucom, *Specters of the Atlantic*, 51).

24   Quoted in John L. Dorman, "Barry Unsworth, Writer of Historical Fiction, Dies at 81," *New York Times* (8 June 2012): A25.

25   Bernard Mandeville, *The Fable of the Bees: Or Private Vices, Publick Benefits*, intro. Philip Harth (1723; London: Penguin Classics, 1989): 75.

hollow Tree / Blest with content and honesty."[26] In other words, virtue leads to economic stagnation and social apathy, whereas selfishness fosters economic progress and social dynamism. This is a stance that neither Kireku nor the other entrepreneurs in the settlement would disallow. Kireku does not elaborate on how trade is going to make everybody "'happy an' rich,'" but Mandeville goes to great lengths to demonstrate that public benefits can be derived from self-interest. Although Mandeville dismisses altruism as hypocrisy, he believes in the ability of the government to cajole prosperous individuals into sharing their profits: "Private Vices by the dextrous Management of a skilful Politician may be turned into Publick Benefits."[27] Mandeville's recourse to state intervention is closer to mercantilism than to uncontrolled laissez-faire. There is no "invisible hand" in Mandeville's society, and legal constraint, especially written law, is given significant weight as the cement that holds the community together. The law also determines whether a private vice is good (useful) or bad (harmful) to society. The difficulty with such a system is that all notions of good and bad are unstable, arbitrary, and divisive. What is fair to some is unfair to others. The case of Erasmus Kemp, the son of the unfortunate William Kemp who committed suicide after the loss of the *Liverpool Merchant*, is a good illustration of the moral instability of law in an era of predatory capitalism.

Erasmus is described as "a man who had come from nothing and nowhere [...] a career meteoric even in these times of opportunity for the clever and unscrupulous" (401). Erasmus has become a wealthy, influential man, and when Captain John Philips reports to him that he saw the wreckage of the *Liverpool Merchant* with his own eyes, and that "The Indians who trade with Cuba from the Florida Keys tell of a kind of settlement somewhere back behind the coast, where white and black live together and no one is chief" (427), Erasmus immediately thinks of financial damage, theft, and legal action. As a man of power from a mighty and conquering nation, Erasmus often invokes the law—a law made for and by people like himself.

Erasmus's smugness shows when he tries to imagine his cousin Paris's life in the settlement of coastal Florida:

> What became of law, of legitimacy, of established order, if a man could assume such attitudes of private morality, decide for himself where his fault lay? It turned everything upside down. [Erasmus] could think of nothing more damnable.
>
> *Sacred Hunger* 452

---

26   Mandeville, *The Fable of the Bees*, 60.
27   *The Fable of the Bees*, 309.

This rhetoric of law merges with notions of justice when it serves Erasmus's interests. While in Florida, Erasmus tells the new governor, Colonel Campbell, that he has come "from England expressly to see justice done" (463), and he hopes that the latter will assist him in raiding the settlement in order to recapture "those negroes [...] and any offspring they may have had," since they are his "by right of purchase" (459). In the world of Erasmus, the law legitimizes profit, translated into punishment when profit has been thwarted. Reflecting on how much money he is going to make with the sale of the *Liverpool Merchant* cargo and their progeny, Erasmus entertains thoughts of "lawful profit and just retribution" (495). There is no big step from justice to justification, and Erasmus finds that "Captain Thurso acted lawfully and within his rights" (608) when he "jettisoned" captives alive because of a shortage of water. Thurso's decision "was a sound one, not only in practical terms, but also more humane, as shortening the sufferings of these wretches" (609).

The legality, rather than the ethics, of a business venture is what Erasmus relies on. When Major Redwood, the commander of the English garrison in Florida, explains how English forces have been pursuing a "policy of terror" (478) in order to set Indian chiefs against one another, Erasmus ignores Redwood's wry humor and reflects: "'Yes, I see [...] It is like dealing with opponents in business [...] You seek to unsettle them and divide their counsels. Quite lawful, of course'"(479). But when Redwood further derides the argument of Colonel Campbell and the Superintendent of Indian Affairs, George Watson, that the trade agreements by which they force Indians to cede their lands are good for Indians, Erasmus is stung by Redwood's sarcasm, since it defies his deep-rooted belief in the virtues of trade:

> Redwood obtruded his views more than a man should, without first making sure they were welcome. And what he was saying was perverse, subversive even. Trade brought benefits to both sides—so much was common knowledge. Erasmus had always disliked people who took a view contrary to what was broadly agreed by men of sense.
>
> *Sacred Hunger* 481

Shortly before he dies, Paris sums up Erasmus's petulance, complacency, and moral corruption when he argues that Erasmus is "a man to whom virtue meant well-cut clothes, a proud bearing, [and] money in the bank" (618).[28]

---

28   Paris's description of his cousin Erasmus could fit Rousseau's definition of the bourgeois, the man who "lives outside himself and can only live in the opinion of others, so that he seems to receive the feeling of his own existence only from the judgment of others concerning him." Rousseau continues: "It is not to my present purpose to insist on the

And Erasmus, echoing Barton's metaphor of babies reaching for anything within their grasp, completes Paris's definition when he tells the latter, at the very end of the story, that "'a man with anything about him knows what he wants and tries to get it'" (619). Such cocksureness and cynicism, often associated with the tenets of a free-market economy, are a far cry from what is afoot in the settlement before the raid, but the underlying ideology is the same: the accumulation of wealth is a fundamental right of the individual, and this right takes precedence over responsibility and allegiance to the community.

3   Age of Unreason and Liberal Involution

Philosophers of the Enlightenment did not all agree on slavery and issues of race, but most of them were in favor of free trade as an alternative to stifling monopolies and government control, and because they believed the virtues of free trade far exceeded its contingent shortcomings. Two decades before Adam Smith published *The Wealth of Nations* (1776), Montesquieu, in *The Spirit of the Laws* (1748), argued that commerce should be the foundation of a democratic state because the "spirit of commerce brings with it that of frugality, economy, moderation, work, prudence, tranquility, order, and regulation."[29] And if excessive accumulation of wealth generates disorder and inequality it is because this "spirit" of commerce has been lost. Hence Montesquieu's argument:

> In order for the spirit of commerce to be maintained, the principal citizens must engage in commerce themselves; this spirit must reign alone and not be crossed by another; all the laws must favor it; these same laws, whose provisions divide fortunes in proportion as commerce increases them, must make each poor citizen comfortable enough to be able to work as the others do and must bring each rich citizen to a middle level such that he needs to work in order to preserve or to acquire.
>
> *The Spirit of the Laws* 48

---

indifference to good and evil which arises from this disposition, in spite of our many fine works on morality, or to show how, everything being reduced to appearances, there is but art and mummery in even honor, friendship, virtue, and often vice itself" (*Discourse*, 50).

29   *The Spirit of the Laws*, 48. Montesquieu was also convinced that "the natural effect of commerce is to lead to peace" (338) among nations, an argument Thomas Paine would borrow to make the case for the independence of the thirteen colonies: "peace with trade, is preferable to war without it." Paine, "Common Sense," in *Paine: Political Writings*, ed. Bruce Kuklick (1776, Cambridge Texts in the History of Political Thought; Cambridge: Cambridge UP, 2nd ed. 2000): 45.

The Erasmus character must be understood in this context: as a staunch prac-
titioner of free trade, he is the child of the Enlightenment; as a rapacious entrepreneur disdainful of the poor and complicit in the slave trade, he is the
negation of the liberal aspirations of the Enlightenment, which the tenets of
both the French Revolution, "liberty, equality, fraternity," and the American
Revolution, "life, liberty, and the pursuit of happiness," encapsulate. Erasmus
and successful individuals like him have done away with Montesquieu's injunction that the laws promoting the "spirit of commerce" must help preserve
a certain level of social harmony. Erasmus belongs to the rising bourgeois class
that advocates hard work and trade in pursuit of private property. Locke, as
shown earlier in this chapter, had already paved the way for the sanctification
of private property in his *Second Treatise* (1689) by arguing that mixing one's
labor with unclaimed land is enough to appropriate that land. In the mind
of Erasmus and his contemporaries, economic freedom (the freedom to trade
without the interference of government laws and regulations) is the same as
individual freedom. The so-called Age of Reason was not always reasonable,
and the freedom it called for would soon degenerate into cutthroat economic
competition and the ruthless exploitation of the many by the few.

The Industrial Revolution and ensuing socio-economic upheavals are at the
heart of *The Quality of Mercy* (2011), Unsworth's last novel and long-awaited
sequel to *Sacred Hunger*. *The Quality of Mercy* begins in 1767 in London, two
years after the raid on the settlement in Florida. Erasmus buried his cousin,
Paris, sold the Africans and their progeny in Charles Town, and "brought the
surviving members of the crew back to London to have their crimes and their
punishment published widely."[30] To Erasmus, however, the trial of the crew is
less important than the civil case regarding his "insurance claim on eighty-five
African slaves, cast overboard while still alive from the deck of the *Liverpool
Merchant* on grounds of lawful jettison" (147).

Erasmus brings his case to court in a peculiar historical context as the abolitionist cause has been gaining momentum. Two years earlier, in 1765, the antislavery lawyer Granville Sharp already made a mark when he and his brother
restored to health and freedom Jonathan Strong, a young slave who had been
severely beaten by his master and left for dead in the street. In 1767—the same
year Erasmus takes his case to court in the story—Strong was kidnapped and
re-enslaved. Sharp, once again, came to the rescue, and, although there was no
legal precedent, managed to save Strong from his abductors. Five years later,
in 1772, the landmark case of James Somerset, which Sharp brought before the

---

30   Barry Unsworth, *The Quality of Mercy* (New York: Random House, 2011): 32. Further page
        references are in the main text.

King's Bench court, made slavery unlawful in England and Wales. This court ruling affected neither the slavery-based economies of British possessions in the New World nor the nation's undisputed domination over the transatlantic slave trade; however, it was a milestone in the campaign against slavery and the slave trade.[31]

When Thomas Pike, the barrister in charge of Erasmus's case, explains to the latter that the argument of the prosecutor, Frederick Ashton, is that "England is the home of freedom and that her laws cannot tolerate one man claiming ownership in another" (27),[32] Erasmus replies in earnest:

> That is all very well [...]. But they don't understand the workings of money, these people. There might be a hundred blacks brought here in the course of a year, all acquired by purchase. Then there are the numbers already here, probably at least a thousand in London alone. It amounts to a very considerable capital sum. Who is going to compensate the owners?
>
> *The Quality of Mercy* 27

Erasmus's litigation exemplifies the ideological conflict between the inviolability of private property and the new discourse on the natural and inalienable rights of individuals. In Erasmus's case, the conflict boils down to two simple questions: if slaves are legal cargo, how can throwing them overboard be illegal? And if they are human beings, how can throwing them overboard be legal?

Ashton is an affluent socialite who has decided to embrace the abolitionist cause, which places him on the right side of history. Yet his self-righteousness and zeal at winning his cases betray a lack of consideration for his clients, who are mere instruments of his legal strategy. What is more, Ashton is a prude who struggles with the thought of Delblanc's racially integrated community:

---

31   Somerset was a slave from Jamaica who, once on British soil, ran away from his American master. He was recaptured, and Sharp decided to take on his defense, arguing that Somerset's presence on English soil guaranteed his freedom. Lord Chief Justice Mansfield concurred and granted Somerset his freedom, stating: "The state of slavery is of such a nature, that it is incapable of being introduced on any reasons, moral or political; but only positive law, which preserves its force long after the reasons, occasion, and time itself from whence it was created, is erased from memory; It's so odious, that nothing can be suffered to support it but positive law. Whatever inconveniences, therefore, may follow from the decision, I cannot say this case is allowed or approved by the law of England; and therefore the black must be discharged." Quoted in Justin Buckley Dyer, *Natural Law and the Antislavery Constitutional Tradition* (Cambridge: Cambridge UP, 2012): 54–55.

32   Ashton's defense, of course, is a slightly anachronistic echo of Lord Mansfield's argument in the above-mentioned 1772 landmark case of *Somerset v. Stewart*.

He felt immediately repelled, and faintly sickened at the thought of it, black and white fornicating together by turns, a thing displeasing to God and man alike, producing a mixed race.

The Quality of Mercy 84

Ashton is also in favor of sending the enslaved back to Africa in order for them "to find dignity and prosperity among their own people" (85). Ashton and Erasmus stand on either side of the slavery debate, but their monomaniacal personalities reduce the distance between them: the former was born to opulence and found a cause into which to pour his excessive riches; the latter is a typical parvenu whose "guiding lights [are] propriety and property" (204). As already evidenced in Erasmus's conversation with Redwood in *Sacred Hunger*, the source of personal enrichment, no less than the acquisition of national sovereignty over overseas territories, is to be questioned. The general feeling is that the law, whether it serves Erasmus or Ashton, is on the side of the wealthy and does not really fulfill its role as a social equalizer.

Social inequality comes to the fore when Erasmus turns his attention to the colliery village of Thorpe in County Durham. England stands at the threshold of the industrial revolution, and Erasmus sees an opportunity for investment and profit in coal mining. His cold financial calculations are met with the solicitude of Jane (his love interest and sister to his arch-enemy Ashton), who talks of improving the lot of these people "who spend their lives toiling in the darkness of the mine" (162). The lives of these miners—their starting work at age seven, and their indigence—are a shocking contrast to the lives of well-heeled Londoners like Ashton and Erasmus whose preoccupations seem suddenly futile. The miners are not slaves (they earn a pittance), yet their living conditions and toil in the mines all over England are reminiscent of slaves' living conditions and toil on the plantations of the New World. Eighteenth-century Britain is a world of haves and have-nots with nothing much in between, and many would argue that today's globalized world, with its blatant and fast-growing injustice, bears an eerie resemblance to these early times of the Industrial Revolution.

When Michael Bordon, a young miner, wins a handball match and is rewarded with three acres of land in the nearby dene by the mine owner Lord Spenton, the local notary Bathgate, working on behalf of Erasmus, who covets the same dene to build a coal shipping route, tries to coax Michael into selling: "With a hundred guineas you could quit the mine for good—no more toiling in the dark, sweating your life away" (275). Bathgate depicts a life diametrically opposed to what the youth's life has been so far, and thinks of the most convincing example his imagination can muster:

> You could set up in some business, manufacturing say— [...]. Or you
> could set up a shop or buy a share in a slaving venture—that is the thing
> nowadays, you acquire a share in a cargo of Africans, you buy sugar and
> rum with the proceeds of the sale, and you make a handsome profit on
> the London Exchange when your ship returns. You increase your invest-
> ment on each voyage and in a few years you find yourself a rich man. I
> have seen it happen to others.
>
> *The Quality of Mercy* 275

At a time when Britain's involvement in the slave trade far exceeds the involvement of all other slave-trading nations put together, Bathgate's piece of advice is practical, reasonable, and obviously unburdened by ethical concerns.
In 1767, the remote, poverty-stricken mining region of Northeast England is
not yet affected by the controversies surrounding slavery and the slave trade in
London. The excesses of the Industrial Revolution, however, will foster greater
awareness of these issues among the working classes throughout Europe, until
the latter connect the dots and see a parallel between their lot and that of the
slaves in the New World. Describing the anti-slavery movement in the wake of
the French Revolution, Robin Blackburn writes that, around 1793–94,

> the sans-culottes were cheering slave emancipation in Paris, and, at
> a Sheffield meeting called to support a wider-franchise and the 'total
> and unqualified abolition of Negro slavery,' thousands of metal workers
> endorsed freedom for the slaves in order to 'avenge peacefully ages of
> wrongs done to our Negro Brethren.'[33]

To some, the comparison between the backbreaking labor of slaves on the
plantations of the Americas and the drudgery of ill-paid workers in Europe is
inappropriate, as chattel slavery, with all its barbarity, stands in a category of
its own. Yet the notion that slavery and capitalism, especially in the nineteenth
century, not only overlapped but could easily amalgamate is far from erroneous. Seth Rockman and Cathy Matson, in their analysis of business practices in
antebellum Baltimore, show that the difference between free and unfree labor
may not have mattered much to a pragmatic employer of that period:

> the system that emerged [...] blurred boundaries between categories
> of labor, assuring the interchangeability of different workers along a

---

33   Robin Blackburn, *The American Crucible: Slavery, Emancipation and Human Rights* (Lon-
      don: Verso, 2013): 239.

continuum of slaves-for-life to transient day laborers—with term slaves, rented slaves, self-hiring slaves, indentured servants, redemptioners, apprentices, prisoners, children, and paupers occupying the space in between.[34]

If employers could so easily overlook the status of those they hired, it stands to reason that free workers in America and Europe could identify with slaves and even support the abolition of the slave trade. The nature of the ties between slavery and capitalism is still being debated today, but from Eric Williams's seminal *Capitalism and Slavery* (1944) to Greg Grandin's *The Empire of Necessity* (2015),[35] most agree that slavery either undergirded or fueled the Industrial Revolution, which made Western Europe and the United States the wealthiest regions of the world—a snowball effect that has arguably continued to the present day.

This trans-historicity underlies Lisa Lowe's hypothesis, in *Intimacies of Four Continents* (2015), according to which "the social inequalities of our time are a legacy of these processes through which 'the human' is 'freed' by liberal forms, while other subjects, practices, and geographies are placed at a distance from the 'human.'"[36] Relying on both postcolonial theories and deconstruction,

---

34   Seth Rockman & Cathy Matson, *Scraping By: Wage Labor, Slavery, and Survival in Early Baltimore* (Baltimore MD: Johns Hopkins UP, 2008): 7.

35   In his chapter on the slave trade, Eric Williams presents the transatlantic slave trade as the launch-pad of early European capitalism: "The seventeenth and eighteenth centuries were the centuries of trade, as the nineteenth century was the century of production. For Britain that trade was primarily the triangular trade. In 1718 William Wood said that the slave trade was 'the spring and parent whence the others flow.' A few years later Postlethwayt described the slave trade as 'the first principle and foundation of all the rest, the mainspring of the machine which sets every wheel in motion'"; Williams, *Capitalism and Slavery*, 51. As for Greg Grandin, he demonstrates that when it comes to benefit from slavery, free northern states and southern slave states were partners in crime: "The expansion of slave labor in the South and into the West was still years away, but slavery as it then existed in the southern states was already an important source of northern profit, as was the already exploding slave trade in the Caribbean and South America. Banks capitalized the slave trade and insurance companies underwrote it. Covering slave voyages helped start Rhode Island's insurance industry, while in Connecticut some of the first policies written by Aetna were on slaves' lives. In turn, profits made from loans and insurance policies were ploughed into other northern businesses"; Grandin, *The Empire of Necessity: Slavery, Freedom, and Deception in the New World* (New York: Metropolitan, 2015): 79.

36   Lisa Lowe, *The Intimacies of Four Continents* (Durham NC: Duke UP, 2015): 2. Further page references are in the main text.

Lowe seeks to expose the logocentricity of Western thought and the resultant cultural, political, and economic marginalization of non-Western others.

The originality of Lowe's argument resides in her locating the source of such domination in the very discourse purportedly committed to "political emancipation, ethical individualism, historical progress, and free market economy" (6). According to Lowe, modern liberalism has spawned "colonial divisions of humanity" (6) that presuppose a progression toward (European) civilization. Such rhetoric has allowed Europeans to make freedom and sovereignty a standard to achieve over time rather than a model immediately and unconditionally bequeathed to all cultures and nations on earth. By arbitrarily ensnaring various cultures and races in a hierarchical framework, Westerners gave themselves license to subjugate non-Westerners. Hence, Lowe argues,

> We can link the emergence of liberties defined in the abstract terms of citizenship, rights, wage labor, free trade, and sovereignty with the attribution of racial difference to those subjects, regions, and populations that liberal doctrine describes as "unfit for liberty" or "incapable of civilization," placed at the margins of liberal humanity.
>
> *Intimacies of Four Continents* 6

Colonialism is over, but the idea that some nations are stuck at lower stages of development has endured and is taken for granted, partly because, Lowe implies, it has helped Western democracies maintain their model of society as the benchmark for the rest of the world:

> The safekeeping and preservation of liberal political society, and the placement of peoples at various distances from liberal humanity—"Indian," "Black," "Negro," "Chinese," "coolie," and so forth—are thus integral parts of the genealogy of modern liberalism.
>
> *Intimacies of Four Continents* 8

In order to illustrate this notion of a developmental process toward civilization, Lowe focusses on G.W.F. Hegel, who posits a teleology of freedom whereby one overcomes enslavement through several stages of personal development, from the initial realization of what the philosopher calls the "truth of self-certainty" to the achievement, in Lowe's own words, of "unity of the particular will of the individual with the collective universality of the whole, or the state" (145). From this dialectic of self-determination, Hegel imagines a hierarchy of civilizations on top of which he situates his own European world. While Hegel is not particularly charitable toward Asians and Mohammedans, he simply excludes Africans from his "category of Universality."[37] Half a century after the debate, featured in *Quality of Mercy*, about the humanity of Africans, three decades after the abolition of the slave trade (1807), and three years after the abolition of slavery in the British colonies (1833), Hegel describes Africa as a "land of childhood" (91), ahistorical and unconnected to the rest of humanity. "In Negro life," Hegel argues,

> the characteristic point is the fact that consciousness has not yet attained to the realization of any substantial objective existence—as for example, God, or Law—in which the interest of man's volition is involved and in which he realizes his own being. This distinction between himself as an individual and the universality of his essential being, the African in the uniform, undeveloped oneness of his existence has not yet attained; so that the Knowledge of an absolute Being, an Other and a Higher than his individual self, is entirely wanting. The Negro [...] exhibits the natural man in his completely wild and untamed state. We must lay aside all thought of reverence and morality—all that we call feeling—if we would rightly comprehend him; there is nothing harmonious with humanity to be found in this type of character.
>
> *The Philosophy of History* 93

Hegel's fanciful knowledge of Africa has been long dismissed in academic circles, but it helped spread many prejudices that have not disappeared from mainstream perceptions of Africa, and have even made their way into the speeches of twenty-first-century politicians,[38] thus confirming the pertinence of Lowe's argument.

---

37   Georg Wilhelm Friedrich Hegel, *The Philosophy of History*. tr. J. Sibree (1837, Mineola NY: Dover Philosophical Classics, 2004): 93.

38   On 26 July 2007, French President Nicolas Sarkozy gave a speech at Cheikh Anta Diop University in Dakar, Senegal in which he talked about Africa, its history and prospects. The tone and content of the speech, unapologetically assumed by the special adviser and speechwriter Henri Guaino, is supercilious, paternalistic, and redolent of '*mission civilisatrice*' ideology. Furthermore, it parrots, two hundred years distant, Hegel's vision of Africa as idolatrous, backward, violent, inward-looking, and irresponsible. Facing his erudite Dakarois audience, an unfazed Sarkozy argued that the African has been mired in traditions, refusing to "thrust himself into the future" and "make his own destiny." Africa is stuck "in nostalgia for a lost childhood paradise," and its tragedy, Sarkozy said conclusively, "is that the African has not fully entered into history" (my translation). Nicolas Sarkozy, "Le discours de Dakar de Nicolas Sarkozy: L'intégralité du discours du président de la

The choice of Hegel to demonstrate the endurance and impact of Eurocentric views of our contemporary world seems almost too facile. But Lowe, following chronological order, assesses her own argument against Marx's theories, which are usually opposed to Hegel's. Surprisingly, Marxism is entangled in the same rhetoric of modern liberalism. Lowe thus dismisses both Marx and Hegel for engaging in the same essentialist logic. Both of them, she argues,

> conceived politics in relation to a universal humanity that may be apprehended through a particular set of normative categories, unities, and teleologies, and posited the transparency and harmony of the realized state, whether bourgeois or communist. In both, there is an inner telos that is re-realized through a progressive history.
>
> *Intimacies of Four Continents* 148

Lowe further argues that neither Marxist nor Hegelian theory is able to discern the violence inherent in "the historical and ongoing coloniality of world development" (148), because, in making the "realization of the state, whether imperial, socialist, or postcolonial" (148) the cornerstone of their philosophy, they ignore "the persistence of contradiction and otherness" (148). These theories deliberately dilute particularisms in a universalizing model obeying a Eurocentric conception of the world, and such a process suppresses attempts at colonial heterogeneity. Furthermore, Lowe claims that although Marxism denies the Hegelian hierarchy of cultures and races, Marxism opposes free labor to slavery and thus "cannot recognize Black slaves and colonized subjects as actors in history and historical change" (149). Finally, Lowe argues that Marx's reluctance to situate "mature capitalism" (149) outside the industrial centers of Europe and North America leads him to discount "slave labor as labor" (149) and to fail to appreciate "the role of slavery as the formative condition for wage labor and industrialization" (149).

The above argument about Marx's failure to acknowledge that slavery triggered the surge of the urban proletariat is challenged by his explicit argument, around the time of the cotton boom in the Old South, that slavery facilitated, and even induced, the industrial revolution, thus enabling the West to become the epicenter of the world:

> Direct slavery is just as much the pivot of bourgeois industry as machinery, credits, etc. Without slavery you have no cotton; without cotton you

---

République, prononcé le 26 juillet 2007," *Le Monde* (9 November 2007): online (accessed 10 March 2018).

have no modern industry. It is slavery that has given the colonies their value; it is the colonies that have created world trade, and it is world trade that is the pre-condition of large-scale industry. Thus slavery is an economic category of the greatest importance. [...] Cause slavery to disappear and you will have wiped America off the map of nations. Thus slavery, because it is an economic category, has always existed among the institutions of the peoples. Modern nations have been able only to disguise slavery in their own countries, but they have imposed it without disguise upon the New World.[39]

Lowe's argument, however, does not confine itself to Marx's ability (or lack thereof) to identify strong links between the plantation and the factory plant. More importantly for Lowe is the fact that Marxist theories have been unable to adapt to the specificities of the colonial world, especially of its race-based structure, which bespeaks not only the rigidity of Marxism as an ideology but also the difficulty of overcoming racial barriers without disregarding the race issue—a conundrum several fictional characters studied in this book, including *Middle Passage*'s Calhoun in the previous chapter and *Sacred Hunger*'s Delblanc in this chapter, grapple with. And as the next chapter will show, Édouard Glissant negotiates the same intricate path, as his concepts of creolization and Relation aim to recognize and transcend problems of race all at once.

Utilitarianism was no more able than Marxism to do away with the "racialized exploitation" (10) of laborers (whether slaves or colonized wageworkers). John Stuart Mill was opposed to slavery, but not to colonialism and its occasional brand of repressive parternalism. His *Considerations on Representative Government* (1861), Lowe argues, "was as much a provision for the colonial state's 'necessary' use of force to educate those 'unfit for liberty,' as it was the argument for liberal representation in Britain" (15). Mill was wary of mob rule and "consistently defined liberty by distinguishing those 'incapable of

39   Karl Marx, *The Poverty of Philosophy: A Reply to M. Proudhon's Philosophy of Poverty*, tr.
       Institute of Marxism-Leninism (*Misère de la philosophie: Réponse à la philosophie de la
       misère de M. Proudhon*, 1847; Moscow: Progress, 1955): 49–50. Sven Beckert's argument
       in *Empire of Cotton: A Global History* (New York: Alfred A. Knopf, 2015), like Marx's, fo-
       cusses on the connection between cotton, slavery, and capitalism in the first half of the
       nineteenth century. As slave-grown cotton from the American South became ever more
       competitive, Beckert notes, "Slavery and the expropriation of native lands, fueled by Eu-
       ropean capital, combined to feed raw materials relentlessly into Europe's core industry.
       The massive infusion of European capital transformed the American countryside; land
       became wealth, and linked across great distances slaves and wage workers, planters and
       manufacturers, plantations and factories. In the wake of the Industrial Revolution, slavery
       had become central to the Western world's new political economy" (133).

self-government' from those with the capacity for liberty" (15). In the context of the British Empire, such a notion became the rationale for an authoritative administration "to maintain 'order and progress'" and implement "modes of surveillance and security to conduct 'free trade'" (15).[40]

The association of Mill with free trade may be misleading, as Mill was neither a follower of Adam Smith's theory of the invisible hand that regulates the market nor a forerunner of today's proponents of neoliberalism. The latter's argument, whereby less government and free enterprise lead to the emancipation of every individual, appears to echo Mill's view that all individuals, including the laboring classes, should be free. However, Mill's desire to limit government was not meant to foster the emergence of a plutocracy. On the contrary, Mill wanted authorities to refrain from intervening in people's everyday life so as to let human energy and creativity blossom to the full. And this could be achieved by fostering universal access to education so that all citizens could become active participants in collective decision making. Mill also believed that the political élite of a nation should be selected from among the most educated, who are also the most apt to govern. As Lowe shows, however, Mill's grand design did not apply to Britain's colonies, which he considered unripe for the experience of political freedom. The extent to which today's neoliberal thinkers harbor similar views is hard to determine, as Mill and his contemporaries' candidness has been replaced by a carefully calibrated ideological discourse supporting the belief that a globalized free-market economy generates greater freedom worldwide.

In *The Black Jacobins* (1938), C.L.R. James compares plantation slaves in the Americas to the industrial proletariat in Europe. Lowe praises James for debunking the myth of the proletarian as "an urban working class within European capitalism" (158), but she faults him for acknowledging a difference between both groups, because "it refuses the simple correspondence between the slaves and the figure of the modern proletarian by continuing to foreground their colonial difference" (158). Lowe then reminds her reader that labor exploitation was not the "primary mode of colonial encounter" (159). Slavery was much more than a mere economic regime, and before the establishment of

---

40   Two years before *Considerations*, in his influential *On Liberty* (1859), Mill had already made it clear that his principle of individual liberty for all did not apply to "those backward states of society in which the race itself may be considered as in its nonage." See John Stuart Mill's *On Liberty, Utilitarianism and Other Essays*, ed. Mark Philp & Frederick Rosen (Oxford: Oxford UP, 2015): 13. For those under British colonial rule, Mill added, "despotism is a legitimate mode of government in dealing with barbarians, provided the end be their improvement" (*On Liberty*, 13).

plantation economies, indigenous peoples were dispossessed of their land, persecuted, and, in some cases, exterminated.

Lowe finally finds a counter-argument to the pernicious rhetoric of modern liberalism in W.E.B. Du Bois's *Black Reconstruction in America* (1935), a definitive account of "the slave foundations of U.S. capitalism" (165) and a compelling analysis of the failure of Reconstruction. In *Black Reconstruction*, Du Bois brings to light a nexus of international commercial exchanges that finds its source in the plantation economy of the South, and unfolds into the manufacturing industry of the North, the factory system of England, and the global world market. The whole structure, whose foundations are the sweat, tears, and blood of Southern black slaves, contributed to the "urbanization of cities throughout western Europe and North America" (167). Du Bois makes the bold argument, Lowe writes, that "slavery was and continued to be systemic and constitutive of U.S. democracy, and of the extension of American power around the world" (167).

Through Du Bois, Lowe questions the very association of the United States with the concept of democracy, as if the nation were born with a defect, a degenerative illness gnawing at its core, an illness its immune system (the founding principles of the nation) tries but fails to allay, either because it refuses to diagnose its existence and perdurance or because, as argued in the last segment of Chapter 2 above, it knows the remedy but won't administer it. The sequela of such illness is a false sense of unity that surfaces time and again. Chapter 1, for instance, showed how new, subtle forms of racial discrimination appeared in the wake of the civil rights movement in the 1960s. The movement was not in vain: negrophobic violence largely subsided and the lot of the African-American community improved in significant ways, but such social advance was met by a conservative backlash meant to restore the racial order that had heretofore prevailed. This backlash was much milder than the one that followed Reconstruction, which, in Lowe's reading of Du Bois, could have been a historic opportunity for radical change.

From Du Bois's perspective, the end of Reconstruction was orchestrated by a joint effort of northern and southern white leaders—an averred fact that constitutes the plot of D.W. Griffith's infamous *Birth of a Nation* (1915). In fact, Du Bois's *Black Reconstruction* may be read as a response to Griffith's film, turning the latter's "happy" ending (the exclusion of blacks from the American democratic experiment) into an "unhappy" ending. Du Bois understood that Reconstruction was not just a problem of race but also a problem of class. Both northern white industrial capital and the southern white planter oligarchy, Lowe contends, felt threatened by the "possible longevity of cross racial worker solidarity" (168), and connived to protect their interests. *Black Reconstruction*, Lowe continues, told a history of [...] ruling-class whites aggressively recruiting poor southern whites as their allies, dividing the black and white workers to prevent their joining in common struggle.

Intimacies of Four Continents 168

Lowe's claim about foiled trans-racial solidarity among the poor in the South should be qualified, for while Du Bois would agree that poor whites were manipulated by the planter class, he might not have been so eager to postulate poor whites' natural propensity to fraternize with slaves and poor blacks in order to form a community of interest.[41] What is undeniable, however, was Du Bois's ability to see beyond the national context. The dismantling of Reconstruction strengthened US capitalism and helped it expand globally, which meant that the black struggle in America was also the struggle of people of color the world over:

The emancipation of man is the emancipation of labor and the emancipation of labor is the freeing of that basic majority of workers who are yellow, brown, and black.

Intimacies of Four Continents 170

Thus, *Black Reconstruction* bears witness to the "emergence of racialized global capitalism" (171). Beyond the national binary oppositions of class and race, Du Bois anticipates a world that will "require relationships across national boundaries, classes, and different racial groups" (171). Du Bois's vision of a future world defined by trans-national, trans-social, and trans-racial relationships may have come to naught, but as the next chapter will demonstrate, it foreshadows Édouard Glissant's vision of a world "in Relation."

• • •

The Quality of Mercy appears to be more hopeful than *Sacred Hunger*, as it endeavors to redeem Erasmus, whose cold-hearted, profit-driven mentality is

---

41   A couple of years before *Black Reconstruction*, in "Marxism and the Negro Problem," Du Bois wrote: "And while Negro labor in America suffers because of the fundamental inequities of the whole capitalist system, the lowest and most fatal degree of its suffering comes not from the capitalists but from fellow white laborers. It is white labor that deprives the Negro of his right to vote, denies him education, denies him affiliation with trade unions, expels him from decent houses and neighborhoods, and heaps upon him the public insults of open color discrimination." William Edward Burghardt Du Bois, "Marxism and the Negro Problem" (1933), in *African American Political Thought, 1890–1930: Washington, Du Bois, Garvey and Randolph*, ed. Cary D. Wintz (New York: Routledge, 2015): 149.

somewhat softened by Jane, the abolitionist wife-to-be with "eccentric ideas" (293). In *Sacred Hunger*, Erasmus is an absolute villain, the epitome of the greedy opportunist of the Industrial Revolution; yet *Sacred Hunger* sheds a more complex light than *The Quality of Mercy* does on that revolution. *Sacred Hunger* takes the reader back to the roots of the debate between proponents of a laissez-faire economy, on the one hand, and a welfare-oriented economy, on the other. But it also suggests that the Industrial Revolution was a time when new ideas of self-affirmation and upward mobility through free enterprise challenged the values of the Middle Ages, in which destinies were sealed at birth. Ironically, Delblanc has created a propitious environment not so much for the advent of an egalitarian society as, rather, for the blossoming of individuals like Kireku, whose story exemplifies this notion that someone at the bottom of the social ladder may achieve success through hard work and perseverance. *Sacred Hunger* is also a reminder that shrewd, ruthless entrepreneurs were not solely European by origin: Kireku, Tongman, Danka, and Tiamoko are all men from the African continent, perfectly cognizant of the arcane practices of commercial trade. Once the settlement is established, these men do not start afresh as Delblanc hoped. They revert to a way of life with which they were most likely familiar prior to their capture back home in Africa. They become involved in a variety of business deals with the purpose of improving their lot; and, just like their European counterparts, they engage in morally questionable practices if it helps them reach their goals. Unlike Erasmus, Kireku's stance is not informed by any specific ideology. He does what he thinks is right, which gives credence to Barton's theory that men, by nature, are greedy, and that such greed is salutary; as Barton argues, with his metaphor of babies trying to grab anything they see, "when we stop reachin' out, we are done for" (582)—an attitude Kireku shares with Erasmus. Kireku, as Barton reminds Paris, "hasn't had the benefits of a lib'ral eddication" (581); but neither did Erasmus, whose upbringing in a struggling, arriviste bourgeois household in Liverpool taught him that those on top do not indulge in altruism. The capitalist creed that emerges in mid-eighteenth-century England is given tremendous currency, and shapes the culture of Erasmus and his generation.[42]

---

42   This form of capitalism is often referred to as industrial capitalism, which is characterized
     by privately owned and operated businesses. Historically, it followed an era of mercan-
     tilism in which states regulated and supported the economy, so as to increase national
     power. In such a system, the state and the merchants worked in partnership for both na-
     tional and personal profit. Thus, the triangular trade started as a national enterprise, but
     really soared when slave-trading governments in Europe abandoned their prerogatives
     and let individual entrepreneurs take over. While the end of mercantilism in England
     is often dated to Adam Smith's 1776 *The Wealth of Nations*, mercantilist regulations had

The contrast between Delblanc's humane, egalitarian community and Erasmus's ruthless, capitalist world is at the heart of Peggy Knapp's "Barry Unsworth's *Sacred Hunger*: History and Utopia" and Greg Forter's "Barry Unsworth's Utopian Imaginings." The latter argues that the originality of *Sacred Hunger* resides in its "contention that a collective avowal of woundedness opens up counterhegemonic possibilities."[43] Indeed, the empowerment of each and every individual in the settlement hinges not on "mastery of others" but on "self-*dis*possession" (148). Taking up Knapp's exploration of the links between history and utopia in *Sacred Hunger*, Forter invokes "the book's utopian dimension," which enables a lucid mapping of the "injuries of early capitalism" and helps "reclaim from the margins of history an untold story of human possibility" (153). *Sacred Hunger* may thus be interpreted as a counter-narrative to the history of humanity understood as an account of capitalist expansion and domination.[44] Knapp concurs but is more measured than Forter, pointing out that even though "there is a trenchant and sustained critique of capitalism" in *Sacred Hunger*, there is "a critique of intellectual certainty (even enlightened liberal certainty) as well."[45] Such a questioning of intellectual vanity comes to the fore when Paris, in the face of growing resentment, speculates that the state of nature in which he and Delblanc have found happiness may well just be "a notion of Eden, a nostalgia of educated, privileged men" (541). Thus, *Sacred Hunger* may not be reduced to a mere indictment of free-market ideology. Delblanc's ideal community is intrinsically flawed, as its lack of a binding social contract and its resistance to social and economic changes lead to internecine conflicts auguring complete and inexorable disintegration, which Erasmus's fateful raid only precipitates.

---

      already been steadily relaxed; it is in this atmosphere of new private business opportunities that Erasmus's father embarks upon the *Liverpool Merchant* venture.

43   Greg Forter, "Barry Unsworth's Utopian Imaginings," *Raritan* 32.1 (Summer 2012): 148. Further page references are in the main text.

44   While the notion of utopia helps Knapp and Forter uncover the counter-historical potentialities of Delblanc's experiment, it should be remembered that the latter is also a *sui generis* political endeavor grounded in historical reality, as it prefigures actual undertakings that started to proliferate not half a century later. Thus, as early as 1794, the Romantic poets Samuel Taylor Coleridge and Robert Southey considered establishing a Pantisocracy: i.e. a system of government with power and property shared equally among all the community members. The Pantisocratic venture, like countless others, never materialized, but some did, and the core ideas of such societies (abolition of hierarchy and private property, shared possessions and resources, and self-sufficiency) have endured and inspired heterodox enterprises across the ages, from anarchist projects of the late nineteenth century to present-day communes in the United States and elsewhere.

45   Peggy A. Knapp, "Barry Unsworth's *Sacred Hunger*: History and Utopia," *Clio* 38.3 (Summer 2009): 336.

Paris's lack of popularity with other leaders in the settlement has to do with his remaining the sole proponent of Delblanc's model of society. Nadri, a black Muslim who shares Tabakali with Paris, is another individual who reproaches Paris about his tendency to impose his views on others. The exchange with Nadri is much briefer than the one with Kireku, but it provides access to the key issue of individual freedom and responsibility to the community. Although less antagonistic than Kireku, Nadri also emphasizes his fate as a victim of the slave trade. However, he leaves Kireku's discourse of race aside, and refocusses the debate on the opposition between oppressed and oppressor. Thus, when Paris argues that "we are all here by accident," Nadri retorts that while Paris is there by accident, he, Nadri, was brought over as a captive in the hold and had no choice. As much as Nadri likes Paris, he has not forgotten that Paris, as a surgeon on the *Liverpool Merchant*, was one of his persecutors, and to let Paris impose his views is more than Nadri can bear:

> You say an attempt understanding but it is only an attempt proving your ideas the right ones. First you bringed us, say we are free, then you want to make us serve some idea in your head. But the people cannot serve your idea, you cannot make them do that. (563)

More than a reproof, Nadri's words are a reminder that freedom is not given but gained—an achievement the cargo was deprived of: first, they were victims of the trade, then bystanders in the insurrection, and, finally, participants in a political experiment, the organization of which they were not consulted about. As Forter points out, "many of the settlement's founding acts are formalized before they even take place, planned in advance and communally enacted as binding plots."[46] And Knapp, comparing Delblanc in *Sacred Hunger* to Gonzalo in Shakespeare's *The Tempest*, notes that Gonzalo intends to be the exclusive ruler of his utopia in order to enforce equality.[47] Delblanc is not a tyrant, yet his eagerness to establish absolute equality backfires and turns his settlement into a coercive polity. This is why Nadri—like Kireku but for very different motives—tells Paris that he reserves for himself the right to pull out of a community he no longer feels attached to. Beyond individual cases, this situation leads to a reflection on the very meaning of what a community is, and what the stakes are of living together.

---

46   Forter, "Barry Unsworth and the Art of Power: Historical Memory, Utopian Fictions," *Contemporary Literature* 51.4 (Winter 2010): 805.

47   Knapp, "Barry Unsworth's *Sacred Hunger*: History and Utopia," 332.

4   Self, Alterity, Community

The frustration of both Kireku and Nadri with the organization and rules of the settlement bring to light the major shortcomings of Delblanc's experiment: too much political liberty has proven liberticidal, and the failure to involve community members in the decision-making process has dulled their sense of civic responsibility, which, in turn, has rent the social fabric of the community. But a community boils down neither to the establishment of a suitable political system nor to camaraderie and allegiance to a group for self-gratification. The essence of community has deeper ontological roots; it lies not so much in the strengthening of the self as in the surrendering of that self to others. This abdication of the self as a *sine qua non* for self-fulfillment is the real challenge of community.

In *Communitas*, Esposito presents the paradox of so-called communities of interests—racial, religious, cultural, etc.—which assume that

> community is a "property" belonging to subjects that join them together [*accomuna*]: an attribute, a definition, a predicate that qualifies them as belonging to the same totality [*insieme*], or as a substance that is produced by their union.
>
> *Communitas* 2

As already stated (24; 144), the word 'community' is composed of the Latin *cum* and *munus*. The former means "with," but the latter is polysemous and means, among other things, debt, gift, duty, and office. From this etymology, Esposito explains,

> it emerges that *communitas* is the totality of persons united not by "property" but precisely by an obligation or a debt; not by an "addition" but by a "subtraction": by a lack, a limit that is configured as an onus, or even as a defective modality for him who is "affected," unlike for him who is instead "exempt" or "exempted."
>
> *Communitas* 6

In other words, community members are united by the *munus*, which is something one gives, not something one receives.

This obligation to the community is what an individual like Nadri in *Sacred Hunger* wants to evade, because it goes against his desire for disengagement and personal autonomy. While Kireku cannot think much beyond race and greed, Nadri takes the debate to a higher level by reproaching Paris for "always wanting to make some kind of *laws* for people" (563)—laws that reduce individuals' independence and compel them to take part in the community more than they intend to. In other words, Nadri questions the very notion of the mutual gift that integration in a community requires. And this is precisely the kind of insularity Esposito warns about:

> Therefore the community cannot be thought of as a body, as a corporation in which individuals are founded in a larger individual. Neither is community to be interpreted as a mutual, intersubjective "recognition" in which individuals are reflected in each other so as to confirm their initial identity; as a collective bond that comes at a certain point to connect individuals that before were separate. The community isn't a mode of being, much less a "making" of the individual subject. It isn't the subject's expansion or multiplication but its exposure to what interrupts the closing and turns it inside out: a dizziness, a syncope, a spasm in the continuity of the subject.
>
> *Communitas* 7

Esposito's theory, that the community exposes the subject "to what interrupts the closing," challenges the notion that the building of a community is meant to foster mutual recognition and identity formation. It is understood that human beings will live together in some sort of community; but if a human being is incomplete without community, it is not so much because of the mutual bond (*cum*) that the community encompasses as because of the debt (*munus*) that every subject must repay to the community. Metaphorically, the chaos in the early stages of the settlement in *Sacred Hunger* illustrates this universal truth in a tragic manner—those who have chosen to dissociate themselves from the group will pay dearly for it: the selfish, greedy Haines is scalped by Indians; his partner in crime, Barton, has become the minion of Kireku; and the hateful Wilson is sacrificed on the altar of communal unity. If being part of a community is inherent in the human condition, it does not mean that there is no desire to quit the community as well. This is another key issue that Esposito addresses with the concept of *immunitas*, which he develops from the term *communis*, a variant of *communitas*:

> If *communis* is he who is required to carry out the functions of an office— or to the donation of a grace—on the contrary, he is called immune who has to perform no office, and for that reason he remains ungrateful. He can completely preserve his own position through a *vacatio muneris*. Whereas the *communitas* is bound by the sacrifice of the *compensatio*, the *immunitas* implies the beneficiary of the *dispensatio*.
>
> *Communitas* 7

Immunitas, Esposito argues elsewhere, "is the negative or lacking [*privativa*] form of *communitas*."[48] While *communitas* binds its members by the *munus*, which "jeopardizes individual identity," *immunitas* "is the condition of dispensation from such obligations and therefore the defense against the expropriating features of *communitas*."[49] Thus, the temptation to immunize oneself is an attempt to reclaim a loss of subjectivity. And subjectivity is precisely what the captives in the hold of the *Liverpool Merchant* were stripped of in the first place, which explains why the survivors from the hold have grown particularly sensitive to the issue. The feeling, no doubt, has been exacerbated by Delblanc's model of government, which, for all its virtues, has accentuated the dilution of the self in the community—a reminder that a well-balanced social contract with clearly defined responsibilities, rights, and obligations is not incompatible with the realization of the self within the community. Esposito makes clear that relinquishing the comfort of the private for the public is a painful experience:

> Here then is the blinding truth that is kept within the etymological folds of the *communitas*: the public thing [*res publica*] cannot be separated from no-thing [*niente*]. It is precisely the no-thing of the thing that is our common ground [*fondo*]. All of the stories that tell of the founding crime, the collective crime, the ritual assassination, the sacrificial victim featured in the history of civilization don't do anything else except evoke metaphorically the *delinquere* that keeps us together, in the technical sense of "to lack" and "to be wanting"; the breach, the trauma, the lacuna out of which we originate. Not the origin but its absence, its withdrawal. It is the originary *munus* that constitutes us and makes us destitute in our mortal finiteness.
>
> *Communitas* 8

In such a model of citizenship, Greg Bird remarks, our belonging to the community is not determined by a social but a deontological contract, which he defines thus:

> All that is exchanged in this contract is *ourselves*. When we are drawn together in the contract of the *munus* we are expropriated so extensively

---

48   Roberto Esposito, *Bíos: Biopolitics and Philosophy*, tr. & intro. Timothy Campbell (*Bíos: biopolitica e filosofia*, 2004; Minneapolis & London: U of Minnesota P, 2008): 50.

49   Esposito, *Bíos: Biopolitics and Philosophy*, 50.

that we are rendered incapable of appropriating the contract, others, even ourselves.[50]

Indeed, there is nothing in the community that its members can claim as their own: they are, to restate Bird, "ex-propriated," without a *proprius*: i.e. "deprived of their own."

If community members, as Esposito argues, are united by an obligation, it follows that communal unity falls apart when members lose the sense of that obligation, or when they grant themselves, as it were, a *vacatio muneris*; and they do so, in Esposito's words, when they can no longer "accept the violent loss of borders"[51] that participation in the community requires of them.

As argued earlier, Kireku and other merchants see the community as a hindrance to their activities, feeling less and less committed to a society fostering collective values while limiting personal initiative. Paradoxically, Delblanc's society, built on the premise that the absence of a leader and governing institutions will generate more freedom for its citizens, ends up being as coercive as its antithesis—Hobbes's *Leviathan*. This is because the type of society Delblanc experiments with can only work with the complete abandonment of the self to the community; and this abandonment, this self-effacement for the sake of the community, ends up being more constraining than a system based on a social contract with representatives and ruling institutions. Delblanc's community is bound to dissent, injustice, and violence, both because it demands unfaltering commitment to the group from each and every member and because, save for an improvised court of law, there is no reliable authority to regulate the lives of the citizens. This is perhaps what Nadri and others have foreseen, and this is why the settlement starts to disintegrate when Erasmus's attack puts a sudden and brutal end to the experiment.

One can only speculate about how the settlement would have evolved without Erasmus's intervention. What can be ascertained is that trade was the downfall of the settlement, since it is through the development of commercial exchanges that the very existence of the settlement became known. It is also obvious that the community—in the sense of togetherness and solidarity implicit in the morpheme *cum*—is presented as a safeguard against the rise of individualistic (i.e. selfish) interests in the settlement. This, however, is Paris's point of view, and may be challenged on at least two counts. First, it is hard to

---

50   Greg Bird, *Containing Community: From Political Economy to Ontology in Agamben, Esposito, and Nancy* (Albany: State U of New York P, 2016): 156.

51   Esposito, *Communitas*, 8.

imagine how this tiny self-sufficient colony could have gone on without commerce and contact with the outside world. Second, it is legitimate to wonder what happens to a world closed in on itself for too long.

In the preface to *The Inoperative Community* (1991), Jean-Luc Nancy warns against the kind of lapses that lie in wait for a community that sees itself as a monolith cut off from outside influences:

> The community that becomes a *single* thing (body, mind, fatherland, Leader...) necessarily loses the *in* of being-*in*-common. Or, it loses the *'with'* or the *'together'* that defines it. It yields its being-together to a being *of* togetherness. The truth of community, on the contrary, resides in the retreat of such a being.[52]

As Nancy says elsewhere, "Being cannot be anything but being-with-one-another, circulating in the *with* and as the *with* of this singularly plural coexistence."[53] Thus, a community tolerates the diversity of views, forms of behavior, and tastes among its members, and is open to influences from outside. This is the type of community Nancy calls for in "Conloquium," an essay prefacing the French translation of Esposito's *Communitas*. In "Conloquium," Nancy argues that "the *cum* links [...] or joins [...] the *munus* of the *communis*" and works as a "springboard" for the whole of Esposito's argument, as the *cum*

> is the sharing of a charge, a duty, or a task, rather than the community of a substance. The being-in-common is defined and constituted by a charge, and in the final analysis it is in charge of nothing other than the *cum* itself.[54]

In other words, a community must learn to cultivate its *cum* (i.e. its togetherness) through the fulfillment of its *munus* (i.e. members' debt or obligation to the community)—for it is the *munus* that ultimately forges the community as an entity. Delblanc's fault, perhaps, is the demands he makes on the *cum*, stemming from the idealistic notions burgeoning at the time of the Enlightenment: brotherhood and the natural goodness of human beings.

---

52   Jean-Luc Nancy, *The Inoperative Community*, xxxix.
53   Jean-Luc Nancy, *Being Singular Plural*, 3.
54   Jean-Luc Nancy, "Conloquium" (1999), tr. Janell Watson, *Minnesota Review* 75 (2010): 105.

5   **Community: Getting to the Root of the Problem**

The conversations that Paris has with Kireku and Nadri reveal that Delblanc's
theories of unimpeded freedom and equality do not stand the test of reality,
and they force Paris to concede that what seems ideal to erudites like Delblanc
and himself may not be ideal to others. The changes the settlement is going
through shortly before Erasmus's raid belie Delblanc's conviction that, given
the right circumstances (i.e. an environment free of real property, cupidity,
and competition), human beings are willing to live in perfect harmony and
fairness. Human beings may be predisposed to live in community with all the
constraints that such a life implies, but they are not predisposed to altruism.
The survivors of the *Liverpool Merchant* come together out of necessity, but
the group loses its cohesion as soon as some of its members feel that the very
community that saved them from a certain death no longer serves their personal interests. It does not mean that these individuals have suddenly lost their
gregarious instincts; it means that, throughout history, binding rules and moral
principles were developed as safeguards against such dissenting attitudes as
well as against coercion, corruption, and selfishness. It also means that the notion of community must constantly be reconsidered lest humanity fall into
patterns detrimental both to individual and collective freedom.

In this perspective, Édouard Glissant's concept of Relation, explored in the
next chapter in parallel with Jean-Luc Nancy's notion of being-with, should
be read as an attempt to question the foundation of community and devise a
new model of human interactions capable of withstanding the onslaught of
economic globalization. Glissant argues that our world has entered a process
of creolization in which constant and teeming artistic and cultural exchanges
are already reshaping the nature of our relations to others, and he situates the
dawn of that process in the hold of the slave ship. In "The Open Boat," the short
prelude to his seminal *Poetics of Relation* (1990), Glissant compares the hold to
a womb whence a new people sprang and blossomed into a myriad of "composite cultures" free from the myth of genesis and other rigid characteristics of traditional cultures. Nancy's key notion of coexistence as pre-existing any social
(de)formation echoes Glissant's image of the captive in the hold, naked to the
world and exposed to new beginnings, but Nancy does not rely on a timeline to
describe the evolution of mankind. Rather, he argues that our mutual exposure
to one another is already there, and he sees in the undoing of our current world
the opportunity to create a (better) world out of nothing.

Tellingly, the much-touted term "community" vanishes from Glissant's and
Nancy's lexicons as their theories progress toward alternative modes of existence. Despite Glissant's claim that his theory of Relation, which is modeled

on the Deleuzian rhizome, still acknowledges the presence and necessity of an original enrooting, Relation seems to facilitate the dilution of the self into a world without solid reference points and horizons. In a similar fashion, Nancy's deconstruction of the idea of community does not seem to provide a clear, convincing, and reassuring reconstruction project. Thus, while Glissant and Nancy open our eyes to the shortcomings of our world and the urgent need to address its faults, their heterodox approach to community runs the risk of undermining their respective projects. The forces that have left our contemporary world in a state of dereliction are the same forces that once made the exponential growth of the slave trade possible. Hence, cutting the roots of these negative forces to start elsewhere may not be enough, for these roots will grow again. It may be more advisable to control their growth, prevent them from becoming parasites, and even remold them into virtuous instruments of communal harmony.

CHAPTER 4

Rethinking the Slave Trade/Rethinking Community: Édouard Glissant's "Relation" and Jean-Luc Nancy's "Being-With"

Our boats are open, we sail them for everyone.[1]

∵

The first three chapters of this book have analyzed the way works of fiction depict various forms of community with the purpose of shedding light on the slave trade and its historical ramifications in the present. Even *Roots*, despite Haley's claim to the contrary, is a story with imaginary characters and events. All these works aim at making the reader reflect on the history and legacy of the slave trade, but none of them has pretensions beyond entertaining, enlightening, and stirring the imagination; and even when such a work intends to unsettle the reader, it is to tell a truth to which more conventional forms of knowledge may not readily grant access. Fictional works may stimulate the intellect, but they rarely elaborate theories or calls for action. However, Glissant's "The Open Boat" is different. Like *Tamango*, *Roots*, *Middle Passage*, and *Sacred Hunger*, it too explores the slave trade in conjunction with the notion of community, but it goes beyond them, as it lays the ground for an ambitious philosophical project that Glissant calls a "poetics of Relation," which encompasses both a set of principles laid down to understand the world (theory) and a method to apprehend it (praxis).

"The Open Boat" is a short piece comprising fourteen paragraphs running over five pages. At once poetic prose fiction, historical account, and metaphysical rumination, it constitutes an exordium to Glissant's seminal *Poetics of Relation* (1990), a philosophical treatise in which he either defines, develops, or revisits some of his key concepts, such as filiation, opacity, errantry,[2]

---

1 Édouard Glissant, "The Open Boat" ("La barque ouverte"), in *Poetics of Relation*, tr. Betsy Wing (*Poétique de la Relation*, 1990; Ann Arbor: U of Michigan P, 1997): 9. Further page references are in the main text.

2 Not a few readers may be pulled up short by the term "errantry" for Glissant's *errance*, as it is historically freighted in English and almost universally relates to the paradoxically random and purposive wandering of medieval knights seeking opportunities to prove their mettle.

worldliness, and, of course, creolization and Relation. "The Open Boat" is a complex text that aims both to remember and transcend the trauma of the Middle Passage by reinterpreting the hold of the slave ship as a womb from which a new humanity has emerged. The survivors of the Middle Passage are thrown into the "absolute unknown" of the New World, and this unknown has become knowledge—yet not knowledge already framed in cultural certainties and reduced to Glissant's own Afro-Caribbean community. Glissant postulates an all-encompassing knowledge (a common awareness, a mutual recognition) conducive to what he defines as Relation. Relation, which started in the "non-world" (*non-monde*), has grown into something new that Glissant calls the "total world" (*tout-monde*). The total world refutes the predictable, the definitive, and everything that opposes communication and heterogeneity. It is a quest to reveal the world in all its diversity. It is a world in Relation.

Glissant presents his theory of Relation (and the process of creolization related to it) as a bulwark, and even a corrective, against the tyranny of a profit-oriented world order. Yet, the recent intensification of forced migrations, racial and social polarizations, and cultural and religious clashes across the world seem to belie Glissant's theory: the prediction, in *Poetics of Relation*, that the "massive and diffracted confluence of cultures" (153) heralds the creolization: i.e. the "limitless *métissage*" (34), of humanity[3] has been disproved by an unprecedented worsening of identitarian closure, including among Glissant's own Caribbean community, whose peculiar legacy of racial and cultural mixing is supposed to be a template for creolization. The first section of this chapter will explore the Glissantian notions of creolization and Relation, and then demonstrate how and why the latter permeates "The Open Boat" both in form and in content.

Through the concept of Relation, Glissant not only questions racial and cultural essentialism but also reappraises the notion of community in ways that resonate with Jean-Luc Nancy's own reworking of the same notion through the central concept of "being-with." Nancy's concept of being-with originates in,

---

"Errancy," of course, would be a trap of transliteration, relating as it does exclusively to error. "Errantry" will be discussed at length in the following pages, but attention should be drawn at this juncture to Betsy Wing's comment on this word as her chosen rendering of *errance*: "While *errance* is usually translated as 'wandering,' 'errantry' seems better suited to Glissant's use of the word, and there is precedence in translations of Césaire. *Errance* for Glissant, while not aimed like an arrow's trajectory, nor circular and repetitive like the nomad's, is not idle roaming, but includes a sense of sacred motivation"; Wing, "Notes" to Glissant, *Poetics of Relation*, 211.

3   In French, the term *métissage* does not necessarily carry a pejorative connotation and is often used in such expressions as *métissage culturel*: i.e. cultural interbreeding, and *métissage musical*: i.e. musical cross-breeding.

and then revisits, the Heideggerian notion of *Dasein* (being-there) by embracing Heidegger's contention that *Mitsein* (being-with) is the ontological condition of human existence, while rejecting Heidegger's conflation of *Mitsein* with national destiny and the political ideology it is associated with.[4] By making the "with" of being-with the foundation of human experience, Nancy makes co-existence, rather than existence, primordial. The individual is in relation with others *a priori*, not as the result of a rational decision.[5] Moreover, plurality is embedded in every singularity beforehand, so that, as Nancy puts it,

> The One as purely one is less than one; it cannot be, be put in place, or counted. One as properly one is always more than one. It is an excess of unity; it is one-with-one, where its Being in itself is copresent.
> *Being Singular Plural* 40

Both Glissant and Nancy invoke this communal bond *ante omnia* against a conception of community in which the "I" surrenders to a wider, reassuring, and totalizing "We." In such a community, based on the exclusion of those who do

---

4   In the 26th section of *Being and Time* (1927), Heidegger clearly states that *Mitsein* plays an essential part in *Dasein's* uncovering of itself: "Being-with is in every case a characteristic of one's own Dasein; Dasein-with characterizes the Dasein of Others to the extent that it is freed by its world for a Being-with. Only so far as one's own Dasein has the essential structure of Being-with, is it Dasein-with as encounterable for Others"; Heidegger, *Being and Time*, tr. John Macquarrie & Edward Robinson (1927; Oxford: Blackwell, 2001): 157. And a bit later, Heidegger adds: "Not only is Being towards Others an autonomous, irreducible relationship of Being: this relationship, as Being-with, is one which, with Dasein's Being, already is" (162). Nancy agrees but, as Ignaas Devisch makes plain, Nancy finds the precedence of *Dasein* over *Mitsein* in *Being and Time* objectionable: "Heidegger introduced the co-originality of *Mitsein* [...] only after he extensively elaborated the originality of *Dasein*. If the 'with' really is accorded the status of being co-original with the 'there,' Nancy asks, why did Heidegger take so long to elaborate the 'with'?"; Devisch, "A Trembling Voice in the Desert: Jean-Luc Nancy's Rethinking of the Space of the Political," *Cultural Values* 4.2 (2000): 242. Devisch goes on to demonstrate how Nancy steers clear of Heidegger's ideological waywardness by calling for the transformation of Heidegger's "ontological project [into] a 'social ontology,' an ontology in which the question of the *socius*, the question of our being-with-each-other, has primary status" (243). Simon Critchley echoes Devisch when he writes that, from Nancy's vantage point, "*Being and Time* must be rewritten without the *autarkic telos* and tragic-heroic *pathos* of the thematic of authenticity, where, in Paragraph 74, *Mitsein* is determined in terms of 'the people' and its 'destiny'"; Critchley, "With Being-With? Notes on Jean-Luc Nancy's Rewriting of *Being and Time*," *Studies in Practical Philosophy* 1.1 (1999): 54.
5   In *The Inoperative Community* (1986), Nancy writes: "Community means [...] that there is no singular being without another singular being, and that there is, therefore, what might be called, in a rather inappropriate idiom, an originary or ontological 'sociality' that in its principle extends far beyond the simple theme of man as a social being (the *zoon politikon* is secondary to this community)" (28).

not belong, the individual identity is closed upon itself. Glissant uses the term "filiation," and Nancy the term "immanentism," to describe the actual or potential violence inherent to such a community, and both redefine community, through their respective notions of Relation and being-with, as originary and preceding free will. As the second section of this chapter will show, Nancy does not so much devise an ideal community as provide tools to build a community free of immanentism. He does so first by rejecting all at once the fusional communities typifying twentieth-century fascism and the exacerbated atomization of our present world, and second by postulating an absolute equality in the diversity of all experiences. We are all ontologically equal by virtue of our constitutive differences.

Glissant and Nancy developed their theories of community in the political context of the 1980s and 1990s, when the collapse of communism seemed to vindicate the proponents of a global, free market economy, and this may account for some of the analogies between their works. Both Glissant and Nancy condemn economic globalization for commodifying all aspects of life and increasing disparities, and both see globalization, which they rename *mondialité* (worldliness) and *mondialisation* (world-forming) respectively, as an opportunity to reevaluate the global world and the notion of community all at once. Glissant suggests the possibility of an alternative world in *Sartorius: le roman des Batoutos* (1999), a novel in which the mythical Batouto tribe embodies the concept of errantry, and invites us to envisage the advent of a creolized world. Nancy also encourages us to confront globalization by deconstructing it through his own concept of "struction," which looks at the disintegration of our knowable, predictable, and controllable world not only as a fatality but also as an opportunity to rebuild from nothingness. Glissant and Nancy, through their analyses of community, deliver a lucid, if somber, diagnosis of our crumbling world. They identify the symptoms, but when it comes to the cure they reach an aporia, suggesting that, despite our foundational exposure to others, it is still as political animals: i.e. rational individuals who can and will participate in social practices, that our interactions with others must be understood. The final argument of this chapter relies on Nicolas Bourriaud's *The Radicant* (2009), a study that reinvents identity and community in the whirlwind of our globalized world. The radicant, a botanical metaphor presented as a substitute for the Deleuzian rhizome, exemplifies "altermodernity," a term Bourriaud coined in order to express the continuance of modernism, albeit in a revamped form, in the twenty-first century. Bourriaud's theory of the radicant is as much an apologia of heterogeneity as Glissant's Relation and Nancy's being-with are, but unlike those two, it dismisses the multicultural ethics of postmodernism, which it depicts as neocolonialism in disguise. Bourriaud, like Glissant before him, embraces Victor Segalen's aesthetics of diversity, and is particularly interested in the figure of the Exot, which he sees as the incarnation of a successful creolization in which cultural difference is preserved after encounter. Bourriaud defines the Exot as "one who manages to return to himself after having undergone the experience of diversity."[6] The Exot does not seek to hybridize but to "translate" the Other through movement, exchange, and negotiation. Glissant would deny it, but his concept of creolization partially forfeits this ability to translate as its promotion of a dispersed and rhizomatic network of relations tends to underplay individual subjectivity. With the radicant, Bourriaud restores the subject to its central role, thereby providing a viable alternative to the de-subjectivizing effects of both neoliberal globalization and its counter-models as conceived by Glissant and Nancy.

1   Glissant's Creolization and Relation

Glissant, a French citizen, is often remembered as a Martinican thinker—a label that has pigeonholed him as a francophone: i.e. a non-metropolitan and non-white author of postcolonial theory—the soulmate of such fellow Martinican thinkers as Frantz Fanon and Aimé Césaire. Glissant may not have balked at such illustrious kinship, although his political and intellectual trajectory differs from both Fanon's and Césaire's.[7] Notwithstanding separatist leanings in his early years, Glissant never fully emulated the former's dogged political engagement, and he never sought public office as the latter did. Glissant would embrace Fanon's call to arms no more than he would extol Césaire's choice to become one of Martinique's representatives to the French parliament. Glissant backed out of direct political action after General de Gaulle put him under house arrest in 1961 for the creation of, and involvement in, the

---

6   Nicolas Bourriaud, *The Radicant*, tr. James Gussen & Lili Porten (*Radicant: pour une esthétique de la globalisation*, 2009; Berlin & New York: Lukas Sternberg, 2009): 65.

7   Glissant's view of Fanon and Césaire requires qualification. Assessing Glissant's own intellectual trajectory against that of these two compatriots, Anjali Prabhu notes: "Frantz Fanon, proclaimed Marxist in his early association with François Tosquelles as well as with his revolutionary work in Algeria; the other, Aimé Césaire, representative in the French Constituent Assembly on the Communist Party ticket. Both figures with mythical status within Martinique as well as in the postcolonial world. Césaire only resigned from the French Communist Party in 1956 to form the Parti Progressiste Martiniquais. It was around this time that Glissant would be expelled from Martinique for his work with the Algerians. If Glissant, in his public persona, resisted the type of huge monumental 'arrival' that the revolutionary figures of both Fanon and Césaire evoke, this gesture can also be read as an attempt to differentiate his career and image from those of these figures"; Prabhu, "Interrogating Hybridity: Subaltern Agency and Totality in Postcolonial Theory," *Diacritics* 35.2 (Summer 2005): 84.

Front des Antilles-Guyane pour l'Autonomie (FAGA). Glissant may not have been a man of action, but he never completely dodged political responsibility either. Just a few years before he passed away, Glissant co-authored, with Patrick Chamoiseau, *Quand les murs tombent* (2007), a political pamphlet denouncing President Sarkozy's new Ministry of Immigration, Integration, National Identity and Co-Development, which targeted, first and foremost, illegal immigrants. Glissant's oeuvre spans five decades, and although he remained a postcolonial thinker firmly attached to his Antillean heritage, he also expanded his view of the world far beyond the limits of the Caribbean and its culture. From *Les Indes* (1965), a counter-historical epic poem about the fate of Martinique at the hands of Christopher Columbus, to *10 mai: Mémoires de la traite négrière, de l'esclavage et de leurs abolitions* (2010), Glissant's writing is suffused with the inaugural violence of the Middle Passage and slavery, but also with the importance of collective memory, reconciliation, and the inevitable and auspicious synergy of arts, cultures, and people in a globalized world—a phenomenon Glissant describes through such concepts as Relation, *tout-monde*, and mondialité.[8]

The above concepts are related to the core concept of creolization, which Glissant introduced in *L'intention poétique* (1969) and expanded in *Le discours antillais* (1981; tr. as *Caribbean Discourse*, 1989). Creolization, however, became the linchpin of Glissantian thought in *Poétique de la Relation* (1990; tr. as *Poetics*

---

8   The following reflection on the notion of identity in *Quand les murs tombent* may serve as a compendium of early and late Glissantian thought: "For a long time, the very notion of identity has been used as a wall either to establish what is one's own, or to distinguish it from what is other, to finally turn it into an ill-defined threat tinged with barbarism. The wall of identity has spawned endless confrontations between peoples [as well as] empires, colonial expansion, the trafficking of Negroes, the atrocities of American slavery and all genocides. Identity as a wall has always existed, and still exists among all cultures and peoples, but it is in the West, spurred by science and technology, that it has been most devastating. Still, the world has become total world. Cultures, civilizations, and peoples have come into contact, clashed, permeated, and enhanced one another, often without knowing it"; Édouard Glissant & Patrick Chamoiseau, *Quand les murs tombent: L'identité nationale hors la loi?* (Paris: Galaade editions, 2007): 8–9; (tr. mine). And this passage from Glissant's manifesto "Tous les jours de mai," which he dedicated to Césaire and Fanon, clearly illustrates the importance of simultaneously remembering and transcending the past through Relation: "Memories of slavery do not seek to revive claims and grievances. In today's total world [...], the poetics of sharing, accepted difference, [and] emerging cultural solidarities [...] urge us, individuals and communities, from wherever we are, to bring our memories together, extend our generosity toward one another, and let knowledge blossom impetuously [...]. To unite our memories so that they liberate one another is to open the paths of a world in Relation"; Glissant, "Tous les jours de mai, ... Pour l'abolition de tous les esclavages," *Institut du Tout-Monde* (2008): online (accessed 8 November 2016) (tr. mine).

of Relation, 1997), and remained prevalent in *Introduction à une Poétique du Divers* (1996), *Traité du tout-monde* (1997) and *La Cohée du Lamentin* (2005). The term "creolization" is not new; it hearkens back, at least in the French-speaking world, to the late nineteenth century, and was then understood as a phenomenon resulting from both environmental factors and race mixing.[9] In postcolonial times, however, creolization became an intricate concept first fully theorized by Edward Kamau Brathwaite in *The Development of Creole Society in Jamaica 1770–1820* (1971). Chris Bongie notes that Brathwaite, despite the violence of slavery and the yoke of colonialism, "found a great if virtually unexplored, potential in the confluence of the two worlds of Europe and Africa, master and slave, white and black."[10] Although Brathwaite's questioning of the polarizing opposition of colonizer and colonized was groundbreaking, Bongie points out that Brathwaite later reinstated "the continued presence [...] of the original cultures that one would suppose the creolization process to have utterly transformed."[11] Glissant is indebted to Brathwaite, but while acknowledging the unique dialogical encounter of languages, races, and cultures typifying the Caribbean, he also moves beyond the persistence of ancestral cultures to celebrate creolization as a process, which, without denying the fragments of the past, has yielded a new form of identity characterized by rootlessness.

Glissant's own view of the past, present, and future of the Caribbean brings him to contrast creolization with creoleness (*créolité*):

> Creolization as an idea is not primarily the glorification of the composite nature of a people: indeed, no people has been spared the crosscultural process [...] To assert peoples are creolized, that creolization has value, is to deconstruct in this way the category of 'creolized' that is considered as halfway between two 'pure' extremes.[12]

Hence, Glissant cannot wholly agree with his epigones Jean Bernabé, Patrick Chamoiseau, and Raphaël Confiant when they stress, in their manifesto *In Praise of Creoleness* (1989), the need to move beyond Aimé Césaire and Léopold Sédar Senghor's Négritude on the basis that it is too afrocentric and fails

9   Jean-Luc Bonniol, "Au prisme de la créolisation: Tentative d'épuisement d'un concept," *L'Homme* 207–208 (2013): 238–240.

10   Chris Bongie, *Islands and Exiles: The Creole Identities of Post/Colonial Literature* (Redwood City CA: Stanford UP, 1998): 53.

11   Bongie, *Islands and Exiles*, 59.

12   Édouard Glissant, *Caribbean Discourse: Selected Essays*, sel., tr. & intro. J. Michael Dash (*Le discours antillais*, 1981; Charlottesville: UP of Virginia, 1989): 140.

to accurately reflect their Creole identity. Bernabé, Chamoiseau, and Confiant define creoleness as racially and linguistically diverse, and oppose it to the totalizing and devitalizing effects of the dominant French culture. Glissant shares their rejection of both Négritude and the French hegemon, but he sees in creoleness yet another attempt at recreating a self-contained, homogeneous, and exclusionary identity. And to the *créolistes'* claim that creoleness is an "annihilation of false universality, of monolingualism, and of purity,"[13] Glissant responds that "the principles of creoleness regress toward negritudes, ideas of Frenchness, of Latinness, all generalizing concepts—more or less innocently."[14] Creolization originates in, but is not confined to, the Caribbean and its history. It has neither spatial nor temporal limits, and neither is it morally or politically motivated. Rather, creolization is an ongoing process characterized by its unpredictable and protean nature. It is an ethics of alterity that posits a parity of cultures as a prerequisite to exchange. It is a celebration of diversity whereby the Other is not to be assimilated but acknowledged for his difference.

Glissant's reflection on diversity owes much to Victor Segalen's posthumously published *Essay on Exoticism: An Aesthetics of Diversity*. Echoing the latter's argument that "the sensation of Exoticism [...] is nothing other than the notion of difference, the perception of Diversity, the knowledge that something is other than one's self,"[15] the former writes that diversity is

> neither chaos nor sterility, [and] means the human spirit's striving for a cross-cultural relationship, without universalist transcendence. Diversity needs the presence of peoples, no longer as objects to be swallowed up, but with the intention of creating a new relationship.[16]

In *Introduction à une Poétique du Divers*, a collection of four essays intended as a tribute to Segalen, Glissant elaborates these reflections further:

> creolization requires that the heterogeneous elements brought into Relation value each other—i.e. there should be neither external nor internal

---

13   Jean Bernabé, Patrick Chamoiseau & Raphaël Confiant. *Éloge de la Créolité / In Praise of Creoleness*, tr. M.B. Taeb-Khyar (1989; Paris: Gallimard, 1993): 90. See also Holly Collins, "*La querelle de la Créolisation*: Creolization vs. *Créolité* in Glissant, Condé and the Creolists," *Nottingham French Studies* 56.1 (March 2017): 67–81.

14   Glissant, *Poetics of Relation*, 89.

15   Victor Segalen, *Essay on Exoticism: An Aesthetics of Diversity*, ed. & tr. Yael Rachel Schlick (*Essai sur l'exotisme: une esthétique du divers* (notes), 1904–18; Durham NC: Duke UP, 2002): 19.

16   Glissant, *Caribbean Discourse*, 98.

debasing and demeaning of Being—while they are in contact and in the process of mixing.[17]

Mixing (*mélange* in the original) should be interpreted neither as amalgam nor as fusion of cultures. Rather, it describes the encounter of disparate cultures that nurture but never absorb one another. Mixing, in this definition, evokes a mosaic, or perhaps the ever-changing and random variegation of a kaleidoscope. In *Poetics of Relation*, Glissant insists that creolization "brings into Relation but not to universalize" (89), for the point of creolization is not for each culture to lose its particularities in a unifying whole, but to respect difference while fostering exchange. François Noudlemann captures this difficult notion in everyday language: "the world changes by exchanging, I can change through exchanging with the other, without losing or distorting myself," adding: "Instead of the universal, Glissant presents us with the principle of an extensive relation which ceaselessly reconfigures the definition—the limits—of the world."[18]

The idea of cultures, communities, groups, and individuals preserving their identity while engaging in cultural exchange is so central to Glissant's poetics that he claims, as early as *Caribbean Discourse*, "a right to opacity" (11). Glissant then clears away all ambiguity about the term "opacity":

> No longer the opacity that enveloped and reactivated the mystery of filiation but another, considerate of all the threatened and delicious things joining one another (without conjoining, that is, without merging) in the expanse of Relation.
>
> *Poetics of Relation* 62

Later on, Glissant adds that opacity "is not enclosure within an impenetrable autarchy but subsistence within an irreducible singularity" (190). Accepting others' opacity, Glissant argues a few years later, is even more important than accepting their difference:

> I no longer need to 'understand' ['*comprendre*'] the other: that is, to reduce him/her to the model of my own transparency, in order to live with or build with him/her.
>
> *Introduction à une Poétique du Divers* 71–72 (tr. mine)

---

17   Glissant, *Introduction à une Poétique du Divers* (Paris: Gallimard, 1996): 18. (My tr.)
18   François Noudlemann, "Édouard Glissant's Legacy: Transmitting Without Universals," tr. Celia Britton, *Callaloo* 36.4 (Fall 2011): 871.

In the original, Glissant puts *comprendre* in ideational quotation marks, for *com-prendre* (from the Latin *cum-prendere*, to take hold of, to take with) denotes inclusion or incorporation. When Glissant claims the right of every individual to opacity, he means that assimilating the other to make him/her become part of oneself is neither necessary nor recommended, for the cardinal virtue of opacity is to allow individuals to keep aspects of their identity out of reach, unknowable, and mysterious. By preserving the complexity of the individual, opacity is constitutive of identity. It protects the individual from assimilation in a context of cultural domination (colonialism), and from erasure in a context of extreme standardization (globalization). It is a form of resistance to transparency—the surrendering of the self to control and uniformization imposed by repressive cultures. As Glissant puts it,

> The thought of opacity distracts me from absolute truths whose guardian I might believe myself to be, [and] saves me from unequivocal courses and irreversible choices.
>
> *Poetics of Relation* 192

Opacity ensures otherness and thus fosters diversity. And Glissant, anticipating the objection that opacity may hinder sincerity and create distrust, argues: "Opacities can coexist and converge, weaving fabrics" (190). Thus, opacity is a core element of diversity, creolization, and Relation.

Relation can be defined as the advent of creolization, which does not mean that Relation is a completed process, as Celia Britton explains:

> Relation envisages human reality [...] as a dynamic network of connections and interactions between elements (especially communities and cultures) such that the elements are constantly changing in ways that are impossible to predict.[19]

Relation is not a cure-all solution, but it can be considered a method for identifying and addressing the symptoms that obstruct the kind of cultural interactions conducive to what Glissant calls *mondialité* (worldliness, or the coming together of cultures in all their diversity) as opposed to *mondialisation* (globalization as cultural standardization from below). Thus, creolization as the fosterer of Relation is what Glissant calls, in *La Cohée du Lamentin* (2005), a "processive reality,"[20] and such a reality realizes itself in what Glissant calls

---

19   Celia Britton, "In Memory of Édouard Glissant," *Callaloo* 34.3 (Summer 2011): 670.
20   Glissant, *La Cohée du Lamentin* [*Poétique V*; Paris: Gallimard, 2005): 138. (My tr.)

tout-monde (total world), which he defines as "our universe as it changes and goes on by exchanging, and, at the same time, the 'vision' we have of it."[21]

As the world is always reinventing itself, and as the constant intermingling of cultures leads to situations that confound any prediction, Glissant also calls his *tout-monde* concept *chaos-monde*, which does not refer to disorder or turmoil but, rather, to a rejection of rectilinear modes of thinking and calcified models of community. *Chaos-monde*, Glissant explains,

> is neither fusion nor confusion: it acknowledges neither the uniform blend—a ravenous integration—nor muddled nothingness. Chaos is not 'chaotic.' But its hidden order does not presuppose hierarchies or precellencies—neither of chosen languages nor of prince nations. The *chaos-monde* is not a mechanism; it has no keys.
>
> *Poetics of Relation* 94

Relation, which is "the *chaos-monde* relating (to itself)" (94), opposes fixity, certainty, and predeterminability.

"The Open Boat," prelude to *Poetics of Relation*, does not dwell on Relation as a concept, but it heralds it. The polytropic quality of the text conveys the omneity, unforeseeability, and fluidity of Relation. This precariousness typifying Relation manifests itself in the way the opening paragraph destabilizes the reader's expectations. First, the paragraph, in its original French version, does not begin with a personal but a relative pronoun suggesting the objectivity of a history book.[22] Yet, the way in which the pronoun is used is not neutral, as it forcefully underscores the idea it introduces: "What is petrifying about the experience of the dislocation of Africans to the Americas is, no doubt, the unknown confronted without preparation or challenge" (my translation from *Poétique de la Relation*, 17). There is a hint of brusqueness in this first line. First, the cumulative force of "What is petrifying," "unknown," and "without preparation or challenge" is that of the situation of Kafka's K., suddenly arraigned by an unknown authority for a crime that is unspecified and that he

---

21   Glissant, *Traité du tout-monde* [*Poétique IV*; Paris: Gallimard, 1997]: 176. (My tr.)

22   It should be noted that Betsy Wing, who translated *Poetics of Relation* into English, chose not to keep the relative pronoun at the beginning of the sentence, and changed the tense from present to past. Glissant writes: "Ce qui *pétrifie* dans l'expérience du déportement des Africains vers les Amériques, sans doute *est*-ce l'inconnu affronté sans préparation ni défi" (*Poétique de la Relation*, 17; emphasis added). Wing's translation goes thus: "For the Africans who *lived* through the experience of deportation to the Americas, confronting the unknown with neither preparation nor challenge *was* no doubt petrifying" ("The Open Boat," 5; emphasis added).

is unaware of; second, it is unclear who, the reader or the captive in the hold, is petrified; finally, the absence of an antecedent to the sentence plunges the reader *in media res*, as if Glissant were in the middle of a lecture. This feeling of spontaneity is enhanced by the adverbial phrase "no doubt" and the relative liberty taken with the choice of words: the word for deportation in the original (*déportement*) amounts, on the face of it, to a barbarism,[23] which suggests either the improvisational style and arbitrariness of oral performance or a conscious decision on the part of the speaker to jolt the audience awake by using a term slightly out of kilter with what is expected. If *déportement* (as indicated in footnote 23) means a swerve or a veering, it may evoke, in the mind of the reader, the idea of dislocation, which etymology (bones out of joint; put out of place) conveys a stronger sense of violence than *déportation* does. Glissant luxates the language, as it were, in order to make the fracture of the Middle Passage more vivid and painful. Furthermore, the choice of the verb "petrify," for all its cogency, suggests a poetic license at odds with a dispassionate description of the slave trade. And the collocation of the verb "petrify" and the word "unknown" is outlandish without a detailed description of what is meant by "unknown"—a key term Glissant will develop at length in the paragraphs that follow. Finally, the surprise effect of that opening is heightened by a footnote referring to the transport of Africans to the New World. On the one hand, the footnote compares the Middle Passage to a fibril (a "creature" represented by a pencil sketch); on the other, it reflects on how the deterritorialization of African orality, from the hold to the plantation, has led to the "creolization of the West" (5).[24] By and large, this first paragraph bears witness to Glissant's unabated concern with the traumatic beginnings of the Caribbean, while also prefiguring the way "The Open Boat" as a text bridges the present and the past, and stands at the crossroads of history, fiction, and philosophy, between a candid account of a shocking past, a poignant response to it, and a transformative theorization of it.[25]

---

23   *Déportement* in French means neither deportation nor deportment. *Déportement* is commonly used in the plural form and means misdemeanor or misbehavior. In the singular, *déportement* means a swerve or a veering, but it is unusual. In that case, the word *embardée* is more common. In French, the word for deportation is, simply, *déportation*.

24   The "West," here, does not designate "Western civilization" and its European roots, but the earth's western hemisphere: i.e. the New World, including the Caribbean and the American continent. This idea of the "creolization of the West" (5) exemplifies Glissant's combination of separate branches of knowledge, as the historical and geographical reality of creolization is, of course, the starting point for Glissant's own concept of creolization (*contra* creoleness).

25   The footnote is a good illustration of how Glissant's work conflates various registers of language and narrative styles. Thus, the schoolbook tone generated by the fibril image

While the introductory paragraph dispenses with personal pronouns (apart from the implied authorial "I"), the rest of the text hinges upon a skillful use of personal pronouns that blurs the lines between the captives, their descendants, and the rest of humanity, putting them all, as it were, in Relation. While the second paragraph follows the style of the first, juxtaposing pedagogical tone and flights of poetry ("The first dark shadow was cast by being wrenched from their everyday, familiar land," 5), it suddenly addresses the reader directly with the second-person plural, enjoining the reader to imagine the living conditions of the captives in the hold:

> *Imagine* two hundred human beings crammed into a space barely capable of containing a third of them. *Imagine* vomit, naked flesh, swarming lice, the dead slumped, [and] the dying crouched.
> "The Open Boat" 5 (emphasis added)

The third paragraph repeats the pattern ("What is terrifying partakes of the abyss," 5), but it now addresses the captives in the hold of the slave ship with the familiar second-person singular "tu," suggesting familiarity and, perhaps, kinship.

This paragraph also introduces the key notion of the "unknown," which Glissant breaks down into three separate ordeals over the following paragraphs. The unknown first designates the hold, where human beings are turned into commodities. In the fourth paragraph, the unknown is linked to the ocean depths, where so many captives, dead or alive, are jettisoned. The text, which has reverted to the third-person singular, now pays tribute to the victims of the Middle Passage with a potent representation of the "deeps" and "their punctuation of scarcely corroded balls and chains [...] gone green" ("The Open Boat," 6)—words that echo Derek Walcott's famous lines, "Bone soldered by coral to bone" and "white cowries clustered like manacles/on the drowned women."[26] The last actualization of the unknown, detailed over the fifth, sixth, and seventh paragraphs, is the New World where survivors are faced with the brutal eradication of their cultural references and the nearly impossible task of remembering. Glissant goes back to the captives, their suffering and confusion, through their anxious questioning of the "unknown," in the form of indirect

---

vies with the less impersonal tone of such lines as "The Slave Trade came through the *cramped doorway* of the slave ship" (5; emphasis added) in the first paragraph, and "Within the ship's space *the cry of those deported was stifled* [...]" (5; emphasis added) in the second paragraph.

26   Derek Walcott, "The Sea Is History" (1979), in *Selected Poems*, ed. Edward Baugh (New York: Farrar, Straus & Giroux, 2007): 137.

speech: "What kind of river, then, has no middle? Is nothing there but straight ahead? Is this boat sailing into eternity toward the edges of a nonworld that no ancestor will haunt?" (7) Glissant calls these three instances of the unknown the abyss (*gouffre*), and the knowledge of this abyss, this maelstrom of bewilderment, shock, and agony, has spawned Relation.

The eighth paragraph begins with a line from Lautréamont's *Les Chants de Maldoror* (1868): "Je te salue, vieil Océan!" (7).[27] But the Lautréamont legacy is already there in the poetic prose of "The Open Boat" and the non-linear narrative style. It is also there in the way Glissant interrupts the flow of the narrative, as he does in the second paragraph, exhorting the reader to engage with the text and imagine what they cannot imagine (the inhumanity of the Middle Passage). In *Les Chants de Maldoror*, the phrase "Je te salue, vieil océan" is used as an antiphon in the First Canto, punctuating ten consecutive paragraphs with the anaphora "Vieil océan!" (22–27) The semantic field of Lautréamont's morbid exploration of suffering and cruelty suffuses Glissant's "The Open Boat." Glissant has borrowed specific words, phrases, or images and readapted them to his own theme of the Middle Passage, suggesting, perhaps, that the sickening trade in human bodies is as contemptuous of humanity as is the evil Maldoror. Thus, such words as *abîme* (abyss, depths), *inconnu* (unknown) or *ténèbres* (darkness, dark shadow) abound in both texts. And if "the ocean has engulfed everything into its belly" after a sea disaster in *Maldoror*,[28] the belly of the boat "swallow[s] up," "devour[s]" and "dissolves" the captives in "The Open Boat" (6). As for the description of a young man tortured by his mother and wife with "whips with leaden lashes" and tar in *Maldoror*,[29] it finds an echo in the "tar-streaked wounds" (7) of the Middle Passage survivors in "The Open Boat," although that painful experience, in the latter, initiates a new life. "The Open Boat" shares neither the assumed nihilistic design nor the gothic idiosyncrasies of *Maldoror*, but Glissant reminds us of Lautréamont in his endeavor to discourage passive reading. Through the proliferation of potent evocations, Glissant repeatedly unsettles his readers' complacent attitude toward

---

27 Lautréamont [Isidore Ducasse], *Maldoror: Les Chants de Maldoror*, "Chant premier," passim. Glissant chose to capitalize "Océan," as if to anthropomorphize the ocean more than Lautréamont did. As for Betsy Wing, she advisedly draws attention to the Lautréamont reference by leaving it in French in her translation. The repeated address is translated as "I salute you, ancient ocean!" in Lautréamont, *Maldoror: Les Chants de Maldoror*, tr. Guy Wernham (1868; tr. 1943; New York: New Directions, 1965): 10, while Paul Knight has the rendering "I hail you, old ocean!" in *Maldoror and Poems* (tr. 1978; London: Penguin Classics, 1988): 42–47 passim.

28 Lautréamont, *Maldoror*, tr. Wernham, 23.

29 *Maldoror*, tr. Wernham, 174.

the experience of the Middle Passage and compels them to use their imagination to challenge their own certitudes. Furthermore, the protean quality of the text recreates the changeability and unpredictability of Relation, thus making the reader a participant in said Relation. Glissant has always given precedence to imagination over theory, for at least two reasons: first, he believes that the plurality of imagination is an antidote to universalizing thought and a conduit to Relation; second, he endows imagination, and more specifically literature, with the power to change the world.[30] As Alessandro Corio puts it, the purpose of Glissant's stylistic strategies is to create a language "capable of breaking free of the shackles of any systemization of thought; of searching, even in the most 'philosophical' prose, for a continuous contact with the life-giving force of poetry and the imagination."[31]

The eighth paragraph is also characterized by a communal "we" that denotes identification between Glissant's Afro-Caribbean community and the victims of the Middle Passage. Glissant addresses the ocean as he would a close acquaintance and calls it "our own unconscious, furrowed with fugitive memories" (7). But the ocean is more than a repository of memories, and Glissant, in the next paragraph, erases the caesura between those who succumbed to the Middle Passage and those who survived it by establishing a continuum between death at sea and life ashore, by turning the ordeal of the dead into the crucible of the survivors, who, after profound hardships, made the new land theirs. Glissant also keeps the connection between past and present by switching tenses from *passé simple*, which is the preterite of historical accounts, to *passé composé*, which is not only an informal preterite but also a present perfect denoting the consequences of past events in the present time. The abyss, whether it is the hold of the slave ship as womb or the bottom of the ocean as sepulcher, has become knowledge, "not just a specific knowledge, appetite, suffering, and delight of one particular people" (8), Glissant argues in the next paragraph, "but knowledge of the Whole, greater from having been at the abyss

---

30   In *Introduction à une Poétique du Divers* (Paris: Gallimard, 1996): 91–92, Glissant argues: "I dream of a new approach, a new appreciation of literature, of literature as a discovery of the world, as a discovery of the *Tout-Monde*. I think that all peoples today have an important role to play in the non-system of relations of the *Tout-Monde*, and that a people that lacks the means to think about this function is indeed an oppressed people, a people that is kept in a state of infirmity. Thus, I dream, since I am a writer, I dream of a new approach to literature in this excess that is the *Tout-Monde*"; translated thus in Bernadette Cailler, "Totality and Infinity, Alterity, and Relation: From Levinas to Glissant," *Journal of French and Francophone Philosophy / Revue de la philosophie française et de langue française* 19.1 (2011): 143–144.

31   Alessandro Corio, "The Living and the Poetic Intention: Glissant's Biopolitics of Literature," *Callaloo* 36.4 (Fall 2013): 920.

and freeing knowledge of Relation within the Whole" (8). As Stanka Radović puts it, this knowledge of the abyss has generated "not only the specificity of the cultures sprung from slavery, but also their profound and enduring connection to the world as a whole."[32] Glissant illustrates this key point by redefining the meaning of the communal "we" at the end of "The Open Boat."

In the penultimate paragraph, Glissant argues that while the Middle Passage has made "you, original victim floating toward the sea's abysses, an exception, it became something shared and made us, the descendants, one people among others" (8). Glissant's emphasis on the continuum between "you, the original victim" and "us, the descendants" still seems restrictive, but he immediately mitigates this initial impression by reinscribing this phylogenetic view of his people in a much wider whole. Also, Glissant insists that the unique, harrowing experience of the Middle Passage yielded more than despair and death: from that chaos, a people has emerged—not a people defined solely by the stigmata of its tragic origins, but a people among other peoples. Glissant's endeavor to free his people from the scarring of the past is not meant to erase that past but to prevent his people from defining themselves as a martyred people—which, because of the especial destiny implied, would embrace the kind of ethnocentric attitudes that once characterized those who had put Africans and their descendants under their yoke. As he argues in the preceding paragraph: "Peoples who have been to the abyss do not brag of being chosen. They do not believe they are giving birth to any modern force" (8). Earlier, in the third paragraph, when addressing the captive in the hold, Glissant compares the Middle Passage to a violent birth and offers the captive (and the reader) a rather confounding explanation for the phenomenon: "Although you are alone in that suffering, you share in the unknown with others whom you have yet to know" (6). While the traumatic experience of the matrix hold, of the "absolute unknown," does inflict utter suffering, it also generates "all the coming unanimity" (6), which is eventually described, in the tenth paragraph, as "knowledge of the whole" (8). The transformation from the forlorn captives' sharing of their torment to the knowledge of Relation is not a unifying process of separate entities. In Relation, every individual preserves and shares their specificity simultaneously. Relation is "understanding"—standing amidst; it is neither the fusion nor the appropriation and refashioning of one by the other. Relation is not negotiation but reciprocity, hence Glissant's remark at the close of the paragraph: "This experience of the abyss can now be said to

---

32   Stanka Radović, "The Birthplace of Relation: Édouard Glissant's *Poétique de la Relation*," *Callaloo* 30.2 (Spring 2007): 475.

be the best element of exchange" (8).[33] Relation is a way of apprehending the world that defies both filiation and what Glissant calls "continental thinking," which thwarts diversity and soon degenerates into various forms of exclusion, domination, and conflict.

2   From Glissant's Relation to Nancy's Being-With

Poetics of Relation can be read as a warning about the dangers of identitarian closure and as an indictment of what Glissant calls "filiation," the ideology on which European cultures have built their dual view of the world and justified their subjugation of cultures deemed inferior. Glissant suggests that filiation has always defined European mythologies, including Christianity, of which the central figure, Jesus Christ, is both the incarnation and the extension of God's paternal authority over the entire Church and the universe. As Glissant argues,

> The retelling (certifying) of a 'creation of the world' in a filiation guarantees that this same filiation—or legitimacy—rigorously ensues simply by describing in reverse the trajectory of the community, from its present to this act of creation.
>
> *Poetics of Relation* 47

Contrasting Christianity and other cultures based on a genesis with Buddhism, a faith characterized by cycles of birth, death, and rebirth, Glissant argues as follows:

> Thinking about One is not thinking about All. These myths express communities, each one innocently transparent for self and threateningly opaque for the other. They are functional, even if they take obscure or devious means. They suggest that the self's opacity for the other is insurmountable, and, consequently, no matter how opaque the other is for oneself (no myth ever provides for the legitimacy of the other), it will always be a question of reducing this other to the transparency experienced by one-self. Either the other is assimilated, or else it is annihilated. That is the whole principle of generalization and its entire process.
>
> *Poetics of Relation* 49

---

33   Although Betsy Wing chose a passive form to convey this thought, Glissant uses the first-person plural "nous" in the original: "Nous pouvons dire maintenant que cette expérience du gouffre est la chose la mieux échangée" (*Poétique de la Relation*, 20). By now, this "nous" no longer stands for Glissant's people alone—Glissant's people is "one people among others" ("The Open Boat," 8).

Glissant calls such cultures that rely on a creation myth for self-legitimization and violence "atavistic cultures," and he opposes them to "composite cultures": i.e. cultures which, like his own, are the result of a mixing of disparate atavistic cultures: "the genesis of Creole societies of the Americas," Glissant contends in *Traité du tout-monde*, "vanishes into this other obscurity, that of the belly of the slave ship. I call this digenesis [*digenèse*]."[34] Glissant's digenesis is the antidote to what he calls "root-identity," which would be similar to what Gilles Deleuze and Félix Guattari call "arborescence" (the opposite of the rhizome) in *A Thousand Plateaus* (1980).[35] Root-identity is characterized by sedentarization, and limits contact and exchange with the outside. It confers power on one group over other groups, and leads to the birth of particularisms. Western civilization, with its history of expansion and acculturation of others, is Glissant's prime suspect, but he never indulges in facile finger-pointing, warning:

> Most of the nations that gained freedom from colonization have tended to form around an idea of power—the totalitarian drive of a single, unique root—rather than around a fundamental relationship with the Other.
> *Poetics of Relation* 14

Glissant's idea of a "fundamental relationship with the Other" is also central to Jean-Luc Nancy's reappraisal of community, and the former's fight against

---

34   Glissant, *Traité du tout-monde*, 36 (tr. mine). A decade later, in *Faulkner, Mississippi* (2000), Glissant returns to this notion of digenesis, describing the specific formation of creolized cultures, which are not based on a unifying, foundational story: "The word in the tale cannot pretend not to know that at the birth of the Antillean or Caribbean people there was no Genesis, but a historical fact established over and over again and erased over and over again from public memory: Slavery. The holocaust of the slave trade and the belly of the slave ship (millions and millions of people displaced, killed, mutilated, raped, belittled, and made degenerate) confer a much more imperative Genesis, even if the origin proceeds from a point that is hybrid. [...] This new type of 'origin,' which is not about the creation of a world, I will call a 'digenesis'"; Glissant, "The Deferred—The Word" (1986), in Glissant, *Faulkner, Mississippi*, tr. Barbara Lewis & Thomas C. Spear (Chicago: U of Chicago P, 2000): 194. In *Traité du tout-monde*, the fourth, as yet untranslated volume of *Poetics*, Glissant explains how Europeans have used Christianity and what they believe to be their special relationship to God in order to claim for themselves the right to expropriate, subjugate, and exploit non-Christian cultures, and he condenses his definition of filiation thus: "Filiation and legitimacy are the lifeblood of this kind of Divine Right of property, at least as far as European cultures are concerned" (35; tr. mine).

35   In *Poetics of Relation*, Glissant writes: "Gilles Deleuze and Félix Guattari criticized notions of the root and even, perhaps, notions of being rooted. The root is unique, a stock taking all upon itself and killing all around it. In opposition to this they propose the rhizome, an enmeshed root system, a network spreading either in the ground or in the air, with no predatory rootstock taking over permanently. The notion of the rhizome maintains, therefore, the idea of rootedness but challenges that of a totalitarian root" (11).

filiation coincides with the latter's against immanentism. Both Glissant and Nancy find in the moral corruption of European cultures a starting point from which to elaborate their theories. In *The Inoperative Community* (1986), Nancy focusses on European cultures and their proclivity to exclude or discriminate against outsiders, but he chooses the totalitarian experiments of the twentieth century—Nazism and Soviet communism—to make his point. Nancy uses the term "immanentism" to describe the inward-looking attitude of such communities. As Ignaas Devisch explains,

> the longing for 'immanence' [...] is the communal equivalent of the individual aspiration to incorporate its own limit, the subjective striving towards an immanent or enclosed presence with oneself.
> "A Trembling Voice in the Desert" 240

And Nancy situates this longing in nostalgia for a lost community:

> The natural family, the Athenian city, the Roman Republic, the first Christian community, corporations, communes or brotherhoods—always it is a matter of a lost age in which community was woven of tight, harmonious, and infrangible bonds and in which above all it played back to itself, through its institutions, its rituals, and its symbols, the representation, indeed the living offering, of its own immanent unity, intimacy, and autonomy.
> *The Inoperative Community* 9

Nancy's description of this "lost community" bears a striking resemblance to Glissant's description of creation myths, and both agree that there cannot be one common source and one common destiny. Furthermore, Nancy's deconstruction of immanentism is reminiscent of Glissant's deconstruction of filiation. As a pursuit, Glissant explains, Relation is "the sum total of *all the differences* in the world."[36] In Relation, Glissant argues at the beginning of *Poetics of Relation*, "each and every identity is extended through a relationship with the Other" (11), but this whole is not synonymous with oneness, as the multiplicity of exchanges generates multiplicity. In Glissant's poetics, totality is opposed to the universalizing flow of root thinking. Totality embodies diversity: it is the advent of a world in Relation. As Lorna Burns puts it, "the functioning of Relation is an attribute of the totality, the movement through which the

---

36   Glissant, *Philosophie de la Relation: Poésie en étendue* (Paris: Gallimard, 2009): 42. (My tr.)

totality realises and diversifies itself."[37] Relation differs from totality, Glissant explains, in that

> Relation is active within itself, whereas totality, already in its very concept, is in danger of immobility. Relation is open totality; totality would be relation at rest. Totality is virtual [...]. Relation is movement.
>
> *Poetics of Relation* 171

Relation is the catalyst of totality; it is limitless, and it precludes immanentism. Glissant, in words echoing those of Nancy, writes that "the idea of totality alone is an obstacle to totality" (*Poetics of Relation*, 192). In other words, to be in Relation does not mean belonging to a finite entity. The "I" does not dissolve in an all-embracing "We." Relation is not a social contract that a subject decides to adhere to in order to belong to a community. Nancy never refers to Glissant's Relation *sensu stricto*, but for Nancy, the idea of being related to others preexists any social or political involvement. In Nancy's view, there is no being without being-with, and this is the meeting-point of his and Glissant's thought.

Glissant's notion of a universal knowledge born out of the unknown and conducive to Relation is difficult to grasp. In the original version of "The Open Boat," the word Glissant uses for "knowledge" is *connaissance*. The metaphor of the hold as womb in the text invites one to err, as Paul Claudel once did, on the side of Cratylism and read *connaissance* as "co-naissance" (to be born together),[38] but etymology teaches otherwise: the word *connaissance* comes from the Latin *cognoscere*, with the prefix co- from *cum-* for "with," and the root *gnocere*, for "knowledge." In other words, "co[n]-naissance" means "to know with" or "to know in common," implying that knowledge, including knowledge of self, is contingent on alterity. Relation, Glissant argues in "The Open Boat," "is not made up of things that are foreign, but of shared knowledge" (8). As shown earlier, Relation starts in the hold where the captive, in his/her solitude

---

37   Lorna Burns, "Becoming-postcolonial, Becoming-Caribbean: Édouard Glissant and the poetics of creolization," *Textual Practice* 23.1 (February 2009): 106.

38   In "Traité de la co-naissance au monde et de soi-même," the second part of *Art poétique*, Claudel writes: "Nous ne naissons pas seuls. Naître, pour tout, c'est connaître. Toute naissance est une connaissance"; *Art poétique* (1907; Paris: Mercure de France, 1913): 62. Cf. "We do not come into the world alone. To be born for everything, means to be born in affinity with everything. All birth is knowledge (naissance-connaissance)," in "Discourse on the affinity with the world and on oneself," in Claudel, *Poetic Art*, tr. Renee Spodheim (tr. 1948; Port Washington WA: Kennikat, 1969): 40.

and pain, is already "shar[ing] in the unknown with others" (6). Glissant's statement is puzzling because the idea of sharing has been associated with the idea of mutual agreement and choice on the part of the individual. But Glissant challenges this idea by foregrounding the isolation of the subject, as the second-person plural *vous* of the second paragraph has given way to the second-person singular *tu* in the third paragraph. This pronoun *tu* cannot be the embodiment of free will, since falling "in the belly of the boat" (6) is not a matter of choice but a matter of circumstance. Of course, the particular experience of the Middle Passage exacerbates the subject's total lack of agency, but what Glissant seeks to make manifest is that this bareness of the subject is not contingent on occurrences but constitutive of the human experience. As Nancy argues, following Heidegger's reflection on *Mitsein* (being-with) and *Dasein* (being-there), there is no being without being-with: i.e. no existence without coexistence—a notion that underlies his whole theory of community. Nancy defines community thus:

> Community means [...] that there is no singular being without another singular being, and that there is, therefore, what might be called, in a rather inappropriate idiom, an originary or ontological 'sociality' that in its principle extends far beyond the simple theme of man as a social being.
> *The Inoperative Community* 28

In *The Experience of Freedom* (1988), Nancy reflects on the meaning of sharing in ways that strikingly overlap with Glissant's own understanding of that notion when describing the lone, alienated captive in the hold:

> Being-*in*-common means that being is nothing that we would have as common property, even though we are, or even though being is not common to us except in the mode of *being shared*. Not that a common and general substance would be distributed to us, but rather, being is *only* shared *between* existents and *in* existents (or between beings in general and in beings [...] but it is always according to existence as such that being is at stake as being). Consequently, on the one hand, there is no being between *existents*—the space of existences is their spacing, and is not a tissue or a support belonging to everyone and no one and which would therefore belong to itself—and on the other hand, the being of each existence, that which it shares of being and by which it *is*, is nothing other [...] than this very sharing. Thus, what divides us is shared out to us: the

withdrawal of being, which is the withdrawal of the properness of self and the opening of existence as existence.[39]

Nancy also calls this "being-*in*-common" being-together, being-in-the-world or being singular plural. The sense of our existence is not determined by a preexisting world but by the fact that we coexist and are exposed to one another. To paraphrase Nancy's terminology, we are always already thrown into the world, which does not mean that, as a collective "We," we form a community. On the contrary, Nancy argues that instead of unity, there is a plurality of singularities, and that each singularity is complex, different, and diverse. Marie-Ève Morin clarifies Nancy's approach thus:

> Because no identity is pure, Nancy will prefer to speak of a *mêlée* instead of a *mélange*. The idea of mixture presupposes the isolation of pure substances and the operation of a mixture. There are no bloods, no races, no subjects to be mixed, but there are still identifiable elements that entangle and disentangle themselves. Thanks to the concept of *ipseity*, it is possible to think of a style, a language, a culture, a city, not as unity, but as a certain identifiable tone that is never contained in any fixed set of features and that, consequently, always remains at the same time unidentifiable, inimitable.[40]

Just as Nancy prefers *mêlée* to *mélange*, Glissant prefers the idea of creolization to that of *métissage*, a term he rejects as pejorative because it denotes forced crossbreeding in the plantation culture of the New World. As Glissant argues in *Poetics of Relation*, "The long list of martyrdoms is also a long *métissage*, whether involuntary or intentional" (67). And it is against this notion of *métissage* that Glissant defines his notion of creolization:

---

39   Jean-Luc Nancy, *The Experience of Freedom*, tr. Bridget McDonald, foreword by Peter
      Fenves (*L'Expérience de la liberté*, 1988; Stanford CA: Stanford UP, 1993): 69–70 (italics in
      the original).

40   Marie-Ève Morin, "Putting Community Under Erasure: Derrida and Nancy on the Plural-
      ity of Singularities," *Culture Machine* 8 (2006): online (accessed 26 October 2016). Focus-
      sing on Nancy's *Being Singular Plural* (1996), Morin describes Nancy's concept of ipseity
      as follows: "Nancy's singular plural does not only mean that there is always a plurality of
      singularities; it means first and foremost that a singularity is itself always plural or mul-
      tiple. There are singular differences in that which we call 'identity,' but those differences,
      or this plurality within singularity, does not prevent identification from taking place. It is
      those 'identifications' that Nancy will name 'ipseity.'"

If we posit *métissage* as, generally speaking, the meeting and synthesis of two differences, creolization seems to be a limitless *métissage*, its elements diffracted and its consequences unforeseeable. Creolization diffracts, whereas certain forms of *métissage* can concentrate one more time. Here it is devoted to what has burst forth from lands that are no longer islands. [...] Creolization carries along [...] into the incredible explosion of cultures. But the explosion of cultures does not mean they are scattered or mutually diluted. It is the violent sign of their consensual, not imposed, sharing.

> *Poetics of Relation* 34

The original French title for Nancy's *Inoperative Community* is *La communauté désoeuvrée*, in which "désoeuvrée" means, literally, "unworked." For Nancy, to unwork the community is to rethink community by transcending immanentism. To unwork the community is to reinvent the world, and such a world, Morin argues, is a world that "make[s] room for all singularities [so as] to create a world in which every singularity can expose itself."[41] Glissant's image of the hold as the "non-world" is a potent illustration of a world that has been erased, a world that can no longer be represented as a reassuring, determined, and unified whole. But instead of longing for such a world, Glissant sees in its demise the possibility for a total world—a world in Relation—to rise. This is not very different from Nancy's notion of *mondialisation*—i.e. globalization—not the capitalist globalization orchestrated by and for the West, but globalization understood as a decentered, chaotic, and "liberating process of creation."[42] Glissant coined the aforementioned term *mondialité* to designate the same phenomenon.

Mondialité is modeled on the historical process of creolization that occurred in the Caribbean as a result of the slave trade, slavery, and colonization. Only now, the accelerated encounter of cultures is the result of the exponential growth of the free-market economy on a world scale. The dialectic of oppressed vs oppressors is the same, but Glissant believes that against the standardizing effects of economic globalization, *mondialité*, which respects the diversity of cultures, can play the role of a counter-hegemonic power and foster the blossoming of a constantly evolving world based on cultural and artistic exchanges. What Nancy and Glissant aspire to is a world of sharing rather than dominance. As Glissant reminds his reader at the end of "The Open Boat": "Our boats are open, we sail them for everyone" (9).

---

41   Morin, "Putting Community Under Erasure."
42   Marie-Ève Morin, in *The Nancy Dictionary*, ed. Peter Gratton & Marie-Ève Morin (Edinburgh: Edinburgh UP, 2015): 102.

3   From Slave Trade to Globalization: Errantry and Struction

While Glissant developed his central notions of creolization and Relation from the concrete, historical destiny of his own creole community in the Caribbean, his conception of the "creolized individual" has become more abstract because his shifting from historical events to a prototype applicable to the whole world contributes to disembodying his subject. In the novel *Sartorius: le roman des Batoutos* (1999),[43] Glissant features the Batouto tribe, which, like the Allmuseri tribe in Charles Johnson's *Middle Passage*, is the stuff of legend. The Batoutos are trans-historical and ubiquitous; and they are never weak or at the mercy of circumstances. Unlike the Allmuseri, however, the Batoutos, as fictional characters, do not seem to evolve. This lack of character development is not fortuitous. First, chapters tend to be short, and each chapter features a different Batouto in a situation that is not necessarily related to the preceding or following chapter. Thus, the narrative thread is tenuous, and the same otherworldliness that made the Allmuseri an intriguing tribe makes the Batoutos an artificial and contrived one. Second, while the Allmuseri soon prove to be as flawed as any other people, the Batoutos seem to be infallible, arguably because, from a narrative perspective, their feelings and personalities do not count as much as what they bear witness to. *Sartorius* is a fable in which the Batoutos are the vehicle of Glissant's theories—first and foremost creolization, which opposes hierarchy, linearity, and predictability. The story of the Batoutos puts an infinite variation of temporalities and spatialities in relation, without preconceived sequencing. They embody the idea of multiplicity as a founding principle of creolization.[44]

---

43   As in *Faulkner, Mississippi*, Glissant, in *Sartorius*, is engaging with what Michael Wiedorn calls "the quasi-totality of Faulkner's work" and seeking the universal in the particular; indeed, the title *Sartorius* "alludes to Faulkner's novel of almost the same name, *Sartoris* (1929)"; Wiedorn, *Think Like an Archipelago: Paradox in the Work of Édouard Glissant* (Albany: State U of New York P, 2018): 35, 36. There is a further possible consideration: "sartorius" is the name given to a muscle, crossing the front of the thigh obliquely, which assists in rotating the leg to the cross-legged position in which the knees are spread wide apart; it derives from Medieval Latin *sartor* "tailor" and alludes to the constricted position adopted while mending. The word would serve Glissant as a bitterly ironic indication of the position slaves are forced into when shackled in the hold.

44   My view concurs with Christopher Miller's when the latter describes *Sartorius* as "kaleidoscopic, adhering to the 'fractal' poetics that Glissant sees as Creole: bouncing around the globe and back and forth in history, with flashes of autobiography, winks to the author's friends, snippets of anthropology, and gleaning from history—but still, continually returning to the story of the Batoutos"; Miller, *The French Atlantic Triangle: Literature and Culture of the Slave Trade* (Durham NC: Duke UP, 2012): 350. However, my view diverges from Miller's when, putting *Sartorius* on a par with Johnson's *Middle Passage*,

In *Sartorius*, the epigraph by Gilles Deleuze heralds Glissant's project:

> Health as literature, as writing, consists in inventing a people that is miss-
> ing. It is the task of the fabulating function to invent a people. We do
> not write with memories, unless it is to make them the origin and collec-
> tive destination of a people to come still ensconced in its betrayals and
> repudiations.[45]

The role of literature is to imagine new horizons to challenge pre-established
ideas, as well as to expand and refine our understanding of the world, and
Glissant's Batoutos are Deleuze's "missing people." Christopher Miller, warning of the "dangerous hypothesis of a 'happy' Middle Passage," notes that the
Batoutos are the "guardian spirits of the slave trade, mythic figures who pass
imperceptibly through the crucible of the Middle Passage and slavery, emerging unscathed, invisible, and 'singular' wherever they go";[46] and Hans Ulrich
Obrist describes them as a utopian people "deriving its identity not from its
own genealogy, but solely from being in constant exchange with others."[47] The

---

he maintains, in particular: "The function of the Batoutos [...] is similar to that of the
Allmuseri" (350). Miller blows hot and cold with regard to *Sartorius*. After a few unspar-
ing paragraphs informed by Peter Hallward's censorious critique of Glissant and other
postcolonial thinkers, Miller dissociates himself from Hallward, arguing that it "would
be reductionist" to read *Sartorius* as "a manifesto of the emergent Tout-Monde" (356).
And Miller concedes: "Perhaps because I admire the novel, and because it has important
things to say about the slave trade, I would like to 'save' it, so to speak, from Glissant's
own theorizing—from the homogeneization of the Tout-Monde" (356). Miller rightly describes *Sartorius* as the first "major, modern novel in French that is principally concerned
with the slave trade" (349); but he might have given a bit more credit to François Bourgeon's *Les passagers du vent* (first series 1979–84), a well-informed and informative five-
volume *bande dessinée* about the slave trade that amounts to much more than a "form
of adventure romance" whose iconography is characterized as "soft pornography" (410).
Miller's overall assessment, however, is accurate: "What is lacking in France is the equivalent of a Barry Unsworth, whose *Sacred Hunger*, through the power of literature, makes
the involvement of Liverpool in the Atlantic slave trade (fictively) real and compelling"
(389). Since Miller wrote *The French Atlantic Triangle* (2012), Léonora Miano's *La saison
de l'ombre* (2013) has somewhat made up for this shortcoming in French and francophone
literature, although Miano's endeavor remains singularly isolated at a time of intense debate about the slave-trading and colonial past of France.

45   Gilles Deleuze, "Literature and Life," in Deleuze, *Essays Critical and Clinical*, tr. Daniel W.
      Smith & Michael A. Greco (Minneapolis: U of Minnesota P, 1997): 4.
46   Miller, *The French Atlantic Triangle*, 354.
47   Hans Ulrich Obrist & Édouard Glissant, *Édouard Glissant & Hans Ulrich Obrist: 100 Notes
      – 100 Thoughts / 100 Notizen - 100 Gedanken* (DOCUMENTA (13): №038 Series; Ostfildern:
      Hatje Cantz, 2012): 5.

idea of lineage, so central to Alex Haley's *Roots*, is here invalidated, as lineage bespeaks root thinking. Cécile Chapon Rodriguez compares the story of the Batoutos to a "counter-genealogy" and, alluding to Glissant's notion of a "prophetic vision of the past," argues that the "utopian potential of the Batoutos," like the total world, appears as a "prophetic inversion of the absolute negativity of the slave ship."[48] Suzanne Crosta describes *Sartorius* as "an actualized myth where illusion, vision, dream, and nightmare make us oscillate between absence and presence."[49] The story of the Batoutos, Crosta further argues, is a "mode of resistance" to the "inexorable progression of empire," to which Glissant's total world is the antidote.[50] If Maldoror is our bad conscience, the Batoutos are our utopian conscience, which helps us envision what a world in Relation could be. Echoing Ernst Bloch's notion of "concrete utopia," which "is concerned to deliver the forms and contents which have already developed in the womb of present society,"[51] Glissant claims, in *La Cohée du Lamentin,* that "utopia is not a dream. It is what is missing in the world."[52] Bloch calls this kind of utopia "a realistic anticipation of what is good,"[53] implying that a possible future is already here, in the making. It is therefore a matter of making that future tangible so that it can become real.

Although the Batoutos remain a very elusive people, their main attributes are displayed in the preamble to *Sartorius*. The Batoutos appeared five hundred years ago somewhere in Africa. They are a nonviolent people interested neither in conquest nor in oppression, and they have conceived Éléné! as "a place in time where humanities will finally come together."[54] Éléné! is the result of an evolution from the global world to the total world. It is Relation realized, but still in the form of an ongoing process, neither to a standstill nor to an end. The story, the narrator indicates, is based on "what [the Batoutos] told a few of us," but this veneer of authenticity is immediately downplayed as the narrator emends what has just been stated: "we dream them more than

---

48   Cécile Chapon Rodriguez, "Entre utopie et chaos: la pensée du Tout-Monde comme alternative à la mondialisation chez Édouard Glissant," *Notes de la communication du mardi 15 décembre 2015: Séminaire Les Armes de la Critique,* Université Paris-Sorbonne (24 May 2017): online (accessed 11 November 2017): 4, 5.

49   Suzanne Crosta, "Des poétiques de relation et de globalisation dans la Caraïbe francophone," *Thamyris* 8 (2001): 47. (Tr. mine.)

50   Crosta, "Des poétiques de relation et de globalisation dans la Caraïbe francophone," 37.

51   Ernst Bloch, *The Principle of Hope,* vol. 2: *Outlines of a Better World,* tr. Neville Plaice, Stephen Plaice & Paul Knight (*Das Prinzip Hoffnung,* 1959; Cambridge MA: MIT Press, 1995): 623.

52   Glissant, *La Cohée du Lamentin,* 16.

53   Bloch, *The Principle of Hope,* 623.

54   Édouard Glissant, *Sartorius: le roman des Batoutos* (Paris: Gallimard, 1999): 15. (My tr.)

we know them."[55] As in a dream, the Batoutos reveal themselves to us in fragments, and their story is not presented in a linear fashion: unrelated situations and scenes follow one another without any apparent logic. The Batoutos are the repository of all the misery Africa and its people went through across the ages on the seven continents.

Chapter after chapter, the Batoutos are featured in historical events great and small, illustrating another Deleuzian concept dear to Glissant, nomadology. Nomadology, Deleuze and Guattari write in *A Thousand Plateaus* (1980), is the opposite of history: i.e. official history as it is "always written from the sedentary point of view and in the name of a unitary State apparatus."[56] The Batoutos give shape to a form of nomadism that contrasts with what Glissant calls the "invading nomadism" of the Huns, the Vandals or the Conquistadors, "whose goal was to conquer lands by exterminating their occupants" (*Poetics of Relation*, 12). But Glissant is concerned not so much with the territorial invasions of these conquering hordes as with what comes after the conquest, for the "arrow-like nomadism" of these hordes, Glissant argues, is a "devastating desire for settlement" (12). In other words, arrow-like nomadism, whose essence is movement, harbors the desire to take root, and it is such a desire that begets nations, their creation of myths to legitimize their "right to possession of a territory," their forging of an identity necessarily defined by opposition to an Other, and the ensuing "passion to impose civilization on [that] Other" (13). Nomadism corresponds to the absence of "a totalitarian root" (11), which Glissant opposes to the rhizome. Rhizomatic thought, Glissant writes, is "what I call the Poetics of Relation, in which each and every identity is extended through a relationship with the Other" (11). Nomadism is often associated with anti-conformism, but this does not mean, Glissant warns, that nomadism is "subversive or that rhizomatic thought has the capacity to overturn the order of the world—because, by so doing, one reverts to ideological claims presumably challenged by this thought" (11–12). Once anti-conformism becomes the norm, it is, by nature, conformist. And once nomadism is accepted or recognized as the path to follow, there is a chance that it will set itself up as the type of dominant model it sought to denounce or destroy in the first place. Finally, Glissant is careful not to romanticize nomadism when he asks:

> But is the nomad not overdetermined by the conditions of his existence? Rather than the enjoyment of freedom, is nomadism not a form

55   Glissant, *Sartorius: le roman des Batoutos*, 15.
56   Gilles Deleuze & Félix Guattari, *A Thousand Plateaus: Capitalism and Schizophrenia*, tr. Brian Massumi (*Capitalisme et schizophrénie 2: Mille plateaux*, 1980; Minneapolis: U of Minnesota P, 1987): 23.

of obedience to contingencies that are restrictive? Take, for example, circular nomadism: each time a portion of the territory is exhausted, the group moves around. Its function is to ensure the survival of the group by means of this circularity.

Poetics of Relation 12

Glissant has in mind itinerant artists, seasonal laborers, and any other type of individuals whose occupation obliges them to be constantly on the move. Circular nomadism is here understood as a lifestyle. Such "nomads" are not settled, but they are not uprooted either. They have a purpose and their itinerancy is not errancy (aimless wandering).

Soon, Glissant leaves Deleuze and Guattari's notion of nomadism behind and introduces his own notion of *errance*, which has been translated as "errantry."[57] Errantry corresponds to a state of exile, but Glissant, rather than expatiating upon the hardships of such a life, likens it to a project, or even, in the words of Betsy Wing, "a sacred mission" (*Poetics of Relation*, xvi). Errantry, Glissant contends, "is constitutive of Relation,"[58] and just as he sees today's globalization as the opportune moment for Relation to be implemented, he situates errantry on a historical timeline. Historically, errantry materialized after the "period of invading nomads" (14) and their "passion for self-definition" (14). Errantry is an advanced form of nomadism, and the thought of errantry "bucking the current of nationalist expansion" (14) was already there, in gestation, "disguised 'within' very personalized adventures" such as that "of a troubadour or that of Rimbaud" (15) whose experience was "an arrant, passionate desire to go against a root" (15). In other words, the likes of Rimbaud are already imbued with Relation even though they are not conscious of it. Glissant adds that all the "great founding books of communities," including "the *Old Testament*, the *Iliad*, the *Odyssey*, the Chansons de Geste, the Islandic Sagas, the *Aeneid*, or the African epics" (15), tell of "errantry as temptation" because, "when the very idea of territory becomes relative, nuances appear in the legitimacy of territorial possession" (15). These sacred books, according to Glissant, not only refute "massive, dogmatic, and totalitarian certainty" (15) but also go "beyond the pursuits and triumphs of rootedness required by the evolution of history" (16). The quest for totality starts "from a nonuniversal context of histories of the West" (18), and in its latest stage the "dialectic of totality turns out to be driven by the thought of errantry" (17).

---

57   See also this chapter, fn. 2 above.
58   Glissant, *Philosophie de la Relation: Poésie en étendue*, 61. (Tr. mine.)

The Batoutos, who express their sense of identity and community neither through filiation nor through an omnipotent notion of the universal, are the reification of errantry. As Glissant argues,

> This thinking of errantry, this errant thought, silently emerges from the destructuring of compact national entities that yesterday were still triumphant and, at the same time, from difficult, uncertain births of new forms of identity that call to us.
> *Poetics of Relation* 18

Glissant does not see uprooting as something with fatal consequences. On the contrary, he believes that it "can work toward identity and [that] exile can be seen as beneficial, when they [uprooting and exile] are experienced as a search for the Other" (18). This new way of building identity through exchange is what the narrator of "The Open Boat" refers to when he tells the captive in the hold of the slave ship: "Although you are alone in this suffering, you share in the unknown with others whom you have yet to know" (6). Errantry is yet another way for Glissant to re-imagine our relationship to others outside the Eurocentric (i.e. dualistic) view of the world.[59] Errantry, Glissant writes, "is at variance with territorial intolerance, or the predatory effects of the unique root" (20).

Errantry is above all a state of mind. As Glissant puts it,

> errantry [...] does not proceed from renunciation nor from frustration regarding a supposedly deteriorated (deterritorialized) situation of origin; it is not a resolute act of rejection or an uncontrolled impulse of abandonment.
> *Poetics of Relation* 18

Rather, it is a leap toward the Other, and even those who "have never experienced the melancholy and extroverted luxury of uprooting" (19) may still experience errantry, for errantry is a disposition present in each and every one of us. Errantry is inherent, but it lies dormant and needs to be externalized. Those

---

59   Glissant makes clear that the dualistic view of the world is not the preserve of European cultures, even if the latter are the most salient illustration of it: "Most of the nations that gained freedom from colonization have tended to form around an idea of power—the totalitarian drive of a single, unique root—rather than around a fundamental relationship with the Other. Culture's self-conception was dualistic, pitting citizen against barbarian. Nothing has ever more solidly opposed the thought of errantry than this period in human history when Western nations were established and then made their impact on the world" (14).

who undergo this stationary errantry, Glissant argues, "may suffer the torments of internal exile" (19), which

> strikes individuals living where solutions concerning the relationship of a community to its surroundings are not, or at least not yet, consented to by this community as a whole. These solutions, precariously outlined as decisions, are still the prerogative of only a few, who, as a result, are marginalized.
>
> *Poetics of Relation* 19

Unlike exile, which is a form of banishment, or errancy, which evokes roaming about, losing one's way, and even being in error, errantry has a purpose: it is a will to challenge the root: i.e. any form of monolithic thinking imposed on the self and the community. As Glissant puts it, the errant individual "challenges and discards the universal—this generalizing edict that summarized the world as something obvious and transparent, claiming for it one presupposed sense and one destiny" (20).

The French term *errance* has also made its way into the Nancean corpus, although Nancy, unlike Glissant, has not turned *errance* into a mindset whereby individuals seek to redefine their identity as an act of self-liberation. Nancy concurs with Glissant on the dangers of universalizing principles and policies, but Nancy's *errance* is neither a quest nor an ethos. Rather, it is an occurrence defined by its facticity, without cause or reason, and devoid of either a positive or a negative valency. Whereas Glissant's *errance* is translated as "errantry," Nancy's *errance* is translated as "errancy," which, as I have intimated, denotes "wandering aimlessly" or "being in error," because it is associated with the indeterminacy of being thrown into the world (much like Heidegger's *Geworfenheit*). Nancy's errancy marks the groundlessness of being—the uncontrolled, accidental, and inoperative relation to others. *Errance* is, so to speak, *ab-errant*: i.e. a deviation from the norm and thus from any social construction, institutional authority, and economic subjection. As such, *errance* is the gate of creation, and creation is the way out of the oppressive forces of globalization.

Nancy's reference, in *The Creation of the World* (2007), to "the absolute errancy of the creation of the world"[60] is reminiscent of Glissant's *chaos-monde*, but Nancy and Glissant pursue divergent paths in response to globalization. The latter considers that globalization, for all its wrongs, has helped spread cultural

---

60   Jean-Luc Nancy, *The Creation of the World, or Globalization,* tr. & intro. François Raffoul & David Pettigrew (*La Création du monde ou la mondialisation,* 2002; Albany: State U of New York P, 2007): 111.

exchanges on an unimaginable scale—an auspicious phenomenon that he calls *mondialité* (worldliness) and that allows him to conceive of a transition from the current situation toward the achievement of total world through Relation. The former foresees a much bleaker future: the world is beyond repair and in need of a fresh start. The encroachment of economic power on the *polis* is such that the community has lost agency over its destiny—a phenomenon that Nancy, together with Philippe Lacoue-Labarthe, once described as the "retreat of the political" whereby political reflection and debate—the instruments of political contestation in democracy—have become dulled as a result of a generalized acceptance of the established order: once politics has helped fashion the social community, it is used by the community to regulate itself and preserve its homogeneity, but never to question itself. The community has become a-political, as it were. Significantly, Nancy and Lacoue-Labarthe identified this disturbing trend in politics in the 1980s, after the oil crises of the 1970s and the ensuing paradigm shift away from social democracy and toward the neoliberal model of economic development that spawned globalization and replicated, *mutatis mutandis*, the type of economic and ideological environment that paved the way, in the mid-eighteenth century, for the exponential growth of the transatlantic slave trade.

In *The Creation of the World*, Nancy dubs this world in which we live *ecotechnology*, which could be described as the end state of Foucault's and Agamben's *biopolitics*. In this age of ecotechnology, the "natural life" of which the state has taken control has become "inseparable from a set of conditions that are referred to as 'technological.'"[61] As Nancy puts it, "*bios*—or life as a 'form of life,' as the engagement of a meaning or of a 'being'—merges with *zōē*, bare life, although such life has, in fact, already become *technē*" (94). According to Nancy, globalization has denatured humanity and deprived individuals of their basic rights. Life understood as "auto-maintaining" and "auto-affecting" has been absorbed and obliterated in this "technological management of life" (94), which implies that human existence has lost its value and its sense of purpose, merely perpetuating itself "through finalities that remain the secrets of power, unless they are simply blind or purposeless finalities of the eco-technological totality in motion" (94). Hence, Nancy proposes nothing less than a tabula rasa from where individuals shall regain their autonomy and freedom, and his reflexion on a new humanity begins by calling into question the very notion of "sovereignty."

In "*Ex Nihilo Summum*," Nancy contrasts the suzerain of the feudal era with the sovereign of the modern political age. The suzerain, Nancy explains,

---

61   Nancy, *The Creation of the World, or Globalization*, 94.

perpetuates the family line and is believed to derive his power from God. As such, he "occupies a certain height within an ordered system" in which "vassal and suzerain are bound to each other by a reciprocal oath of allegiance and assistance."[62] Conversely, the power of the sovereign is neither hereditary, nor divine, nor mutually binding. The sovereign exercises authority "in the precise sense that the sovereign is the author of the law" (98), which implies that sovereignty is founded on itself, on its own creation. Transposing this idea to that of the "sovereign people" in democracy, Nancy argues that "the sovereign people possess nothing less and nothing more than the absolute monarch: namely, the very exercise of sovereignty" (99), and this exercise, he continues, "is nothing other than the establishment of the State and of its law, or of the law that makes a State. It supposes that nothing either precedes it or supercedes it, that no authority or instituting force has been exercised before it" (99). Finally, Nancy gainsays Carl Schmitt's theory of "political theology," arguing that modern sovereignty "is not the secularization of a divine sovereignty, precisely because divine sovereignty contains, by definition, the supreme reason and power that modern sovereignty is assigned with giving" (99).

A sovereign state is thus the opposite of a theocratic state, but this emancipation from the religious toward the secular generates what Nancy calls the "sovereign contradiction"—the most telling example of which he finds in Jean-Jacques Rousseau's notion of the "sovereignty of the people." As sovereign, Nancy argues,

> the people must be understood as the subject or the body that forms itself: such is the object of the contract that becomes, in Rousseau, in addition to a pact of security, the very institution of the contractors and their body, in other words, humanity itself [...]. The sovereign people are a people who constitute themselves as subjects in all senses of the word: namely, as the self-relation of each in the relations of all to the others and as the subjection of all to this relation. But since the relation to self is infinite, the people is also infinitely lacking to, or in excess of itself.
> "*Ex Nihilo Summum* (Of Sovereignty)" 100

The "contradiction" Nancy identifies is that the sovereign people has established itself as subject by submitting itself to a (social) contract which purpose is to achieve harmony and unity: i.e. finitude. As Devisch states in *Jean-Luc Nancy and the Question of Community* (2013), "Sovereignty is the power of

---

62   Jean-Luc Nancy, "*Ex Nihilo Summum* (Of Sovereignty)," in Nancy, *The Creation of the World, or Globalization*, tr. Raffoul & Pettigrew, 98.

self-completion, without being subordinated to any other end."[63] This ratio-nale is, however, flawed because sovereignty, like the self, can only co-exist. Sovereignty cannot stand isolated, impervious to exposition and plurality. Not-withstanding its aspiration to absolute autonomy, it is infinite. Even when it encloses itself (e.g.: within national borders), it is exposed to others, involved in some act of communication by its very claim to separateness. The only way for sovereignty to achieve real power would be to transition from infinity to finitude, which is a quest for immanence. According to Nancy, sovereignty is cut off from its base and "stands exclusively and straightaway at the height of absolute value."[64] The danger of such an endeavor lies in the fact that the sov-ereign may rule that the freedom of the community is best achieved by depriv-ing it of freedom. Schmitt calls this paradox whereby the sovereign makes, but also remains above or outside, the law the "state of exception," which becomes a normal legal order and is never questioned. There is a fundamental violence involved in the making and enforcement of the law, and sovereignty, as it im-poses and yet stands outside the law, has a problem of legitimacy. Regarding the "absence of superior or foundational authority" overseeing sovereignty, Nancy comments:

> For the sovereign, authority must be essentially occupied with founding itself or with overcoming itself in order to legislate prior to or in excess of any law. In a rigorous sense, the sovereign foundation is infinite, or rather sovereignty is never founded. It would, rather, be defined by the absence of foundation or presupposition.
>
> "*Ex Nihilo Summum* (Of Sovereignty)" 103

Sovereignty is the embodiment of self, and since, as Nancy argues above, "the relation to self is infinite," that is irremediably exposed to an outside, the sense of autonomy and finitude associated with sovereignty is questionable. As Nan-cy notes,

> A self is nothing other than a form or function of referral: a self is made of a relationship to self which is nothing other than the mutual referral between a perceptible individuation and an intelligible identity.[65]

---

63   Ignaas Devisch, *Jean-Luc Nancy and the Question of Community* (London: Bloomsbury, 2013): 139.

64   Nancy, "*Ex Nihilo Summum* (Of Sovereignty)," 102.

65   Jean-Luc Nancy, *Listening*, tr. Charlotte Mandell (*A l'écoute*, 2002; New York: Fordham UP, 2007): 8.

The self has no completion: it is neither a subject nor an essence. As already stated in the second section of this chapter, "being" is always "being-with," which means that the sovereign as a singularity cannot exist outside its co-presence or the spaces it shares with others. As Devisch puts it, "there is no sovereignty that precedes this exposure unless it is an always already shared [...] sovereignty."[66]

This isolation characterizing sovereignty leads Nancy to argue that sovereignty is "a detached summit,"

> without any contact with the outside of the whole structure built upon the base: and since this outside is nothing, and there can be no question of access, or an access that can be immediately experienced as a penetration into nothing, sovereignty turns out strictly to be that nothing itself.
> "*Ex Nihilo Summum* (Of Sovereignty)" 102

Nevertheless, this nothingness of sovereignty, Nancy goes on, is something:

> it is that very particular thing that *nothing* [rien] is. Not 'the nothing,' as if it was an entity, and specifically, the entity of a negation of being. That is what is called, 'nothingness' ['*le néant*']. Nothingness is not nothing [*rien*]: it is that which being turns into as soon as it is posited for itself and as unilateral.
> "*Ex Nihilo Summum* (Of Sovereignty)" 102

From this perspective, being oneself is a contradiction in terms, and, Nancy concludes, "one must resolve to think of being as its own effacement that negates it and, while negating it, allows for the spacing of the concrete" (102). As each singularity is necessarily plural, exposure and sharing of a space of co-presence is the apodictic condition of each singularity. As Nancy has always claimed, there is no ontology but the ontology of being-in-common.

Since the 1980s, the sovereignty of the state has been severely eroded by the triumphs of the free-market economy and the self-serving plutocracy that now presides over the destiny of the globalized world. Violence no longer emanates from the sovereign state and the laws it enacts. Violence is the consequence of the accumulation of wealth, which has become immune to regulation and unaffected by borders. Capital, Nancy writes, "no longer has a need of the State (or in a limited way), and the State no longer knows on what to found itself or what it founds."[67] Earlier in *The Creation of the World*, Nancy describes this

---

66   Devisch, *Jean-Luc Nancy and the Question of Community*, 144.
67   Nancy, *The Creation of the World, or Globalization*, 105.

phenomenon as "the conjunction of an unlimited process of eco-technological enframing and of a vanishing of the possibilities of forms of life and/or of common ground."[68] In order to counter this process, Nancy does not wish to restore sovereignty, but he nonetheless detects in the "principle of the *nothing* of sovereignty" a potential for an alternative:

> Being nothing, or being founded on nothing, does not mean being powerless [...]: it means to found and measure power by that *nothing* which is *the very thing* of *the reality* of the people: its nature as nonfoundational, nontranscendent [...] nonsacred, nonnatural etc.
>
> "*Ex Nihilo Summum* (Of Sovereignty)" 104 (emphasis in the original)

The idea of a people constituting itself is key to Nancy: "A people are always their own invention" (104). Thus, Nancy does not dismiss sovereignty, instead imagining two scenarios. First, he advocates

> the reclamation of sovereignty at its roots, which is *nothing* and in this *nothing* the thing itself, which is precisely not a root but the summit, the inverted radicality of the uncompromising, inconsistent, and absolutely resistant summit: the summit as *ex nihilo,* whence a world can emerge— or its contrary.
>
> "*Ex Nihilo Summum* (Of Sovereignty)" 105 (emphasis in the original)

Alternatively, Nancy envisions a separation of politics and sovereignty,

> assuming that 'politics' no longer designates the assumption of a subject or in a subject [...], but designates the order of the subject-less regulation of the relation between subjects: as individual as collective or communitarian subjects, groups of different kinds, families of different sorts, interest groups, whether labor or leisure, local or moral affinities, etc. The main axiom here would be that these groupings are not subsumable under a sole common being of superior rank.
>
> "*Ex Nihilo Summum* (Of Sovereignty)" 105

Nancy calls such a model of politics without a subject "an antisovereignty, [...] a negative sovereignty, [...] a sovereignty without sovereignty" (107), and while he does not provide the tools required for the interpretation of such a model, he looks at the void that the end of sovereignty has created as an opportunity: "This spacing of the world," Nancy argues, "*is itself the empty place*

---

68   *The Creation of the World, or Globalization,* 95.

of sovereignty."[69] As shown earlier in this chapter (Section 2 above), spacing is where a singularity encounters difference, and makes its plurality manifest as it structures and is structured by other singularities. The spacing of the world is where our incompleteness is revealed, and this incompleteness is our finitude.

In such a world, Devisch points out,

> a number of motifs take on privileged positions: togetherness over dividedness, the contractual over the hierarchical, the network over the organism, and plurality and delocalization above unitary and centralization.
>
> *Jean-Luc Nancy and the Question of Community* 141

In *"Cosmos Basileus,"* the short text that concludes *The Creation of the World,* Nancy defines the unity of the world in terms reminiscent of Glissant's own definition of the total world:

> The unity of a world is not one: it is made of a diversity, including disparity and opposition. It is made of it, which is to say that it is not added it to it and does not reduce it. The unity of a world is nothing other than its diversity, and its diversity is, in turn, a diversity of worlds. [...] The world is a multiplicity of worlds and its unity is the sharing out [...] and the mutual exposure in this world of all its worlds.[70]

Nancy does not dwell on the concrete implementation of this "sharing out," but, just as he did for "negative sovereignty," he offers a clear description of what he has in mind: i.e. a world where justice and equality prevail. Playing on the meaning of the French *"rendre justice,"* Nancy argues that "justice [...] must be rendered [...] restituted, returned, given in return to each singular existent,"[71] and he reminds us that

> existence is nothing other than being exposed: expulsed from its simple self-identity and from its pure position, exposed to the event, to creation, thus to the outside, to exteriority, to multiplicity, to alterity, and to alteration.
>
> *"Cosmos Basileus,"* 110

---

69   Jean-Luc Nancy, *Being Singular Plural,* tr. Robert D. Richardson & Anne E. O'Byrne (*Être singulier pluriel,* 1996; Stanford CA: Stanford UP, 2000): 136–137 (emphases in the original).

70   Jean-Luc Nancy, *"Cosmos Basileus,"* in Nancy, *The Creation of the World, or Globalization,* tr. Raffoul & Pettigrew, 109.

71   Nancy, *"Cosmos Basileus,"* 110.

Nancy does not mean to create this "coexisting totality"; he takes it for granted, and thus makes the demand for justice self-evident:

> The law of justice is this unappeasable tension toward justice itself. Similarly, the law of the world is an infinite tension toward the world itself. These two laws are not only homologous; they are the same and unique law of absolute sharing.
>
> *"Cosmos Basileus,"* 112

Nancy sees a potential for the coming of this "absolute justice" in globalization—not globalization as ecotechnics but as what he calls *mondialisation*: i.e. world-forming.

Nancy has coined the term *mondialisation* (world-forming) in order to describe an alternative world to the exploitative, deterministic globalization that thwarts efforts to achieve justice. Nancy calls globalization *l'immonde*, a neologism based on the adjective *immonde* (unsavory, foul, filthy), which, once nominalized, translates as the "un-world"—the absence of world, or its negation. Nancy's conclusions on the deleterious effects of globalization are similar to Glissant's, albeit more pessimistic:

> The world has lost its capacity to 'form a world' [*faire monde*]: it seems only to have gained that capacity of proliferating, to the extent of its means, the 'un-world' [*immonde*], which, until now, [...] has never in history impacted the totality of the orb to such an extent. In the end, everything takes place as if the world affected and permeated itself with a death drive that soon would have nothing else to destroy than the world itself.
>
> *The Creation of the World, or Globalization* 34 (emphasis in the original)

In the preamble to *What's These Worlds Coming To?* (2011) Nancy and Aurélien Barrau observe that our world, often described as "'globalized' [*globalisé*] or 'world-formed' [*mondialisé*]—and thus unified,"[72] is actually disorderly and unpredictable. Nancy and Barrau reflect this ongoing turmoil with the plural form: "Our worlds and our ways of life and culture are constantly more diffracted, scattered, heterogeneous, and even unidentifiable" (3). In the end,

---

72   Jean-Luc Nancy & Aurélien Barrau, *What's These Worlds Coming To?* ed. Stefanos Geroulanos & Todd Meyers, tr. Travis Holloway & Flor Mechain, foreword by David Pettigrew (*Dans quels mondes vivons-nous?*, 2011; New York: Fordham UP, 2015): 3. Further page references are in the main text.

Nancy and Barrau argue, "the question of the world must be reconsidered" (3). Unlike Glissant, who perceives the diffraction of the world as a favorable occasion for creolization to blossom, Nancy considers the same phenomenon with much more circumspection. According to Nancy, the world has lost its unity and we have lost our power over the world:

> What is disappearing or being diluted is the more advanced sense of the cosmos or beautiful unity that is composed according to a superior order that directs it and that it also reflects.
>
> *What's These Worlds Coming To?* 52

That world, Nancy argues, "constantly escape[s] the grasp of every construction" (52). The assemblage of the bits and pieces that form the world, Nancy adds,

> does not refer to a first or final construction but rather to a kind of continuous creation where what is constantly rekindled and renewed is the very possibility of the world—or rather the multiplicity of worlds.
>
> *What's These Worlds Coming To?* 52

In order to demonstrate that the world is no longer a finite, organized, and identifiable structure, Nancy isolates the term "struction" (from the Latin *struere* "to amass," "to heap," "to build") from its usual affixes (con-, de-, in-).[73] Struction, Nancy argues, is a structural paradigm "relative to an assembling that is labile, disordered, aggregated, or amalgamated rather than conjoined, reunited, paired with, or associated" (49). Struction, he adds, "would be the state of the 'with' deprived of the value of sharing, bringing into play only simple contiguity and its contingency" (49). Struction is the world in our technological age, a bare world characterized by absolute indeterminacy. And in such a chaotic environment, Nancy sees liberation and an opportunity to re-create the world from the nothingness it has become.

---

73 Nancy describes our globalized world thus: "We are no longer in the process of discovering a world that has remained in part unknown; we are in a spiraling, growing pile of pieces, parts, zones, fragments, slivers, particles, elements, outlines, seeds, kernels, clusters, points, meters, knots, arborescences, projections, proliferations and dispersions according to which we are now more than ever taken hold of, interwoven into, absorbed into, and dislodged from a prodigious mass that is unstable, moving, plastic, and metamorphic, a mass that renders the distinction between 'subject' and 'object' or between 'man' and 'nature' or 'world' less and less possible for us"; *What's These Worlds Coming To?*, 52. The discussion of struction first appeared as "Of Struction," *Parrhesia* 17 (2013): 1–10.

In *The Creation of the World*, Nancy turns his attention to the motif of creation, which is recurrent in the Western and monotheist traditions: "If 'creation' means anything, it is the exact opposite of any form of production in the sense of a fabrication that supposes a given, a project, and a producer."[74] The idea of creation, Nancy adds, is "the idea of the *ex-nihilo*" (51), which does not mean that some superior power (God) created the world but, rather, that *nothing* has grown as *something*. "In creation," Nancy argues, "a growth grows from nothing and this nothing takes care of itself, cultivates its growth" (51). Globalization has drained the world of its old meaning, and Nancy proposes no less than a strategy to rebuild that world on a better foundation:

> *To create the world* means: immediately, without delay, reopening each possible struggle for a world, that is, for what we must form the contrary of a global injustice against the background of general equivalence. But this means to conduct this struggle precisely in the name of the fact that this *world* is coming out of nothing, that there is nothing before it and that it is without models, without principle and without given end, and that it is precisely *what* forms the justice and the meaning of a world.
>
> *The Creation of the World, or Globalization* 54–55 (italics in the original)

Nancy's *mondialisation* (world-forming) is as much a bulwark against globalization as Glissant's *mondialité* is, but unlike Glissant, Nancy sees no potential in globalization. Nancy advocates a struggle against capital, but the purpose of the struggle is neither "the exercise of power—nor property—whether collective or individual" (55). He envisions the act of creation itself as a struggle that

> seeks itself [...] and its contagious communication and propagation of an enjoyment that, in turn, would not be a satisfaction acquired in a signification of the world, but the insatiable and infinitely finite exercise that is the *being in act of meaning* brought forth in the world [...].
>
> *The Creation of the World, or Globalization* 55 (emphasis added)

Struction is the underlying assumption of this *poiesis*, this act of creation whereby individuals will transform and regain agency over their own world. In *What's These Worlds Coming To?* Nancy defines struction thus:

---

74   Nancy, *The Creation of the World, or Globalization*, 51.

> Struction offers a dis-order that is neither the contrary nor the destruc-
> tion or ruin of order: it is situated somewhere else in what we call con-
> tingency, fortuity, dispersion, or errancy, which could equally be called
> surprise, invention, chance, meeting, or passage. It is nothing but the
> copresence or better yet the appearing-together of all that appears, that
> is, of all that is.
>
> *What's These Worlds Coming To?* 54

Struction is not just a soothing concept meant to expose the intricacies of
the globalized world. It is a reminder, if not an injunction, to exercise moral
and political responsibility toward others. We have lost the reassuring, fixed
framework of a well-ordained, divine order, but rather than passively endure
the contingency of our "naked existence" we ought to take advantage of it and
produce new forms of bonding and community. Nancy, however, does not provide a concrete methodology for doing so.

Similar criticism may be leveled at Glissant. Despite his foresight about
the pitfalls of globalization, his poetics of Relation has proved inefficient as
an instrument of change. One way of explaining this apparent failure is that
Relation, along with cognate notions of creolization, diversity, and totality
owes more to Glissant's fertile imagination and ideological leanings than to
reality. Peter Hallward, in the preface to *Absolutely Postcolonial* (2001), derides
Glissant's version of creolization, which "comprehends and moves beyond all
possible contraries" and makes "the notions of centers and peripheries [...]
obsolete."[75] According to Hallward, these notions have been replaced by "a
kind of universal 'erratics'" (xvii) that seems to have been conceived to fit Glissant's vision rather than to provide a thorough and objective assessment of globalization. Hence, Hallward excoriates Glissant, whose *tout-monde* "can only
be a 'chaos-world' [...] a 'completely erratic' anti-system" (xvii). Hallward goes
on to argue that, in Glissant's cosmogony, *tout-monde* is not characterized by
cosmopolitanism "but rather [by] the deterritorialising exuberance of chaos
itself. The 'erratic dimension has become the dimension of the *tout-monde*'
and 'today's *errances* no longer seek to establish a territory'" (xvii). This highly
critical comment is followed by a hypophora:

> Why should they? There is no need for territorial security since—as the
> inhabitants of *systematically* exploited countries may be surprised to

---

75   Peter Hallward, *Absolutely Postcolonial: Writing Between the Singular and the Specific*
      (Manchester: Manchester UP, 2001): xvi.

learn—'absolute [...] unpredictability is the law as regards the relations
between human cultures.'

Absolutely Postcolonial xvii

From Hallward's perspective, Glissantian creolization and similar theories en-
trap the postcolonial subject in an essentialist discourse.

What Hallward fears, Lorna Burns explains, is "entropic stagnation in which
all that is specific and particular aims to dissolve in unity with the undiffer-
entiated totality."[76] In Hallward's view, Burns goes on, "the postcolonial will
tend toward the elimination of specific histories, locations, or cultures as independent, contextualising forces" (105). Burns concedes that Glissant's concept of totality and Relation do constitute a philosophy of immanence, but
she also demonstrates, particularly by means of a close analysis of the notion
of *échos-monde*, that Glissant makes room for identities to maintain coherence and stability in the vortex of creolization. *Échos-monde*, Burns argues,
"are not 'models,' fixed and essentialised entities, resistant to change: they are
not substances" (109) but, rather, unities that "express cultural identities" (110).
They play a role similar to that of opacity: they protect subjectivities from utter
dissolution, but while opacity is an attribute the subject strives to preserve in
order to ward off transparency, *échos-monde* are "defensive strategies against
the overwhelming force of Relation" (109). *Échos-monde*, Burns contends, are
"necessary in order to express an opinion or take a position to 'construct unities'" (109), but such unities "are not absolute and infinite, but finite, partial,
and subject to further change or creolizations through the continued process
of Relation" (109). *Échos-monde,* unlike opacity, are contingent on the change-
ableness of Relation, and yet their presence introduces a level of stability and
coherence in the chaos of a world in Relation. Finally, their transitory coexistence and active role in the process of creolization portend the emergence of
composite cultures.

Échos-monde are not the only strategy Glissant developed in anticipation of
the type of criticism Hallward levels against him. Glissant actually spends a lot
of time defining Relation in contrast to what it is not. Early in *Poetics of Relation*, Glissant writes that "the poetics of Relation remains forever conjectural
and presupposes no ideological stability" (32); and a couple of pages further
on:

---

76   Burns, "Becoming-postcolonial, Becoming-Caribbean," 105.

> Relation is not an absolute toward which every work would strive but a totality [...] that through its poetic and practical and unceasing force attempts to be perfected, to be spoken, simply, that is, to be complete.
>
> *Poetics of Relation* 34

Later, Glissant establishes a parallel between his Relation and Einstein's Theory of Relativity in order to make two points. First, Relation, no more than Relativity, is "purely relative" (134); and second,

> The totality within which Relativity is exerted and to which it is applied, through the workings of the mind, is not totalitarian, therefore: not imposed a priori, not fixed as an absolute. And, consequently, for the mind, it is neither a restrictive dogmatism nor the skepticism of probabilist thought.
>
> *Poetics of Relation* 134

According to Glissant,

> Consent to cultural relativism ('each human culture has value in its own milieu, becoming equivalent to every other in the ensemble') accompanied the spreading awareness of and adherence or at least habituation to, the idea of Relativity.
>
> *Poetics of Relation* 134–135

This detour through Einstein's famous theory also allows Glissant to admit that "cultural relativism has not always come without a tinge of essentialism" (135)—an important concession made at the right moment, just when Glissant has established the validity (and perhaps the necessity) of cultural relativism. Toward the end of *Poetics of Relation*, Glissant returns to the topic of totality in order to contrast his own notion of it with that of Western thought, which is "threatened with immobility" (192). Relation, Glissant reminds his reader, "is an open totality evolving upon itself" (192), which means that Relation "is the principle of unity that we subtract from this idea" (192). In Relation, Glissant goes on, "the whole is not the finality of its parts: for multiplicity in totality is totally diversity" (192). By embracing Relation, Glissant implies, one is able to forge, protect, and preserve one's identity from external influences: "I will take care of [my identity] myself. That is, I shall not allow it to become cornered in any essence; I shall also pay attention to not mixing it into any amalgam" (192). And he concludes:

The rule of action (what is called ethics or else the ideal or just logical relation) would gain ground—as an obvious fact—by not being mixed into
the preconceived transparency of universal models. The rule of every
action, individual or community, would gain ground by perfecting itself
through the experience of Relation.

Poetics of Relation 193

To those who object that Relation, with all its rules, risks becoming a universal
principle or a doctrine, Glissant replies that the constitutive changeability of
Relation makes such a threat unlikely.

Glissant's considerable effort to define Relation from every conceivable angle does not convince Hallward, who considers the very concept of Relation to
be intrinsically flawed:

my argument against Glissant's 'Relational' *créolisation* and its various
postcolonial equivalents in no sense depends on the denial of the actual reality and growth of inter-cultural relations as such. My resistance
concerns their allegedly exemplary status and their apparently political
implications.

Absolutely Postcolonial 252

Hallward does not object to the idea of relationality per se: "Identities are ba-
nally relational" (252), he quips. What he objects to is the premise on which
relationality is based:

there is nothing in this condition [relationality] that orients the expression of these differences toward an anarchic dissemination any more
than toward a disciplined coordination.

Absolutely Postcolonial 252

Relationality, Hallward implies, is factual: we are related to others and this re-
latedness may evolve in many different ways. Relationality is not a course set
by a theory, a program, or a practice. Relation, Hallward argues contra Glissant,
"is not made up of anything more primitive than itself, and has no substance
other than the individuals it relates" (252). Hence, Relation, according to Hallward, cannot be theorized or made into a poetics.

The inherent nature of Relation is not the only point Hallward wishes to
challenge. He also identifies a dichotomy between Glissant's theory, which
foregrounds a world of incessant, ever-changing, and unforeseeable exchanges,

and the reality of the global world. The latter favors the free movement of goods and capital for profit, and it bears witness to the proliferation of fertile cultural encounters, but it remains conspicuously ineffective at facilitating the movement of people across the borders of nation-states, when it is not actively unwilling to do so. Hallward acknowledges "the results of a growing 'interconnection and inter-dependence' of diverse cultures" (62) in the globalized world, and he agrees that, "compared to earlier times,"

> cultural production has been progressively uncoupled from earlier territorial and social moorings, 'released from its traditional determinism in economic life, social class, gender, ethnicity, and region.'
> *Absolutely Postcolonial* 62

However, Hallward refutes the argument according to which borders across the world are being abolished, paving the way for creolization:

> Global capitalism is no doubt the most aggressively singularising force the world has ever seen. But like any singularity, its operation is *hierarchical* through and through: it proceeds through the exploitation of differences and gaps, and its impact has proved as polarizing as Marx predicted. Segregation by poverty, insecurity and lack of opportunity— both internationally and intra-nationally—is probably more severe today than ever before.
> *Absolutely Postcolonial* 62–63 (emphasis in the original)

To the claim that "the whole world is becoming an archipelago"[77] Hallward retorts that the increase in cultural interactions generated by globalization is not sufficient to defeat capitalist exploitation and lead to a postnational era free of limits, hierarchies, and taxonomies. Describing *Tout-monde* (1993), a novel in which Glissant imagines a "mise en Relation" of the world, Hallward jeers: *Tout-monde* "is one of the most stridently enthusiastic fictional incantations of a borderless world ever written" (102). From Hallward's perspective, Glissant's vision of a creolized world lies somewhere between naive optimism and sophistry. Yet, Glissant is aware that creolization is a protracted process:

---

77   Édouard Glissant & Patrick Chamoiseau, "The Unforeseeable Diversity of the World," in *Beyond Dichotomies: Histories, Identities, Cultures, and the Challenge of Globalization*, ed. Elisabeth Mudimbe-Boyi (Albany: State U of New York P, 2002): 290.

the World is becoming creolized. This is to say that the culture of the
world is furiously and knowingly coming into contact with each other,
changing by exchanging, through irremediable collisions and ruthless
wars—but also through breakthroughs of moral conscience and hope.

Introduction à une Poétique du Divers 15

In this passage from 1996, Glissant calls for, rather than prophesies, the advent
of a creolized world. However, this clear-cut distinction between an anticipa-
tive and a romantic vision of a creolized world will subside as the years go
by, and Glissant's growing reliance on the imagination rather than observation
and rationality accounts for the wrath he incurs from such critics as Hallward.
Chris Bongie situates this retreat from political activism in favor of the alleged
power of the imagination in a chronological framework:

> Glissant's work, from the 1990 *Poétique de la Relation* onward, seems to
> have declined away from [...] the sort of partisan position-takings that
> characterized his interventions from the 1960s and 1970s, many of them
> produced in Martinique and collected in 1981 as *Le discours antillais*.[78]

Focussing on *La Cohée du Lamentin* (2005), the fifth and last of the *Poetics* vol-
umes, Bongie describes the evolution of Glissant's argument in favor of the
transformative power of the imaginary:

> Glissant's late work [...] occasionally presents the poetics of relation as a
> necessary but not sufficient condition for some never articulated politics,
> but more often gives the impression that this poetics is sufficient unto

---

78   Chris Bongie, *Friends and Enemies: The Scribal Politics of Post/colonial Literature* (Liver-
      pool: Liverpool UP, 2008): 338. Bongie supports his argument thus: "In the words of Peter
      Hallward, the most vocal and philosophically rigorous critic of Glissant's turn away from
      principled politics and toward utopian poetics, if there was 'no *sudden* break in Glissant's
      work, no sharply defined before and after' [...], there has nonetheless been 'a major shift
      in his priorities' since the publication of the *Discours*, one that is perhaps most noticeable
      in the gradual sidelining, and eventual erasure, of arguments on behalf of the Martini-
      quan nation and the regional concept of *Antillanité*, this latter term being one of the few
      key Glissantian neologisms not to have made the passage into his later work [...]" (338).
      And Bongie adds a bit later: "It is not so much that Martinique and the greater Caribbean
      become a lesser presence in Glissant's later work, as Hallward somewhat unfairly sug-
      gests, but that the nation and the region have simply ceased to function as the conceptual
      ground upon which 'a specific political position with respect to global trends' can be ad-
      opted [...]" (339).

itself and, as a consequence, that it is not politicians, or people armed with principles, who will be of the most help to us in our dealings with the forces of globalization and Empire but poets. It is poets, he asserts near the end of the section on Empire [in *Cohée*], who are especially attuned to the 'trembling truth' of the Tout-Monde; it is they who on the basis of their (un)common sense of globality augur the imminent failure of those totalizing forces to achieve their destructive ends [...].

Friends and Enemies 337

Glissant places creolization and all his theories under the umbrella term "poetics," which denotes a creative rather than an empirical approach to the various ills of the world. While the year 1990 is a watershed in the Glissant corpus, the role Glissant accords to imagination as an instrument of change predates the publication of *Poetics of Relation*. Already in *Caribbean Discourse*, Glissant is advocating the recourse to the arts of imagination (i.e. the fine arts qua product of the imagination and the imagination qua arts itself) in order to produce "a prophetic vision of the past" meant to restore a history purposefully overlooked by the colonizers in the Caribbean:

The past, to which we were subjected, which has not yet emerged as history for us, is, however, obsessively present. The duty of the writer is to explore this obsession, to show its relevance in a continuous fashion to the immediate present. This exploration is therefore related neither to a schematic chronology nor to a nostalgic lament. It leads to the identification of a painful notion of time and its full projection forward into the future, without the help of those plateaus in time from which the West has benefited, without the help of that collective density that is the primary value of an ancestral cultural heartland.

Caribbean Discourse 63

Imagination not only informs Glissant's work but also comes as an alternative to established, institutional, and official knowledge. Glissant argues in "Creolization in the Making of the Americas" that creolization "probably has no political or economic power. But it is precious for mankind's imagination, its capacity for invention."[79] In *Poetics of Relation*, Glissant develops this idea and makes explicit the link between imagination and action:

---

79 Édouard Glissant, "Creolization in the Making of the Americas," *Caribbean Quarterly* 54.1–2 (2008): 88.

No imagination helps avert destitution in reality, none can oppose op-
pressions or sustain those who 'withstand' in body or spirit. But imagination changes mentalities, however slowly it may go about this.

Poetics of Relation 183

As Glissant admits in *Introduction à une Poétique du Divers*, Relation is "neither
virtuous nor 'moral' [and] a poetics of Relation does not presuppose the immediate and harmonious end of domination" (106). But practicing Relation is not
a mere self-gratifying discipline. It seeks to have an ethical, social, and political
impact—a point Glissant hammers home:

Let us not stop with this commonplace: that a poetics cannot guarantee us a concrete means of action. But a poetics, perhaps, does allow us
to understand better our action in the world. We consider, for instance,
how our requirement for cultural responsibility, inseparable from political independence, is to be related to the prophylactic violence of forms
of deculturation.

Poetics of Relation 199

Glissant's poetics of Relation relies on the transformative power of the imagination—a notion the pragmatic world we live in finds difficult to support. And
Glissant's original phrase, *l'imaginaire des peuples* (*Poétique de la Relation*, 12),
can be misleading: as an adjective, *imaginaire* translates as "imaginary" and denotes illusion, fantasy, and myth. But Glissant uses *imaginaire* as a noun, which
translates as "imagination." *Imaginaire*, however, is more than imagination: it
may be understood as collective imagination, mind, or consciousness. Also,
while *imaginaire* is not the real, it is not completely disconnected from either
the real or reason, since it produces images or ideas from experience. Unlike
imagination, it is already anchored in the reality of the subject. As Glissant
puts it: "The imaginary does not bear with it the coercive requirements of idea.
It prefigures reality, without determining it a priori" (*Poetics of Relation*, 192).

In a 1998 interview, Glissant, referring to social tensions in France, dismisses
unemployment as the cause of racism and intolerance. Rather, he believes in
the key role of *imaginaires* and wonders whether it is

possible to change *imaginaires*, that is, not only the consciousness, but
also the unconscious and the imagination of people so as to definitively
curb their propensity to return to the old exclusions.[80]

---

80   Quoted in Andrea Schwieger Hiepko, "L'Europe et les Antilles: Une interview d'Édouard
       Glissant," *Mots Pluriels* (8 October 1998): online (accessed 5 August 2017). (My tr.)

But to some, changing the way people think is not a very practical answer to such pressing issues as income disparities and xenophobia. Once a separatist under house arrest in France (1961–65) and a signatory of the *Manifesto of the 121* (1960) for the independence of Algeria, Glissant never ceased to advocate for justice, but the nature of his commitment to political struggles changed over time. The transition from creolization as a social-historical phenomenon to creolization as a system of thought meant transcending crippling particularisms; this has created a distance between the gritty reality of creole life in the Caribbean and the theorizing thereof. Bongie describes this evolution in Glissant's theory as "the hyper-aestheticizing embrace of creolization" and laments Glissant's "increasingly cynical (or 'sceptical humanist') depreciation of any and all forms of principled politics."[81]

Glissant's disdain for traditional political channels shows at the end of *Traité du tout-monde* (1997) in a brief chapter called "Martinique" in which he enjoins Caribbean nations to come together, think as an archipelago, and emancipate themselves either from multinational corporations or, as in the case of Martinique, Guadeloupe, and Guyane, from the tutelage of a faraway motherland that subjects them to bureaucratic control and thwarts their capacity to think, make their own decisions, and develop their economic potential as they see fit. Focussing on his beloved Martinique, Glissant suggests transforming the whole island, as well as the rest of the Caribbean, into the lungs of the earth:

> Let's begin the cleaning, and let Martinique, for example, proclaim and maintain itself, in its entirety, as a bright and ecological land [...] Let us seek elsewhere in the world the places where goods that we will have selected, developed, and produced in common could be marketed and purchased. In the world there is a place (of buyers, enthusiasts, people eager to exchange) for all that would spring from a place of light, for all that would arise from a will to clean the waters and clouds, the Gardens and Sands. [...] Let's talk to France neither to battle her nor to be her servants or appointed representatives, but simply to tell her we're going to start something different.[82]

Glissant's plea is ambitious and full of good intentions, but it does not say how to proceed. Without a clear political plan and financial support, a self-sufficient, independent, and unified Caribbean is a chimera. Glissant has reinvented the notion of utopia, replacing its prescriptive ideals of Western culture with the "mise en Relation" and equivalence of all things, people, and cultures.

---

81   Chris Bongie, *Islands and Exiles*, 341–342.
82   Glissant, *Traité du tout-monde*, 227–228. (My tr.)

Thus, for Glissant, utopia is not a nowhere of perfection, but an elsewhere of possibilities. Glissant's utopia is the total world, and it can be achieved by changing people's "imaginaire"—an approach typical of what Bongie calls "late Glissant."

Edelyn Dorismond deplores this loss of touch with reality and focusses on the lack of practical application characterizing Glissant's vision. He argues that Glissant's poetics fails to engage with politics, as it "leaves the question of the political organization of a future Creole society [...] hanging."[83] Indeed, the creolization Glissant calls for posits a world without cultural hierarchies and without a power structure to preside over the community. In this perspective, Glissant's total world is no more than a "fantasized" community in which so-called "atavistic cultures" relying on a creation myth for self-legitimation and the subjugation of others have given way to "composite cultures." The latter, as they arose from a mixing of disparate atavistic cultures, are deprived of a genesis, and are arguably less inclined to conquest and more open to cultural exchange, since they are already creolized. Yet, as Dorismond points out, the creolization of cultures in what Glissant calls Plantation-America was not the result of mutual understanding. As Glissant himself admits, "elements of African and black cultures were routinely treated as inferior."[84] Hence, Dorismond takes a stance opposed to that of Glissant: "Creolization proceeds from inequality among cultures."[85] With the concept of creolization, Glissant challenges the principle of political authority and its unifying force, but he does not provide the model for what would be, in effect, a creole world.

Dorismond is also skeptical of Relation, as it tends to ignore the specificities of the individual subject at a time when some individuals feel they are being deprived of subjectivity. In a later essay, he tackles this very issue through his analysis of creolization. Creolization, which is characterized by change, transformation, and evolution, presupposes the absence of a unique root, a fixed origin, and even selfhood (at least in a pure, intrinsically individuated form) because Relation, as the concretization of creolization, implies that there is no self without another self. These postulates, Dorismond argues, imply that the process of Relation "must be interpreted as an ex-propriation of what belongs to the Other while also depriving the self of any claim to privileges."[86]

---

83   Edelyn Dorismond, "Créolisation de la politique, politique de la créolisation: Penser un 'im-pensé' dans l'œuvre d'Édouard Glissant," *Cahiers Sens Public* 3.11–12 (2009): 138. (My tr.)

84   Glissant, *Introduction à une Poétique du Divers*, 17. (My tr.)

85   Dorismond, "Créolisation de la politique, politique de la créolisation," 140.

86   Edelyn Dorismond, "Comment Deleuze et Derrida voyagent dans la pensée glissantienne de la créolisation," *Rue Descartes* 78.2 (2013): 35. (My tr.)

The self and the self of the Other, Dorismond contends, are "disseminated in Relation" (35). As a poetics, Relation and its abolition of any dialectical relationship among individuals help envision what an idealized world could be, but such a poetics, as suggested earlier, leads to an impasse when it comes to establishing a politics of creolization, let alone a fully functioning Creole society. A bit further on, Dorismond argues that in Relation "what one retains from others is not their alterity, which is their intrinsic quality, but the process that unceasingly makes them Other" (42). In this perspective, Dorismond goes on, creolization is "a thought of the Other qua other; [creolization] is concerned with the Other becoming Other" (42). Put another way, Relation is endless "othering," in that it hinges on perpetual exchange and difference rather than on the possibility of stability and harmony. Dorismond compares Relation to a form of contamination that "de-essentializes all subjectivities by linking them in relations" (42). By making Otherness its nexus, Relation puts any claim to purity (as a discourse of filiation would) under erasure, but it also weakens the idea of subjectivity. In Relation, the quest for equivalence leads to absolute reciprocity: I seek the Other's otherness, and I, in turn, become the Other of an Other. My becoming a full-fledged subject depends on my becoming Other, which means that the I is plural and always on the brink of disappearing in an endless network of mutual recognitions. Dorismond finally takes his criticism of Glissant's concept of creolization a step further:

> Creolization, as it did not make room for the advent of the 'self,' has over-looked the fundamental issues of Caribbean societies, which are made of 'dispossession of the self' [and] marked by a self-reflexive desire for acknowledgement.
>
> "Comment Deleuze et Derrida voyagent dans la pensée glissantienne de la créolisation" 43

The thought of creolization, a vehement Dorismond continues,

> has generated a frivolous, untroubled, inconsistent self, a self that claims no form of injustice or violence since we need a bit of everything to make a world; we need a bit of everything to build the total world.
>
> "Comment Deleuze et Derrida voyagent dans la pensée glissantienne de la créolisation" 43

And Dorismond concludes by wondering whether creolization is not just a "whimsical theory"—a theory full of good intentions but devoid of substance and practical application, a theory that preempts the constitution of the self, even though the latter is precisely what displaced and so called "subaltern" people aspire to most. Dorismond's criticism stems from a Caribbean point of view,[87] but it can be extended to the larger Glissantian concept of creolization, which is conducive to a process of de-subjectivization.

4   The Radicant

Nicolas Bourriaud's *The Radicant* (2009) restores the identity of the subject to prominence. Bourriaud, a curator, tackles the same issues of globalization and identity as Glissant and Nancy do, but he does so through the prism of the fine arts, which yields a less fatalistic—albeit equally insightful—view of the world. Thus, Bourriaud talks about global upheavals primarily in terms of movement rather than alienation and injustice, and he puts "the immigrant, the exile, the tourist, and the urban wanderer" in the same category, calling them "the dominant figures of the contemporary culture."[88] Bourriaud does not ignore the blatant de-subjectivization of individuals as a sequela of globalization, but rather than contemplating a permanent revolution as Glissant does with Relation or the complete reconstruction of a tabula rasa world as Nancy does with struction, Bourriaud introduces, through the concept of the radicant, a new way of understanding and coping with the effects of globalization.

Bourriaud, rather than dwelling on the subject's loss of identity, considers how the nature of identity has been shaped anew by a world in transformation. The radicant is a new aesthetic of alterity that rejects the Deleuzian rhizome as a reliable means by which to confront the disintegrations of social and cultural referents, and to assess the evolution of subjectivities amid the exponential growth of continental and trans-continental movement since the 1970s. Furthermore, the figure of the radicant embodies what Bourriaud

---

87   Glissant's idealization of creole cultures may not elicit unanimity, even among fellow Caribbeans. "In the Caribbean," Glissant once claimed in an interview, "it is obvious that there is no possibility of ethnic massacres or ethnic cleansing because of the very notion of ethnicity found there"; Quoted in Andrea Schwieger Hiepko, "L'Europe et les Antilles: Une interview d'Édouard Glissant," *Mots Pluriels* (8 October 1998): online (accessed 5 August 2017). (My tr.) Dorismond, who is from Haiti, may not agree with such a statement, especially when remembering the 1937 Parsley Massacre on the occasion of which Rafael Trujillo, the dictator of neighboring Dominican Republic, decided to cleanse the border of "darker" Haitians. The Dominican Republic, whose 73 percent of the population is of mixed origin (black and white), has never been very welcoming toward its Haitian neighbors, 95 percent of whom are of African descent.

88   Nicolas Bourriaud, *The Radicant*, tr. James Gussen & Lili Porten (*Radicant: pour une esthétique de la globalisation*, 2009; Berlin & New York: Lukas Sternberg, 2009): 51. Further page references are in the main text.

calls "altermodernity," a concept that decries both twentieth-century modernity for its obsession with roots and its production of myths (e.g., nationalism, imperialism, and capitalism), and postmodernity for its celebration of multiculturalism, which, paradoxically, generates both the self-ghettoization of minorities and the standardization of cultures. Altermodernity brings the question of individual identity back to the fore by exploring its metamorphosis rather than heralding its dissolution in a world characterized by thrusts and shocks, impermanence and volatility.

The radicants, Bourriaud argues,

> resemble those plants that do not depend on a single root for their growth but advance in all directions on whatever surfaces present themselves by attaching multiple hooks to them, as ivy does.
>
> *The Radicant* 51

Botanists call ivy, couch grass, and the suckers of the strawberry plant radicants, and such plants, Bourriaud explains, "develop their roots as they advance, unlike the radicals, whose development is determined by their being anchored in a particular soil" (51). Radicants, Bourriaud goes on,

> grow their secondary roots alongside their primary one. The radicant develops in accord with its host soil. It confirms to the latter's twists and turns and adapts to its surfaces and geological features. It translates itself into the terms of the space in which it moves.
>
> *The Radicant* 51

The liminal nature of the radicant is not a drawback; adaptability is key, as the rest of Bourriaud's definition implies:

> With its at once dynamic and dialogical signification, the adjective 'radicant' captures this contemporary subject, caught between the need for a connection with its environment and the forces of uprooting, between globalization and singularity, between identity and opening to the other. It defines the subject as an object of negotiation.
>
> *The Radicant* 51

Bourriaud's term "altermodernity" makes clear that he did not jump on the bandwagon of the antimodernist crusade.[89] Altermodernity denotes an

---

89   In *Back From Utopia*, Hilde Heynen explains how postmodern thinkers have perceived
      modernism: "In postcolonial theories the interconnections between the Enlightenment

"altered" or "alternative" modernity—a modernity of the twenty-first century that rejects Western élitism and cultural domination. Altermodernity, Bourriaud explains,

> designates a construction plan that would allow new intercultural connections, the construction of a space of negotiation going beyond postmodern multiculturalism, which is attached to the origin of discourses and forms rather than to their dynamics.
>
> *The Radicant* 40

Multiculturalism not only extols but also revels in difference, as it calls for the respect of all cultures, especially "subaltern" cultures. But multiculturalism, in its endeavor to acknowledge and promote difference, maintains alterity and prevents the logic of absolute cultural equivalence, which would lead to the abolition of all hierarchies toward a perfectly creolized world, from being achieved. In other words, multiculturalism thwarts the fulfillment of a world in Relation: i.e. the total world in which Glissant placed his hopes. And just as Glissant warned newly decolonized nations about the dangers of developing inward-looking, hubristic national identities lest they resemble the nations that once colonized them (*Poetics of Relation*, 14), Bourriaud warns his contemporaries of the siren song of postcolonial theory, which, in its eagerness to recognize the other as Other, has led the West to develop a sense of insecurity toward the Other. In the world of art, Bourriaud argues, "we are witness to a postmodern aesthetic courtesy, an attitude that consists of refusing to pass critical judgment for fear of ruffling the sensitivity of the other" (27). The consequence of such an attitude, Bourriaud continues, is that non-Western artists are viewed as guests "to be treated with politeness, and not as full-fledged actors on the cultural scene in their own right" (27). And he concludes:

> In postmodern discourse, 'recognition of the other' generates a kind of reverse colonialism, as courteous and seemingly benevolent as its predecessor was brutal and nullifying.
>
> *The Radicant* 27

---

project of modernity and the imperialist practice of colonialism have been carefully disentangled. Following the lead of Edward Said's *Orientalism*, it is argued that colonial discourse was intrinsic to European self-understanding: it is through their conquest and their knowledge of foreign peoples and territories (two experiences which usually were intimately linked), that Europeans could position themselves as modern, as civilized, as superior, as developed and progressive vis-à-vis local populations that were none of that"; Hilde Heynen, "Engaging Modernism," in *Back from Utopia: The Challenge of the Modern Movement*, ed. Hilde Heynen & Hubert-Jan Henket (Rotterdam: 010 Publishers, 2002): 388.

Hence, Bourriaud is resolved to confront the hypocrisy lurking behind the good intentions of multiculturalism:

> we must move beyond peaceful and sterile coexistence of reified cultures (multiculturalism) to a state of cooperation among cultures that are equally critical of their own identity—that is to say, we must reach the stage of translation.
>
> *The Radicant* 27–28

Bourriaud's notion of translation stems from Segalen's theory of diversity and the figure of the Exot. Bourriaud's uncompromising depiction of postmodern standardization corresponds to Segalen's fear of the dilution of diversity in growing cultural uniformity: "If the homogenous prevails in the deepest reality," Segalen warns,

> nothing prevents one from believing in its eventual triumph over sensory reality [...]. Then the way will be cleared for the Kingdom of the Lukewarm; that moment of viscous mush without inequalities, falls, or reboundings.
>
> *Essay on Exoticism* 57

Segalen calls the loss of diversity "the great earthly threat" (63), and cautions:

> Let us not flatter ourselves for assimilating the customs, races, nations, and others who differ from us. On the contrary, let us rejoice in our inability ever to do so, for we thus retain the eternal pleasure of sensing Diversity.
>
> *Essay on Exoticism* 21

The Exot is the one who preserves and practices diversity. He is, Segalen writes, "a born Traveler, someone who senses all the flavor of diversity in worlds filled with wondrous diversities" (25). The Exot experiences diversity through exposure to the unfamiliar, and through the ability to preserve his/her differences while in contact with others. The Exot, and by analogy the radicant, neither embraces nor rejects the Other's differences. Nor does he/she attempt to dissolve those differences in order to create a homogeneous whole. Rather, the Exot (the radicant) respects and adapts to the Other's differences without losing his/her integrity in the process. The Exot, like the radicant, translates. In the plethora of cultures forming global dialogue and negotiation, Bourriaud makes translation the modus vivendi and modus operandi of his radicants:

Altermodernity promises to be a translation-oriented modernity, unlike the modern story of the twentieth century, whose progressivism spoke the abstract language of the colonial West. And the search for a productive compromise among singular discourses, this continuous effort at coordination, this constant elaboration of arrangements to enable disparate elements to function together, constitutes both its engine and its import.

The Radicant 43–44

Bourriaud compares the various stops on the radicant's trajectory to installations:

one 'installs oneself' in a place or situation in a makeshift or precarious way, and the subject's identity is nothing but the temporary result of this encampment, during which acts of translation are performed.

The Radicant 56

Bourriaud likens the radicant subject to a montage—a juxtaposition of heterogeneous elements, who must translate him/herself into a new environment as he/she follows his/her trajectory. The radicant always seeks temporary harmonization with other cultures, and does so through an "act of translation" (30). Translation does not follow universal codes. It means that one neither blindly accepts the values of another nor imposes one's own values on that other. Translation involves cooperation, concession, and compromise, and as such, it is "inevitably incomplete and leaves behind an irreducible remainder" (30). The result of these interactions is twofold: radicants leave a bit of themselves wherever they go, but they also take a bit of others with them when they leave. This is what the "act of translation" implies: to carry (*latus*) across or beyond (*trans*). Radicants are always in motion, and always in dialogue.

Bourriaud's altermodernity and Glissant's Relation, although very similar, lead to divergent models of society in a global culture. Bourriaud's insistence that the dynamics of "discourses and forms" matter more than their origin echoes Glissant's emphasis on movement once the latter has evolved from its primitive form of nomadism into errantry.[90] As a matter of fact, Bourriaud defines altermodernity in terms reminiscent of Glissant's concept of errantry:

---

90   Initially, Glissant confines the importance of movement over rootedness to the specific
      era of the invading nomads, for whom adventures were a mere instrument for self-defi-
      nition: "Along the route of their voyages conquerors established empires that collapsed
      at their death. Their capitals went where they went. 'Rome is no longer in Rome, it is

The altermodernity emerging today is fueled by the flow of bodies, by our cultural wandering. It presents itself as a venture beyond the conceptual frames assigned to thought and art, a mental expedition outside identitarian norms. Ultimately, then, radicant thought amounts to the organization of an exodus.

The Radicant 77

The radicant, just like errantry, is a mode of resistance to cultural inertia and a conduit toward a world of exchange, a world in Relation. As much as Glissant, Bourriaud deplores the standardization of thought and commodification of culture in a globalized world, and he concurs with Glissant that the modernist pursuit of origin and purity begets radicalism and intolerance. In fact, Bourriaud refers to Glissant's concept of creolization as an important factor in the development of altermodernity: "Today, creolization functions as a conceptual model whose figures could constitute the basis of a globalized modernity, a weapon against cultural standardization" (76).

The point of divergence between Bourriaud and Glissant turns on the notions of rootedness and identity. Jarrod Hayes defines the Glissantian trace as "identity-in-movement," which suggests an ever-changing identity: i.e. an identity that can never put down roots.[91] When Glissant borrows Deleuze and Guattari's rhizome metaphor to describe Relation, he emphasizes the fact that "the notion of the rhizome maintains [...] the idea of rootedness but challenges that of a totalitarian root" (*Poetics of Relation*, 11). Glissant acknowledges the presence, and perhaps the necessity, of rootedness. Yet, the possibility of being rooted is never discussed save in negative terms in his oeuvre except, perhaps, in the notion of trace, which suggests the perdurance of some roots, but also their frailty. The rhizome evokes an endless proliferation of small, entangled roots; similarly, Relation presupposes a horizontal network of infinite, unpredictable exchanges but, in order to guarantee equality, precludes the formation of a vertically hierarchical, rooted identity. Bourriaud also rejects the idea of a static, rooted identity, but his approach to identity formation differs sharply from that of Glissant:

To be radicant means setting one's roots in motion, staging them in heterogeneous contexts and formats, denying them the power to completely

---

wherever I am.' The root is not important. Movement is" (*Poetics of Relation*, 12). Movement, at this stage in history, precedes any conscious desire for settlement and errantry.

91   Jarrod Hayes, *Queer Roots for the Diaspora: Ghosts in the Family Tree* (Ann Arbor: U of Michigan P, 2016): 12.

define one's identity, translating ideas, transcoding images, transplant-
ing behaviors, exchanging rather than imposing. What if the twenty-first-
century culture were invented with those works that set themselves the
task of effacing their origin in favor of a multitude of simultaneous or
successive enrootings?[92]

> *The Radicant* 22

What matters, Bourriaud argues, is not so much the origin as the destination.
The radicant, Bourriaud explains, "can [...] cut itself off from its first roots and
reacclimate itself. There is no single origin but rather successive, simultaneous, or alternating acts of enrooting" (52). Thus, radicant-thinking reconciles
errantry and root. This is why Bourriaud, instead of elaborating a theory that
buries modernity, as Glissant and most postmodern thinkers do, calls for a reinvention of it. According to Bourriaud, the modernist quest for essences or
"return to the root" (50) does not boil down to the "mere assignment of an
identity" (50) as it does in the postmodern age. It can also be the vector for
positive values, as it opens up "the possibility of a radical new beginning and
the desire for new humanity" (50). Altermodernity, Bourriaud contends, "implies the invention of a new *conceptual persona* [...] that would bring about the
conjunction of modernism and globalization" (41).

   While Deleuze and Guattari present the rhizome (the cornerstone of Glissant's theory of Relation) as multiple, unforeseeable, and fluid,[93] Bourriaud
maintains that the rhizome "brackets out the question of the subject from the
beginning" (55). The radicant, by contrast, "implies a subject, but one that is
not reducible to a stable, closed, and self-contained identity" (55). The radicant
is neither what Deleuze and Guattari describe as "a search for arborescence

---

92 James Gussen and Lili Porten, who translated Bourriaud's *Radicant* for Sternberg Press,
    have coined the term "enrooting" for the French "enracinement," perhaps because the
    terms "rooting," "rootedness," and "deep-rootedness" do not properly render the prefix
    "en-," which means "to become" or "to morph into."

93 Deleuze and Guattari, in their introductory chapter to *A Thousand Plateaus*, write that
    "one of the most important characteristics of the rhizome is that it always has multiple
    entryways" (10). Unlike the tree and its roots, of which outcome is "the radicle solution,
    the structure of Power" (15), the rhizome is "alliance, uniquely alliance" (23), and its "traits
    are not necessarily linked to traits of the same nature; it brings into play very different
    regimes of signs, and even nonsign states" (19). The rhizome, Deleuze and Guattari go
    on, "is composed not of units but of dimensions, or rather directions in motion. It has
    neither beginning nor end, but always a middle (*milieu*) from which it grows and which it
    overspills" (19). Finally, the rhizome is an "acentered, nonhierarchical, nonsignifying sys-
    tem without a General and without an organizing memory or central automaton, defined
    solely by a circulation of states" (19).

and [a] return to the Old World"[94] nor a quest for what Glissant calls filiation. Rather, it is characterized by its wandering, and it is movement, Bourriaud concludes, "that ultimately permits the formation of an identity" (55).
Glissant uses the Deleuzian concept of the rhizome in order to express the
horizontal multiplicity of Relation and to go beyond the Cartesian dualism of
the modern age. But Glissant's Relation, as an overarching principle positing
mutual recognition between individuals and absolute equivalence between
cultures, ends up diluting identities in a non-hierarchical but ultimately controlled, coercive, and crippling environment such as the settlement Delblanc
experimented with in *Sacred Hunger* (see Chapter 3 above). The subject is back
at center-stage with Bourriaud's radicant, which posits what could be called
either a state of permanent, globalized errantry or a state of flexible, changing,
transient enrooting.

5   Coda

Earlier in this chapter, the reflection on *Sartorius*, along with Hallward's critical observation about the novel *Tout-monde*, demonstrates that Glissant's fiction sometimes candidly mirrors his theory. The reverse is also true: Glissant's
theoretical writing, both meticulously crafted and flamboyant, sometimes
reads like a belletristic undertaking. And as the analysis of "The Open Boat"
makes clear, Glissant's writing can lie between fiction and non-fiction, abstract
theory and concrete historical narrative, arcane academic prose and playful,
inventive, creolized phraseology. Glissant thus breaks binary oppositions and
unleashes the potentialities of various disciplines heretofore bound by strict
rules and principles. This deconstructionist approach, however, reaches its
limit when Glissant starts fusing poetics and politics: i.e. when the power he
attributes to imagination encroaches on the domain of (concrete) political
action: it yields very little or no result, and relegates Glissant to the rank of
an amiable visionary who is read for the elegance and originality of his prose
rather than for the pertinence and impact of his thought in rethinking community. Nancy's prose is no less elaborate but less adorned, a bit more arid, and
seemingly more academic than Glissant's. Arguably, both Glissant's and Nancy's endeavor to think past traditional, homogenizing, and stifling conceptions
of community has led them beyond and away from community (understood as
a socio-political entity and/or a group of people sharing interests in common)
as the only viable form of human existence. The intention is laudable, but the

---

94   Deleuze & Guattari, *A Thousand Plateaus*, 19.

hurdles both thinkers have faced raise the question of whether their vision of a different world is feasible.

Pace Glissant and his notion of Relation as a "concrete utopia," Relation has heretofore yielded the exact opposite of what it was purported to yield. Even his own Caribbean world, which he presents as the epitome of a composite culture and the cradle of creolization, is not immune to old, atavistic reflexes of other times and places. As Andrea Schwieger Hiepko observes, Glissant does not really

> come to terms with the fact of reterritorializing movements within con-
> temporary Caribbean societies, such as the nationalizing and identitarian
> movements on different islands and the resounding success of religious
> sects over the past few years.[95]

Furthermore, Glissant's warning to decolonized nations not to emulate those who oppressed them in the name of a fantasized innate superiority was all too prescient. Former colonies have rebuilt themselves along norms and values not so different from those upheld by their colonial rulers, often finding in jingoism and ethnocentricity a way of asserting their sense of independence and national identity. Finally, it is in locales most conducive to Relation, where authorities and cultures are most eager to respect the rights and integrity of minorities, that the latter have grown ever more sectarian (as sectarian as those, nativists and identitarians, who reject them). Host nations, in particular, are not absolved of liability for this plunge into ethnic and/or religious particularisms, but nor should they bear the entire responsibility for such failures. Beyond this fundamental debate, it appears that any community, once given the opportunity, asserts itself athwart others, as if the shortest way to achieve recognition and a sense of self were ruthlessness and self-interest. Refugees and migrants, whatever their origins, are as subject as those Glissant calls "invading nomads" to the impervious need to settle somewhere and forge an identity apart from others, preferably in opposition to the dominant culture.

In this sense, the attitude of such minorities echoes that of Nadri, Kireku, and other businessmen in *Sacred Hunger* (Chapter 3 above) who intend to "immunize" themselves. The motives may be different (individual freedom for economic expansion in the case of the dwellers in Delblanc's settlement, and a

---

95   Andrea Schwieger Hiepko, "Creolization as a poetics of culture: Edouard Glissant's 'ar-
      chipelic' thinking," in *A Pepper-Pot of Cultures: Aspects of Creolization in the Caribbean*, ed.
      Gordon Collier & Ulrich Fleischmann (Matatu 27–28; Amsterdam & New York: Rodopi,
      2003): 258.

sense of alienation in the case of minorities in Western democracies), but the result is the same: disengagement from one's allegiance and responsibility to the community. Such disengagement, however, is rarely a step toward absolute individual freedom. It is an engagement elsewhere: Kireku, Nadri, and their cohort, willingly or not, constitute a community of entrepreneurs, and even if they compete with one another, they all want out of the community that saved them from death, because it has become a hindrance to their trading activities. As for members of minorities who reject the national community they live in, these often take refuge in an alternative community (religious, ethnic, cultural, etc.), to whose values they more readily adhere.

Certainly individuals belong to several communities with various degrees of adherence, but the mechanism remains the same: each community (family, business, nation, etc.) behaves like an individual and seeks to protect its own interests by immunizing itself from other communities. In this view, it may be more accurate to define humanity as a system ruled by what Peter Sloterdijk calls "co-immunity." Dismissing the "travelers on the ship of fools that is abstract universalism,"[96] Sloterdijk believes that we have now entered an era of absolute diversity composed of communities that resists categorization and the logocentric forces of the West. Altruism is sacrificed, or at least hampered, on the altar of co-immunity, as each specific community tends to limit altruism to its own members; but, for Sloterdijk, a global co-immunity order must supersede globalization, which he describes as "an actual integration disaster in progress" (447). Sloterdijk describes the members of the world community as "workers on the consistently concrete and discrete project of a global immune design" (451), and suggests that a modus operandi can be found with the right dispositions:

> The history of the own [the self] that is grasped on too small a scale and the foreign [the other] that is treated too badly reaches an end at the moment when a global co-immunity structure is born, with a respectful inclusion of individual cultures, particular interests and local solidarities.
> *You Must Change Your Life* 451

Sloterdijk's concept of co-immunity prefigures Nancy and Barrau's argument in *What's These Worlds Coming To?* As mentioned earlier in this chapter (Section 3 above), Nancy and Barrau argue that "the question of the world

---

96   Peter Sloterdijk, *You Must Change Your Life*, tr. Wieland Hoban (*Du mußt dein Leben ändern*, 2009; Cambridge: Polity, 2013): 451. Further page references are in the main text.

must be reconsidered" (3) because globalization has completely disrupted its organization and unity:

> the world-cosmos is fractured [and] the very idea of "world" (one, ensemble) no longer answers to the investigation of physics or to metaphysical questioning. "Pluriverse" and "multiverse" are now on physicists' agendas, while "multiplicity" and "multitude" permeate sociologies as well as ontologies.
>
> *What's These Worlds Coming To?* 3

Sloterdijk shares this view, and while Nancy sees "struction" (his term for a world with neither order nor coordination) as a tabula rasa from where everything can be built anew, Sloterdijk believes that immunology, which he sees as the founding principle of all cultures, is the conduit through which the global world is apprehended and even shaped. Like Nancy, Sloterdijk wants to tackle the utter chaos of the current world—its transformation from a unified whole to a multiverse—and he believes that communism, for all its past flaws, has been right about "the understanding that shared life interests of the highest order can only be realized within a horizon of universal *co-operative asceticisms*" (451–452) (emphasis added). Sloterdijk's notion of ascetic cooperation ups the ante on Nancy and Glissant's respective notions of being-with and Relation, as it denotes a concerted, disciplined, and repetitive practice toward the realization of global immunology. Finally, Sloterdijk predicts that communism will make a comeback and impose itself as a panacea, for it "presses for a macrostructure of global immunizations: co-immunism" (452)—a prospect Nancy would welcome.

In *Le communisme existentiel de Jean-Luc Nancy* (2013), Frédéric Neyrat argues that Nancy's theory of the originary plurality of each individual may be interpreted as "a supplement at the heart of the subject, [which] may be linguistic, social or ethical."[97] This reading is in accord with the structuralist tenet "before I speak, I am spoken," which assumes that the self is inexistent outside its cultural, social, and political environment. But Neyrat admits that "this social primacy is not really manifest in Nancy's philosophy,"[98] since Nancy's being-singular-plural is antecedent and extraneous to any process of society building. Nancy understands community as an ontological rather than a political concept because, as he claims in *The Inoperative Community*, "it is

---

97   Frédéric Neyrat, *Le communisme existentiel de Jean-Luc Nancy* (Paris: Éditions Lignes, 2013): 36. (My tr.)

98   Neyrat, *Le communisme existentiel de Jean-Luc Nancy*, 36.

the communal fabric, it is immanence that is lacerated. And yet this laceration does not happen *to* anything, for this fabric does not exist."[99] Nancy means that there is "no subject or substance of common being"[100] but, rather, a being-in-common, a "sharing out" of singularities exposed to one another.

In *Birth to Presence* (1993), Nancy calls this inaugural lack of communal foundation "abandonment," which Daniel Matthews describes as an "absolute withdrawal with no return, a permanent banishment from the metaphysical comforts of identity, fixity, permanence, unitariness and so on."[101] To be, Matthews explains, "is to be abandoned, to be without fixity, identity or presence; to be is to be cast outside oneself and exposed in an inoperative relation to others" (83). Matthews sees this irremediable groundlessness as an opportunity to reimagine common law and thus foster justice in a society that has forsaken the well-being of its citizens. According to Matthews, "social and political institutions [...] manipulate subjectivities through [a] debtor-creditor relation" (84), and the "bare facticity of being-in-common" is a reminder that "the ligaments that tie us to the common persist beneath, before or beyond any subsequent social and political constructions of indebtedness" (84). Matthews further argues:

> Social and political obligations—solidarity, trust and the question of the common good—are obscured by the obsession with rights and the quasi-juridical management of social affairs.
> "A Spirit of the Common" 86

And he is convinced that there is a way out of this impasse if, following Nancy, we understand that "being-abandoned calls for an opening of the world, an ongoing fashioning of human relations that must assume, as 'essential,' the groundless being-in-common of our existence" (86). Then and only then can we learn from the medieval era, where, according to Matthews, "we can see a centrally important appeal to the common, to the indubitable connection between the legal form and the creative life of people living and producing together" (86). Matthews's reflection on abandonment—a term that entered the Nancean lexicon in 1993—is a reminder that Nancy, long before the notion of struction (introduced in 2011), only exposed our understanding of community

---

99   Jean-Luc Nancy, *The Inoperative Community*, 30.
100   Nancy, *The Inoperative Community*, 30.
101   Daniel Matthews, "A Spirit of the Common: Reimagining 'The Common Law' with Jean-Luc Nancy," in *Space, Power and the Commons: The Struggle for Alternative Futures,* ed. Samuel Kirwan, Leila Dawney & Julian Brigstocke (New York: Routledge, 2016): 82. Further page references are in the main text.

as a fallacy in order to envision new departures from which to build a better future.

Nancy, by declaring the community "inoperative," has done away with social contract theories, because a social contract inevitably leads to the formation of an "operative" community—that is, a community that works toward establishing a communal identity defined by its difference from others, necessarily in conflict with others, and thus aspiring to immanentism. Nancy advocates the emergence of a new world built upon the ruins of our collapsed world, but he seems more eager to pinpoint the wrongs (withdrawal of the political, sovereignty, ecotechnology) than to come up with solutions. The following comment, in *The Creation of the World*, illustrates Nancy's indeterminacy: "The whole question is whether we can finally manage to think the 'contract' [...] according to a model other than the juridicocommercial model" (111). Nancy goes on to criticize the social contract for taking the bond for granted and thus ignoring the subject's freedom of choice, only to suggest in the last instance that it is impervious to "think the social bond according to another model or perhaps without a model. To think its act, establishment, and binding" (111). Nancy implies that there are alternatives to the world we live in, but he does not devise a method for effecting change.

Ultimately, Nancy's approach to community hints at a reluctance to engage with politics, and more specifically with Aristotle's proverbial *zoon politikon*: i.e. the individual as a thinking, rational being who fully realizes him/herself in the social context of the *polis*. In *Politics*, Aristotle states that "the state is a creation of nature, and [...] man is by nature a political animal."[102] Aristotle goes on to define the *zoon politikon* by its antithesis:

> he who by nature and not by mere accident is without a state, is either above humanity, or below it; he is the 'Tribeless, lawless, heartless one,' [...] the outcast who is a lover of war; he may be compared to an unprotected piece in the game of draughts.
>
> *Politics* 28

The definition anticipates Hobbes's apocalyptic vision of the state of nature, and it refutes Nancy's claim that "the *zoon politikon* is secondary to [the inoperative] community,"[103] for it implies that there is no humanity prior to life in society.

---

102   Aristotle, *Politics*, tr. Benjamin Jowett (1905; Mineola NY: Dover, 2000): 28.
103   Jean-Luc Nancy, *The Inoperative Community*, 28.

Aristotle's vision of community is no less conceptual and idealized than Nancy's vision of a postglobal world where being-in-common has become the driving force of existence. In contrast to Nancy, however, Aristotle puts the city-state at the center of human existence:

> The state is the highest form of community and aims at the highest good. [...] It consists of villages which consist of households. The household is founded upon the two relations of male and female, of master and slave; it exists to satisfy man's daily needs. The village, a wider community, satisfies a wider range of needs. The state aims at satisfying all the needs of men. Men form state to secure a bare existence; but the ultimate object of the state is the good life. The naturalness of the state is proved by the faculty of speech in man. In the order of Nature the state precedes the household and the individual. It is founded on a natural impulse, that towards political association [...].
>
> *Politics* 7

The most salient aspect of Aristotle's state is its natural origin and the fact that it is the site where the gregarious nature of human beings blossoms. Humans come together to satisfy the basic needs of life and to strive toward "the good life." In the Aristotelian cosmogony, humans do more than being co-present: they cooperate—debate, compromise, and finally work together for the good of all. Aristotle gives prominence to the lawgiver, whose role is to establish the city-state and give it an "aristocratic" constitution, by which Aristotle means that the best people (*aristos*) should be in charge of the affairs of the state. The aim is justice and happiness for all. The community that Delblanc builds in *Sacred Hunger* (Chapter 3 above) reveals the limits of such an ideal vision of life in common: although the survivors of the shipwreck unite in the early days in order to survive, and while Delblanc, no doubt a reader of Aristotle, believes in the natural inclination of human beings to live together under a just system of law, the community unravels as soon as living conditions improve. Thriving entrepreneurs are the first to distance themselves from the social affairs of the community, because the community no longer serves their personal interests. These profit-minded individuals are self-absorbed—the opposite of political animals whose rational mind, according to Aristotle, should give priority to the community.

Humans may be social beings by nature, but this predisposition toward others varies across people, times, places, and circumstances both in content and in density. Even if Nancy's theory that we coexist prior to any form of communal consciousness is accurate, it does not mean that this coexistence is fundamentally altruistic. Altruism always competes with selfishness, and whether it is inborn or not, it needs to be stimulated. Altruism must be learned; therefore, it is the responsibility of the community to nurture it. More than a desideratum, altruism is a necessity, which would explain why, in most cultures, altruism is turned into a regulatory device, a social equalizer translated into a moral obligation. Altruism is a problem insofar as it tends to stop at the border of the community (be it political, religious, national, racial, etc.), but it is hard to imagine how altruism, which needs to be triggered, could develop outside a community of individuals bound by a social contract.

Nancy's use of a cautious "perhaps" regarding the reappraisal of the "social bond [...] *without* a model"[104] suggests that he is grappling with the idea of an alternative to a model of society outside a social contract. But Nancy remains confident that the whole social edifice ought to be reimagined and rebuilt primarily because the law the sovereign people has made for itself fails to deliver justice. Nancy contests the legitimacy of popular sovereignty, on the ground that it puts the plurality of existence under the yoke of its unifying power. Furthermore, he deems sovereignty undemocratic because it makes itself immune to the law it has created for its members. This argument, however, can easily be diverted from its intended course. A political philosopher once offered the following view of modern democracy:

> It seems to be the regular course of the development of democracy that after a glorious first period in which it is understood as and actually operates as a safeguard of personal freedom because it accepts the limitations of a higher nomos, sooner or later it comes to claim the right to settle any particular question in whatever manner a majority agrees upon.[105]

Out of context, one may attribute this view to such thinkers as Agamben and Nancy, but scholars of political science will recognize these as the words of Friedrich Hayek, one of the architects of the neoliberal revolution that has shaped precisely that globalized world against which the greater part of Nancy's corpus is pitted. Agamben and Nancy share with Hayek the feeling that citizens of liberal democracies have lost their basic political rights, but the way the former reach such a conclusion differs sharply from the latter's.

---

104   Jean-Luc Nancy, *The Sense of the World*, tr. & intro. Jeffrey S. Librett (*Le sens du monde*, 1993; Minneapolis: U of Minnesota P, 1997): 111. (Emphasis added).

105   Friedrich Hayek, *Law, Legislation and Liberty*, vol. 3: *The Political Order of a Free People* (Chicago: U of Chicago P, 1981): 2.

Agamben argues that, in the West, a state of exception whereby the whole juridical order is suspended has taken over regular democratic procedures. According to Agamben,

> the sovereign is the point of indistinction between violence and law, the threshold on which violence passes over into law and law passes over into violence.[106]

Agamben evokes a "sovereign ban" that echoes Nancy's earlier notion of "abandonment," which, Nancy argues, "does not constitute a subpoena to present oneself before this or that court of the law. It is a compulsion to appear absolutely under the law, under the law as such and in its totality"[107] (*The Birth to Presence*, 44). Abandonment is a form of subjugation: it "respects the law; it cannot do otherwise" (44). In a state of exception, as Agamben describes it, subjects are treated as living human beings (bare life, *zoē*) deprived of their status as citizens (political existence, *bios*) responsible for their own life. Thus, the state of exception is a trap in which the subject is included in the social order through exclusion,[108] and the "only truly political action," Agamben concludes, "is that which severs the nexus between violence and law."[109]

Nancy's solution is perhaps more radical than Agamben's call for political action, as Nancy suggests doing away, purely and simply, with the familiar model of political/juridical sovereignty. In *The Creation of the World*, Nancy argues that "*nomos basileus*," the law of the sovereign, should be replaced with "*cosmos basileus*" (110), the law of the universe:

> The unity of a world is not one: it is made of a diversity, including disparity and opposition. It is made of it, which is to say that it is not added it

---

106   Giorgio Agamben, *Homo Sacer: Sovereign Power and Bare Life*, tr. Daniel Heller-Roazen (*Homo sacer: Il potere sovrano e la nuda vita*, 1995; Stanford CA: Stanford UP, 1998): 32.

107   Jean-Luc Nancy, "Abandoned Being," in Nancy, *The Birth to Presence*, tr. Brian Holmes et al. (Stanford CA: Stanford UP, 1993): 44.

108   In *Homo Sacer*, Agamben writes: "The fundamental categorial pair of Western politics is not that of friend/enemy but that of bare life/political existence, *zoē/bios*, exclusion/inclusion" (8). Further on, Agamben describes the sovereign ban, thus: "The exception is a kind of exclusion. What is excluded from the general rule is an individual case. But the most proper characteristic of the exception is that what is excluded in it is not, on account of being excluded, absolutely without relation to the rule. On the contrary, what is excluded in the exception maintains itself in relation to the rule in the form of the rule's suspension" (17).

109   Giorgio Agamben, *Homo Sacer*, 88.

to it and does not reduce it. The unity of a world is nothing other than its diversity, and its diversity is, in turn, a diversity of worlds.

"Cosmos Basileus" 109

In this perspective, the law is the world, and the world is the law. The world (or the cosmos) is sovereign-free and defined by its "sharing out" (109):

> Its supreme law is in it as the multiple and mobile line of the sharing out that it is. *Nomos* is the distribution, the repartition, and the attribution of the parts. Territorial place, nourishment, a delimitation of rights and duties: to each and each time as appropriate.
>
> *"Cosmos Basileus"* 109

This world in which Nancy places his hopes is the fragmented, uncoordinated, and disunified world that he describes via the concept of struction. Paradoxically, it is from this world in disarray that sense can emerge again. Sense, Nancy tells us, will be found in struction,

> at the place where there is neither end, nor means, nor assembly, nor disassembly, nor top, nor bottom, nor east, nor west. But merely an all together.
>
> *What's These Worlds Coming To?* 58

Unlike Agamben and Nancy, Hayek does not attribute the loss of political rights to a state of exception but to too much democracy, which has led the representative government, arrogating to itself all legislative powers, to trample upon the principles of constitutionalism. The law of the majority has replaced moral principles with the interests of special groups organized to support a particular program. Eventually, the government controls economic life regardless of the "consent of the people," and Hayek concludes that,

> wherever democratic institutions [cease] to be restrained by the tradition of the Rule of Law, they [lead] not only to "totalitarian democracy" but in due time even to a "plebiscitary dictatorship."[110]

Thus, the fundamental difference between Nancy and Hayek is that the former associates the loss of freedom incurred by an excess of sovereignty with accumulation of capital and growing social disparities, whereas the latter associates it with an obstacle to the accumulation of capital and self-interest.

---

110   Friedrich Hayek, *Law, Legislation and Liberty*, vol. 3: *The Political Order of a Free People*, 4.

Nancy and Hayek hold antipodal views about the very meaning of democracy, and yet, the appropriation of the concept of freedom by Hayek should serve as a warning about Nancy's own concept thereof. Struction, despite its emancipating potential, carries in its midst the possibility of its own ruin. Indeed, struction posits a completely disorderly environment in which singularities freely and unpredictably interact with one another—an absence of structure that unfetters singularities from any form of programming, which in turn allows the world to make sense. This absolute autonomy, however, runs the risk of precipitating singularities into chaos and lawlessness, thus creating a fertile ground for the kind of world Hayek and his cohort have created. The best response to such a threat is the establishment of a social contract and new laws. The real challenge lies not in fewer laws for less coercion, but better laws for more freedom, equality, and justice.

Conclusion

The United Nations High Commissioner for Refugees estimates that from 2014 to 2017, 1.6 million men, women, and children, mostly from the Middle East and Africa, tried to reach Europe via the Mediterranean Sea. Of these prospective migrants, over fifteen thousand are considered dead or missing.[1] Their wretched conditions do evoke the Glissantian figure of the "naked migrant"[2]— the captive in the hold of the slave ship who was disembarked in the Americas with nothing on his back, and in a state of utter physical, psychological, and emotional exhaustion. But the situation of today's migrants—the violence of their deracination notwithstanding—remains quite different from that of these captives. Unlike the latter, the migrants chose to risk their lives to make it to Europe. They were not wrested from their homes and communities by raiding parties to be sold off to European traders who would take them across the Atlantic Ocean for a life of slavery in the New World. They paid for their passage across the Mediterranean and set off on frail, rickety vessels chartered by smugglers in ports of the Maghreb. As for those who died during the crossing, they were not thrown overboard because of an epidemic or a captain eager to make an example of a few recalcitrants. They drowned because the miserable dinghies they boarded were overcrowded or taking on water.

A recent piece of news, however, provides a basis for comparison between the migrant crisis and the slave trade. On 14 November 2017, the cable news channel CNN released an undercover video of a slave auction just outside Tripoli, the capital of war-torn Libya, which has become a major transit hub from Africa to Europe.[3] The men being sold are sub-Saharan Africans who were defrauded of their meager life savings, kidnapped, and brought to slave markets while trudging along the North African migrant routes: "There they become commodities to be bought, sold and discarded when they have no more value,"

---

1   United Nations. "Mediterranean Situation," *The United Nations High Commissioner for Refugees* (22 December 2017): online (accessed 31 December 2017).

2   In "Creolization in the Making of the Americas" (1995), Glissant distinguishes three types of migrants to the New World. The first type is that of the "founding" or "armed migrant"—the *Mayflower* settler and his descendants who built "the economic power of the Northern Americas" (87); the second type is that of the "household migrant" who arrived "with his kitchen ranges, [...] family pictures, [and] perhaps a business ability" (87); and the third type is the "naked migrant" whom Glissant describes as "the African deported by the Middle Passage, arriving with only traces of his original country and his languages, and with the difficult and progressively vanished memory of his gods" (87).

3   CNN, "Migrants being sold as slaves," *CNN: International Edition* (14 November 2017): online (accessed 1 January 2018).

explains Leonard Doyle, the chief spokesman for the International Organization for Migration (IOM) in Geneva.[4] The places where these migrants are detained are reminiscent of the barracoons and holding cells of the slave-trade era, with "dreadful sanitary conditions, and food offered only once per day." As for individuals unable to pay their captors, they are "reportedly killed, or left to starve to death." The IOM also reports that, "when somebody die[s] or [is] released, kidnappers return to the market to 'buy' more migrants to replace them." Finally, while men are usually purchased for farm work, women "[are] 'bought' by private individuals [...] and brought to homes where they [are] forced to be sex slaves."

The ease and celerity with which slave traders have taken advantage of the migrant crisis in Libya evokes a bygone age when ruthless entrepreneurs could profit from human trafficking with impunity and the blessing of their national authorities. CNN's video prompted world leaders to express their shock and indignation even though aid workers and NGOs had been sounding the alarm for several months. Wealthy nations of the Northern Hemisphere, which once organized forced migrations for commercial purposes, have been particularly eager to take action. Accordingly, they have deployed an arsenal of international laws to protect the rights of the migrants, and have pledged a substantial amount of money to support humanitarian assistance. But this philanthropic attitude conceals ulterior motives: these nations would rather have the starving poor and war victims of the South and elsewhere stay home, for their priority is to stem the migratory flows threatening the precarious stability of a world order based on economic power.

The real stakes are national security and prosperity, and even though many in Europe and North America stand in principle by what Jacques Derrida calls the "categorical imperative of hospitality,"[5] few are willing to share what they have with those less fortunate in the rest of the world. The European Union is typical of this Janus-faced approach: on the one hand, it has opened its doors to many refugees and asylum seekers; on the other, it has taken strong preventive measures in order to limit the number of migrants entering and staying in Europe. The proverb "charity begins at home" has become a disingenuous way for affluent nations to dodge their moral responsibility and ignore their own inherent contradictions, for the problem at the heart of the recent migrant

---

4   International Organization for Migration (IOM). "IOM Learns of 'Slave Market' Conditions Endangering Migrants in North Africa," International Organization for Migration (IOM): The UN Migration Agency (4 November 2017): online (accessed 31 December 2017).

5   Jacques Derrida, *Of Hospitality: Anne Dufourmantelle Invites Jacques Derrida to Respond*, tr. Rachel Bowlby (Palo Alto CA: Stanford UP, 2000): 75.

crisis is not the migrant; it is the segmentation of the world into nation-states that have lost their sovereignty to the logic of laissez-faire economics and corporate capitalism.

Democracies of the Northern Hemisphere are facing a conundrum: they have written moral principles into laws that regulate their institutions and guarantee a level of political integrity and freedom unimaginable elsewhere. But the linchpin of this freedom is economic prosperity, which is contingent on being successful in a world dominated by economic competition—a world in which the fair redistribution of wealth is a non-binding principle and in which the traditional tools designed to regulate the market have been consigned to oblivion. The leaders of developed nations never miss an opportunity to lecture their counterparts in less developed nations about how democratic reforms constitute the fulcrum of economic growth, when in fact the opposite may be more accurate: economic growth is the fulcrum of democracy, and in a world subject to the sacrosanct logic of the market, the opportunity for poor countries to alter the status quo is scant. The CNN footage has just shown the world the effect of this pitiless reality: Africans are being auctioned off in exactly the same way their ancestors were auctioned off in the era of the transatlantic slave trade.

The difference between then and now remains one of volume, legality, and moral conduct. The transatlantic slave trade, especially after the end of royal charters and the transition from mercantilism to free trade in the mid-eighteenth century, is an early manifestation of the kind of exorbitance unbridled capitalism can bring about. In terms of output, the mass manufacturing of African slave labor for the plantation economy of the New World mirrors the mass-production of factory goods during the Industrial Revolution and into the twentieth century. By contrast, the recent slave auctions in North Africa are sporadic, small-scale, clandestine operations. They are not organized into a trans-continental network of business transactions, and have no intention of expanding much beyond the local market. Yet, these slave auctions answer to the same logic of greed underlying the slave trade and today's global market economy.

As shown in Chapter 3, there is a continuum between slavery, the Industrial Revolution, and today's neoliberal world order. Those who have fallen through the cracks of the prosperity gap are the descendants of those who were once enslaved, colonized, or exploited. If the liberal West, as Lowe believes, is to blame for the economic disparities plaguing the world, it can also be argued that its democratic values, even if they have failed to spread uniformly across nations and cultures, remain the only bastion against wholesale moral chaos and a return to the *bellum omnium contra omnes* of Thomas Hobbes. Liberal democracy, for all its shortcomings, has largely contributed to influencing public opinion over time: the slave trade was abolished on the grounds of morality and justice—principles that eventually became axiomatic. Meanwhile, labor laws were enacted to protect the rights of exploited workers and are now taken for granted (even if hard-won social gains are being dismantled as a result of globalization and its enhancement of the neoliberal agenda). The core notion, in the 1948 United Nations Universal Declaration of Human Rights, that some rights are inalienable has made its way into the minds of populations and political leaders throughout the world. Today, slave trading is considered a crime against humanity and no financial backers, whether public or private, will endorse the slave traffickers in North Africa. These slave auctions in Libya must be understood in light of the post-Gaddafi era: the absence of political leadership and the lack of due process of law, combined with the prioritization of self-interest over the common weal and morality, have created ideal conditions for such commerce to thrive.

But these slave auctions, even though they are geographically circumscribed and the result of exceptional circumstances, are still the symptom of a much larger problem. Advocates of the global economy tell of the success stories of BRICS, MINTS, PINES, MISTS, CIVETS, and EAGLES.[6] These acronyms reflect the economic growth of emerging markets, and bear witness to the capacity of globalization to generate economic activity, but they do not tell of who reaps the benefits of such development. Profit is generated, and yet poverty increases, which means that wealth is not properly re-distributed.[7] In a world controlled

---

6   BRIC: Brazil, Russia, India and China. MINT: Mexico, Indonesia, Nigeria, and Turkey. MIST: Mexico, India, South Korea, and Turkey. PINE: Philippines, Indonesia, Nigeria, and Ethiopia. CIVET: Colombia, Indonesia, Vietnam, Egypt, Turkey, and South Africa. EAGLE: Emerging and Growth Leading Economies (including Brazil, China, Egypt, India, Indonesia, South Korea, Mexico, Russia, Taiwan, and Turkey). Other acronyms used in the business world are MIKT (Mexico, Indonesia, South Korea, and Turkey), and KETU for the East African markets (Kenya, Ethiopia, Tanzania, and Uganda). The term "Fragile Five," which obviously carries less marketing clout, stands for those nations (Indonesia, South Africa, Brazil, Turkey, and India) that have grown dependent on unreliable foreign investments.

7   On 22 February 2007, OECD Secretary General Angel Gurría addressed the Chambers of Deputies in Rome, Italy and described the economic situation of the world in the following terms: "Globalisation has facilitated the creation of enormous wealth, whilst inequality has at the same time increased. Today 1% of the world's adults own 40% of global wealth, while 50% own less than one percent. The 'poor countries' of the planet are four times less productive than the rich ones, and experiencing a significant fall in the incomes vis-à-vis the developed world, an erosion of their competitiveness, structural unemployment and chronic disparities and insecurity"; OECD, "Reaping the Benefits of Globalisation: The Importance of Public Policies," *Remarks by Angel Gurría, Secretary General of the OECD, Foreign Relations Commission, Chamber of Deputies, Rome* (22 February 2007): online (accessed 2 January 2018).

by the shareholders of giant multinational corporations that dodge taxes and are answerable neither to national nor to international law, pauperization increases, the social and communal fabric begin fraying, and populations grow ever more transient.

As shown earlier (Chapter 4), Glissant finds in the impermanence of such diasporic communities the type of cultural synergy he associates with Relation—a stage in the evolution of humanity when the proliferation of artistic and cultural exchanges is able to leap the hurdles of global capitalism and its commodification of human life. However, Glissant's concept of Relation errs on the side of optimism. Globalization does bring cultures of the world in contact, and to some extent fosters diversity. Yet, instead of dampening racial tensions, globalization inflames them and polarizes people around an erstwhile rhetoric of race—the type of rhetoric leading to conservative, bigoted attitudes on either side of the racial divide, as the analysis of *Roots* and *Tamango* (Chapter 1 above) has demonstrated. Today, such sectarianism is often exacerbated by recourse to religious affiliation, which may be either the result of ostracism or a strategy of self-imposed ghettoization.

Concomitantly, political debates are reverting to simplistic binary oppositions that ignore the complexity of social dynamics and stoke the fires of demagoguery, intolerance, and violence. The normalization of extremist ideas in Europe and the United States over the last two or three decades is reminiscent of the dangerous ideologies purveyed respectively by Falcon and Diamelo in *Middle Passage* (Chapter 2 above)—ideologies that Calhoun, who believes in the principles enshrined in the founding texts of the United States, seeks to evade. Much has changed in the century separating the pre-Civil War world of Calhoun from the pre-civil rights world of the Invisible Man, yet both protagonists aspire to the same democratic reforms. Many reforms were adopted in the wake of the civil rights legislation of the mid-1960s, but the new political climate of the post-Obama presidency suggests that both Calhoun and the Invisible Man's claim that the nation does not live up to the values it holds most dear is still relevant.

Nowadays, the idea of a more egalitarian world is widely accepted in Europe and North America, but it is a disembodied idea conforming to harmless, non-committal cosmopolitan values. The small black and white community featured in *Sacred Hunger* (Chapter 3 above) shows how difficult it is to live together even when all possible sources of division and inequality among community members have been ostensibly removed. The failure of Delblanc's settlement in *Sacred Hunger* may be attributed either to the lack of a binding social contract or to the simple fact that human beings, depending on their circumstances, will waver between gregarious and antisocial attitudes. The small settlement does not self-destruct, however. It is brutally destroyed by Erasmus

Kemp—the embodiment of the greedy, merciless capitalist of the early stages of the Industrial Revolution, and a prototype, some would argue, of the neo-conservative entrepreneur of our age.

There is no perfect community, but Glissant always believed that community must be reinvented outside the Western model of filiation, which permanently links a community to its own creation and blunts its capacity to open up to others. Nancy goes even farther, as he likens the Western nostalgia for a lost community that must be restored to a form of totalitarianism, and advocates a "community without communion."[8] Glissant does not go as far as Nancy in his theorizing of community, but in "The Open Boat" he imagines the advent of a new people, which begins in the hold of the slave ship and spreads, through a process of creolization, to the rest of the world. Creolized individuals are not defined by filiation but by their relation to others. As argued in the fourth chapter, however, Glissant's rhizomatic approach soon generates a feeling of groundlessness, a disorientation that leaves the subject without reliable fixed markers. Bourriaud's concept of the radicant, which recognizes randomness and rootedness as a twofold necessity, is introduced as an alternative to Glissant's rhizome, but the radicant, by limiting the scope to the art world, seems to turn a blind eye to the harsh reality of migrants in quest of new beginnings.

The transitory state of most foreign job seekers is a challenge to nation-states, whose stability partially hinges on a strict management of who can stay and who must go. But this international workforce is also manna from heaven for wealthy nations in dire need of a replacement migration to make up for their declining birth rates and finance their pension schemes. The cheap, unqualified, and unprotected foreign workers who knock at the door of affluent nations are either granted temporary status or left undocumented and at the mercy of an exploitative black market that works as a safety valve for the official market. These workers are defenseless and amenable to both their host nations and the big businesses prospering from their expendability. In a context of de-unionization and weakening welfare, the presence of these overseas workers also affects the local workforce, as their labor costs contribute to lowering the national average wage. As Western democracies rely more and more on this new subclass of domestic and non-domestic working poor, the conditions that once made the transatlantic slave trade possible are looming ahead in revenant guise. Not surprisingly, the issues that fictions of the slave trade address bear an eerie resemblance to the issues defining our age.

Liberal democracy in its most complete and noble form—with rule of law, civil liberties, and political freedom—appears to have been a mere hiatus in the history of modernity. As a concept, liberal democracy is the child of the

---

8   Jean-Luc Nancy, The *Inoperative Community*, 144.

Enlightenment, but it really grew strong and imposed itself as a model of society in the three decades following the end of the Second World War. It started to wilt as a result of the oil crises in the 1970s, the dismantling of the welfare state in the 1980s, and the collapse of Soviet communism at the end of that decade. The end of liberal democracy marks the advent of neoliberalism,[9] which, according to Wendy Brown, "involves *extending and disseminating market values to all institutions and social action,* even as the market itself remains a distinctive player."[10] It follows that, in the neoliberal order, "not only is the human being configured exhaustively as *homo œconomicus,* but all dimensions of human life are cast in terms of a market rationality."[11] In such a system, welfare policies are seen as an impediment to the advancement of individual wealth. The neoliberal model of society that now dominates the world economy has at least dispelled the belief that social conscience and selflessness are inborn qualities. Such qualities must be developed and maintained through political will and action, and, as the analysis of *Sacred Hunger* (Chapter 3 above) suggests, it is often born of necessity—a bitter but lucid conclusion that research in the field of anthropology confirms.

From an evolutionary standpoint, altruism is an instrument rather than a quality inherent in human beings. Discussing the socio-political structure of primate societies, Herbert Gintis notes that "many primate species, including humans and our closest living relatives, seek to dominate others and are adept at forming coalitions."[12] In other words, dominating others comes first, and the purpose of forming a group is to dominate. There will be altruistic behaviors within the group, but outsiders will be either excluded or subjugated or, in the worst case, exterminated. We should not find solace in the fact that these

9   In a 1989 essay, Francis Fukuyama interprets the end of communism as a seal of approval on free market capitalism, and prophesies the advent of "Western *liberal democracy* as the final form of human government"; "The End of History?" *The National Interest* 16 (1989): 3 (emphasis added). Three years later, in *The End of History and the Last Man* (New York: Avon, 1992), Fukuyama argues that that there is "no ideology with pretensions to universality that is in a position to challenge *liberal democracy*" (45; emphasis added). The notion that liberal democracy holds the promise of a more equitable world would not be erroneous if it weren't for Fukuyama's play on the double entendre of the word "liberal," which denotes free-trade ideology, on the one hand, and the progressive agenda of the political left, on the other. By fusing these two meanings into one, Fukuyama erases the difference between neoliberalism and liberal democracy, thus deceptively endowing the former with the virtues of the latter.

10   Wendy Brown, *Edgework: Critical Essays on Knowledge and Politics* (Princeton NJ: Princeton UP, 2005): 39–40 (emphasis in the original).

11   Brown, *Edgework,* 40.

12   Herbert Gintis, *Individuality and Entanglement: The Moral and Material Bases of Social Life* (Princeton NJ: Princeton UP, 2016): 18.

scenarios are set in proto-historical times: they are primitive versions of what is happening in our contemporary world.

In fact, Gintis makes this trans-historical link explicit:

> Dominance seeking and coalition formation in humans are not purely cultural. Rather, humans are endowed with the genetic prerequisites for this behavior.
>
> *Individuality and Entanglement* 18

This anthropological approach is also a reminder that, thousands of years before Aristotle's *zoon politikon*, primates displayed rudimentary socio-political forms of behavior: they formed groups "to reduce the risk of predation [...], exchange information about food location [...], and defend food sources and mates against competing groups" (19). Over time, Gintis concludes, humans and their hominid ancestors achieved socio-political cooperation through "reverse dominance hierarchy" and "cooperative child rearing and hunting."

On the one hand, reverse dominance hierarchy was achieved by neutralizing the hegemonic power of the alpha male and replacing it with "a lasting egalitarian order" (43). Leaders, Gintis argues, "were kept weak, and their reproductive success depended on an ability to persuade and motivate, coupled with the rank-and-file ability to reach a consensus with such leadership" (43). On the other hand, cooperative childrearing and hunting was characterized by pro-sociality and norms of fairness (43), but the spread of the human species worldwide, which corresponds to our Holocene epoch, put an end to it:

> This system persisted until cultural changes in the later Holocene fostered material wealth accumulation, through which it became once again possible to sustain a social dominance hierarchy based on coercion.
>
> *Individuality and Entanglement* 43

Through these two distinct models of socio-political cooperation, Gintis presents the paradox of our modern societies: we are inclined to cooperate and form strong communities that will limit hierarchy and create institutions serving the needs of the collectivity, thereby maintaining a reasonable level of equality and justice among citizens; but we also establish hierarchy by encouraging selfishness, especially through the accumulation of wealth, and therefore domination. The ultimate purpose of our communities is to either defend themselves from other communities or to dominate them. It is against this propensity to endless violence that Nancy advocates the creation of the world *ex nihilo*, and Glissant the advent of a world in Relation.

The lessons of anthropology constitute a rebuttal of neither Nancy's nor Glissant's theories. Rather, they confirm that these thinkers have accurately assessed the perilous course the world is pursuing. Nancy's description of the world as a *glomus*—a portmanteau word designating a global *mundus*: i.e. an amalgam of heterogeneous worlds at the mercy of capitalism and ecotechnology—must be read as both a warning and an opportunity to start afresh as if, paradoxically, the homogenizing forces of globalization had uncovered a forgotten ontological reality: namely, that we are singularities thrown into the world and that we exist only in our mutual exposure.

In a way, the loss of the coherence of our world has hurled us back to primitive times and created favorable conditions for what Nancy calls world-forming, a world in which altruism would take precedence over the urge to dominate and subjugate. Glissant, through his concept of Relation, takes this transformation for granted. The world, as a result of *mondialité* (globalization absent savage capitalism), is already engaged in a process of creolization. Following in the steps of Claude Lévi-Strauss, Glissant dismisses the notion of racial superiority and the linear understanding of progress whereby some cultures are advanced whereas others are stuck in infancy. As Lévi-Strauss demonstrates in *Race and History* (1952), European cultures owe their hegemony to the serendipitous confluence of old and contemporary cultures at the time of the Renaissance, which generated exchanges, accumulation of knowledge, and progress. Cultures become cumulative, as opposed to stationary, as a result of collaboration, and Glissant's Relation is nothing other than the systematization of such collaboration on a global scale.

Glissant is adamant, however, that Relation is not homogenization—a position that echoes, once again, that of Lévi-Strauss: "a world civilization could, in fact, represent no more than a world-wide coalition of cultures, each of which would preserve its own originality."[13] In this perspective, Glissant's proposal to turn his native Martinique into a pioneering ecological nation of the twenty-first century is not so extravagant: the idea is to transform Martinique into a cumulative nation rid of its dependence on a faraway *mère patrie* not necessarily supportive of initiatives outside its authority. And while Glissant never made a secret of his nationalist feelings for Martinique, his promotion of it should not be viewed as a contradiction but, rather, as a way of privileging diversity over uniformity.

Beyond the case of Martinique, the point of Relation is to foster working together while preserving particularities—a challenge Lévi-Strauss had already presented in *Race and History*:

---

13   Claude Lévi-Strauss, *Race and History* (Paris: UNESCO, 1952): 45.

> if men are to progress, they must collaborate; and, in the course of their collaboration, the differences in their contributions will gradually be evened out, although collaboration was originally necessary and advantageous simply because of those differences.[14]

In other words, the homogenization that results from collaboration must, at some point, be controlled and curtailed. Cultures must exchange with one another, but at the same time they must protect their specificity from the process of harmonization and standardization that intercultural collaboration generates.

Lévi-Strauss's theory that cross-cultural cooperation must be limited in scope in order to slow down an inexorable process of assimilation becomes controversial once it falls into the hands of opponents of multiculturalism who square Lévi-Strauss's theory to their own anti-immigration agenda. They claim that, in the name of cultural diversity, migrants should stay home lest they undergo a process of westernization that will erase their cultural values and beliefs once they move to Europe or America. This deceptive rhetoric allows them to conceal their hatred of ethnic plurality behind a discourse of rationality and respect for others. Glissant's Relation, which simultaneously promotes respect for the specificity of each culture and reciprocal influence among cultures, may be interpreted as an antidote to such a xenophobic ideology.

The aim of Relation is to create a worldwide mosaic of cultures reminiscent of Nancy's concept of Being-singular-plural, as it implies that a culture can exist only if it coexists (and collaborates) with other cultures. Nancy's premise that there is no being without "being-with," or that there is no meaning if meaning is not shared, may be read as a repudiation of the *homo œconomicus* (as an individual driven solely by the pursuit of self-interest) and a celebration of the *homo reciprocans* (as an individual driven by the desire to cooperate with others and contribute to the well-being of all).

My claim in the Introduction that we are "all in the same boat" referred to the fact that all parties involved in the slave trade—slave-ship captains, financial backers, insurers, ship builders, subcontractors, African traders, sailors, and even captives—are cogs in a vast machinery of interdependent commercial transactions, a tentacular network of interests that seems to elude human agency. The theories of Glissant, and even more so those of Nancy, confirm that we are "all in the same boat," but they also imply that it is our responsibility to take back the helm and steer the boat in the direction we wish our world to go.

---

14   Lévi-Strauss, *Race and History*, 48.

Works Cited

Adams, Russell L. "An Analysis of the 'Roots' Phenomenon in the Context of American Racial Conservatism," *Présence Africaine* 116.4 (1980): 125–140.

Agamben, Giorgio. *The Coming Community*, tr. Michael Hardt (*La comunità che viene*, 1990; Minneapolis: U of Minnesota P, 1993).

Agamben, Giorgio. *Homo Sacer: Sovereign Power and Bare Life*, tr. Daniel Heller-Roazen (*Homo sacer: Il potere sovrano e la nuda vita*, 1995; Stanford CA: Stanford UP, 1998).

Alexander, Elizabeth. "Amistad," in *American Sublime: Poems* (Minneapolis MN: Graywolf, 2005): 61–73.

Alexander, Michelle. *The New Jim Crow: Mass Incarceration in the Age of Colorblindness* (New York: The New Press, 2010).

Anderson, Benedict. *Imagined Communities: Reflections on the Origin and Spread of Nationalism* (1991; London: Verso, 2006).

Aristotle. *Politics*, tr. Benjamin Jowett (1905; Mineola NY: Dover, 2000).

Arnold, James R., & Roberta Wiener, ed. *Cold War: The Essential Reference Guide* (Santa Barbara CA: ABC–CLIO, 2012).

Baker, Houston A., Jr. *Betrayal: How Black Intellectuals Have Abandoned the Ideals of the Civil Rights Era* (New York: Columbia UP, 2010).

Baker, Houston A., Jr. "Failed Prophet and Falling Stock: Why Ralph Ellison Was Never Avant-Garde," *Stanford Humanities Review* 7.1 (Summer 1999): 4–10.

Bakhtin, Mikhail M. *Rabelais and His World*, tr. Hélène Iswolsky (Bloomington: Indiana UP, 1984).

Baldwin, James. "Autobiographical Notes" (*Notes of a Native Son*, 1955), in James Baldwin, *Collected Essays*, ed. Toni Morrison (New York: Library of America, 1998): 5–9.

Balon, Robert E. "The Impact of 'Roots' on a Racially Heterogeneous Southern Community: An Exploratory Study," *Journal of Broadcasting* 22.3 (May 1978): 299–307.

Baucom, Ian. *Specters of the Atlantic: Finance Capital, Slavery and the Philosophy of History* (Durham NC: Duke UP, 2005).

Beckert, Sven. *Empire of Cotton: A Global History* (New York: Alfred A. Knopf, 2015).

Behn, Aphra. *Oroonoko; or, The Royal Slave*, ed. Catherine Gallagher & Simon Stern (1688; Boston MA: Bedford/St. Martin's Classics, 2000).

Bernabé, Jean, Patrick Chamoiseau & Raphaël Confiant. *Éloge de la Créolité / In Praise of Creoleness*, tr. M.B. Taeb-Khyar (1989; Paris: Gallimard, 1993).

Berry, John, dir. *Tamango* (CEI Incom, Da.Ma. Cinematografica, Les Films du Cyclope, France / Italy 1958; 104 min.).

Bird, Greg. *Containing Community: From Political Economy to Ontology in Agamben, Esposito, and Nancy* (Albany: State U of New York P, 2016).

Black, Daniel. *The Coming: A Novel* (New York: St. Martin's, 2015).

Blackburn, Robin. *The American Crucible: Slavery, Emancipation and Human Rights* (London: Verso, 2013).

Blau, Eleanor. "Charles Johnson's Tale of Slaving, Seafaring and Philosophizing," *New York Times* (2 January 1991): C9+.

Bloch, Ernst. *The Principle of Hope*, vol. 2: *Outlines of a Better World*, tr. Neville Plaice, Stephen Plaice & Paul Knight (*Das Prinzip Hoffnung*, 1959; Cambridge MA: MIT Press, 1995).

Bogle, Donald. *Toms, Coons, Mulattoes, Mammies, and Bucks: An Interpretive History of Blacks in American Films* (New York: Continuum, 2001).

Bongie, Chris. *Islands and Exiles: The Creole Identities of Post/Colonial Literature* (Stanford CA: Stanford UP, 1998).

Bongie, Chris. *Friends and Enemies: The Scribal Politics of Post/colonial Literature* (Liverpool: Liverpool UP, 2008).

Bonilla-Silva, Eduardo. *Racism without Racists: Color-Blind Racism and the Persistence of Racial Inequality in the United States* (Lanham MD: Rowman & Littlefield, 2nd ed. 2006).

Bonniol, Jean-Luc. "Au prisme de la créolisation: Tentative d'épuisement d'un concept," *L'Homme* 207–208 (2013): 237–288.

Borde, Raymond. "*Tamango*," *Les Temps Modernes* 146 (April 1958): 1904–1905.

Bourgeon, François. *Les passagers du vent* (1980–84; Tournais & Paris: Casterman, 1994).

Bourriaud, Nicolas. *The Radicant*, tr. James Gussen & Lili Porten (*Radicant: pour une esthétique de la globalisation*, 2009; Berlin & New York: Lukas Sternberg, 2009).

Britton, Celia. "In Memory of Édouard Glissant," *Callaloo* 34.3 (Summer 2011): 667–670.

Brown, Wendy. *Edgework: Critical Essays on Knowledge and Politics* (Princeton NJ: Princeton UP, 2005).

Buckley Dyer, Justin. *Natural Law and the Antislavery Constitutional Tradition* (Cambridge: Cambridge UP, 2012).

Burns, Lorna. "Becoming-postcolonial, Becoming-Caribbean: Édouard Glissant and the poetics of creolization," *Textual Practice* 23.1 (February 2009): 99–117.

Cailler, Bernadette. "Totality and Infinity, Alterity, and Relation: From Levinas to Glissant," *Journal of French and Francophone Philosophy / Revue de la philosophie française et de langue française* 19.1 (2011): 135–151.

Camus, Albert. *The Rebel: An Essay on Man in Revolt*, tr. Anthony Bower, foreword by Herbert Read (L'homme révolté, 1951; tr. 1956; New York: Vintage, rev. ed. 1992).

Chapon Rodriguez, Cécile. "Entre utopie et chaos: la pensée du Tout-Monde comme alternative à la mondialisation chez Édouard Glissant," *Notes de la communication du mardi 15 décembre 2015: Séminaire Les Armes de la Critique,* Université Paris-Sorbonne (24 May 2017): online (accessed 11 November 2017).

Chomsky, Marvin J., & John Erman, dir. *Roots* (Warner Bros., USA 1977; 570 min.).

Christopher, Emma. *Slave Ship Sailors and Their Captive Cargoes, 1730–1807* (Cambridge: Cambridge UP, 2006).

Claudel, Paul. *Art poétique* (1907; Paris: Mercure de France, 1913). Tr. by Renee Spodheim as *Poetic Art* (tr. 1948; Port Washington WA: Kennikat, 1969).

Cliff, Michelle. *Abeng* (1984; New York: Plume, 1995).

CNN. "Migrants being sold as slaves," *CNN: International Edition* (14 November 2017): online (accessed 1 January 2018).

Collins, Holly. "*La querelle de la Créolisation*: Creolization vs. *Créolité* in Glissant, Condé and the Creolists," *Nottingham French Studies* 56.1 (March 2017): 67–81.

Colucci, Lamont C. *The National Security Doctrines of the American Presidency: How They Shape Our Present and Future* (Santa Barbara CA: Praeger, 2012).

Conner, Marc C., & William R. Nash, ed. *Charles Johnson: The Novelist as Philosopher* (Jackson: UP of Mississippi, 2007).

Corio, Alessandro. "The Living and the Poetic Intention: Glissant's Biopolitics of Literature," *Callaloo* 36.4 (Fall 2013): 916–931.

Cotton, John. *The Correspondence of John Cotton*, ed. Sargent Bush, Jr. (Chapel Hill: U of North Carolina P, 2001).

Courlander, Harold. *The African* (New York: Crown, 1967).

Critchley, Simon. "With Being-With? Notes on Jean-Luc Nancy's Rewriting of *Being and Time*," *Studies in Practical Philosophy* 1.1 (1999): 53–67.

Cropper, Corry. "Prosper Mérimée and the Subversive 'Historical' Short Story," *Nineteenth Century French Studies* 33.1–2 (Fall 2004–Winter 2005): 57–74.

Crosta, Suzanne. "Des poétiques de relation et de globalisation dans la Caraïbe francophone," *Thamyris* 8 (2001): 29–41.

Crouch, Stanley. "The 'Roots' of Huckster Haley's Great Fraud," *Jewish World Review* (18 January 2002): 57–62.

Cugoano, Quobna Ottobah. *Thoughts and Sentiments on the Evil of Slavery and Other Writings*, ed. & intro. Vincent Carretta (1787; London: Penguin Classics, 2007).

Curtin, Philip D. *The Atlantic Slave Trade: A Census* (Madison: U of Wisconsin P, 1969).

D'Aguiar, Fred. *Feeding the Ghosts* (Hopewell NJ: Ecco, 1997).

Dabydeen, David. *Turner: New and Selected Poems* (1994; Leeds: Peepal Tree, 2002).

Delany, Martin R. *Blake: or, The Huts of America* (1861–62; Boston MA: Beacon, 2000).

Delbanco, Andrew. *Melville: His World and Work* (New York: Alfred A. Knopf, 2005).

Deleuze, Gilles. "Literature and Life," in Deleuze, *Essays Critical and Clinical*, tr. Daniel W. Smith & Michael A. Greco (*Critique et clinique*, 1993; Minneapolis: U of Minnesota P, 1997): 1–6. Originally published in *Critical Inquiry* 23.2 (Winter 1997): 225–230.

Deleuze, Gilles, & Félix Guattari. *A Thousand Plateaus: Capitalism and Schizophrenia*, tr. Brian Massumi (*Capitalisme et schizophrénie 2: Mille plateaux*, 1980; Minneapolis: U of Minnesota P, 1987).

Derathé, Robert. *Jean-Jacques Rousseau et la science politique de son temps* (Paris: Librairie Philosophique Vrin, 2000).

Derrida, Jacques. *Of Hospitality: Anne Dufourmantelle Invites Jacques Derrida to Respond*, tr. Rachel Bowlby (Stanford CA: Stanford UP, 2000).

Devisch, Ignaas. "The Sense of Being(-)With Jean-Luc Nancy," *Culture Machine* 8 (2006): online (accessed 26 October 2016).

Devisch, Ignaas. "A Trembling Voice in the Desert: Jean-Luc Nancy's Rethinking of the Space of the Political," *Cultural Values* 4.2 (2000): 239–255.

Devisch, Ignaas. *Jean-Luc Nancy and the Question of Community* (London: Bloomsbury, 2013).

Di Giovanni, Julian, et al. "Globalization: A Brief Overview," *International Monetary Fund: Issues Brief* (May 2008): online (accessed 28 December 2016).

Diouf, Sylviane A. *Slavery's Exiles: The Story of the American Maroons* (New York & London: New York UP, 2014).

Doniol-Valcroze, Jacques. "Le Masque et la Plume," *RTF* radio, Michel Polac, host (6 February 1958).

Dorismond, Edelyn. "Créolisation de la politique, politique de la créolisation: Penser un 'im-pensé' dans l'œuvre d'Édouard Glissant," *Cahiers Sens Public* 3.11–12 (2009): 137–146.

Dorismond, Edelyn. "Comment Deleuze et Derrida voyagent dans la pensée glissantienne de la créolisation," *Rue Descartes* 78.2 (2013): 34–47.

Dorman, John L. "Barry Unsworth, Writer of Historical Fiction, Dies at 81," *New York Times* (8 June 2012): A25.

Douglass, Frederick. *The Heroic Slave*, ed. John R. McKivigan, Robert S. Levine & John Stauffer (1853; New Haven CT: Yale UP, 2015).

Du Bois, William Edward Burghardt. *The Souls of Black Folk* (1903), in *Writings: The Suppression of the African Slave-Trade / The Souls of Black Folk / Dusk of Dawn / Essays and Articles*, ed. Nathan Huggins (New York: Library of America, 1987): 357–548.

Du Bois, William Edward Burghardt. "Marxism and the Negro Problem" (1933), in *African American Political Thought, 1890–1930: Washington, Du Bois, Garvey and Randolph*, ed. Cary D. Wintz (New York: Routledge, 2015): 146–151.

Dunbar, Paul Laurence. "We Wear the Mask" (1896), in *The Collected Poetry of Paul Laurence Dunbar*, ed. & intro. Joanne M. Braxton (Charlottesville: UP of Virginia, 1993): 71.

Ellison, Ralph. *Invisible Man* (1952; New York: Modern Library, 1994).

Ellison, Ralph. "Perspective of Literature" (1976), in *The Collected Essays of Ralph Ellison: Revised and Updated*, ed. John F. Callahan (New York: Random House, 2003): 770–786.

Ellison, Ralph. "What America Would Be Like Without Blacks" (1970), in *The Collected Essays of Ralph Ellison: Revised and Updated*, ed. John F. Callahan (New York: Random House, 2003): 581–588.

Eltis, David, Stephen D. Behrendt, David Richardson & Herbert S. Klein. *The Trans-Atlantic Slave Trade: A Database on CD-ROM* (Cambridge & New York: Cambridge UP, 1999).

Emanuel, James A. "The Middle Passage Blues" (1989), in *Black Imagination and the Middle Passage*, ed. Maria Diedrich, Henry Louis Gates, Jr., & Carl Pedersen (New York: Oxford UP, 1999): 3–4.

"Embargo Act of 1807" (nd), *West's Encyclopedia of American Law*, edition 2 (2008): online (accessed 2 July 2014).

Emerson, Ralph Waldo. "Self-Reliance" (*Essays, First Series*, 1841), in Emerson, *Essays and Lectures*, ed. Joel Porte (New York: Library of America, 1983): 259–282.

Equiano, Olaudah. *The Interesting Narrative of the Life of Olaudah Equiano, or Gustavus Vassa, The African, Written by Himself*, ed. Werner Sollors (1789; Norton Critical Editions; New York: W.W. Norton, 2001).

Esposito, Roberto. *Bíos: Biopolitics and Philosophy*, tr. & intro. Timothy Campbell (*Bíos: biopolitica e filosofia*, 2004; Minneapolis & London: U of Minnesota P, 2008).

Esposito, Roberto. *Communitas: The Origin and Destiny of Community*, tr. Timothy Campbell (*Communitas: origine e destino della comunità*, 1998; Stanford CA: Stanford UP, 2009).

Eze, Emmanuel Chukwudi. *Race and the Enlightenment: A Reader* (1997; Oxford & Malden MA: Blackwell, 2005).

Farley, Reynolds. "Trends in Racial Inequalities: Have the Gains of the 1960s Disappeared in the 1970s?" *American Sociological Review* 42.2 (April 1977): 189–208.

Faulkner, William. *Sartoris* (1929; New York: Random House, 1956).

Fishbein, Leslie. "*Roots*: Docudrama and the Interpretation of History," in *American History, American Television: Interpreting the Video Past*, ed. John E. O'Connor (New York: Frederick Ungar, 1983): 279–305.

Forter, Greg. "Barry Unsworth and the Art of Power: Historical Memory, Utopian Fictions," *Contemporary Literature* 51.4 (Winter 2010): 777–809.

Forter, Greg. "Barry Unsworth's Utopian Imaginings," *Raritan* 32.1 (Summer 2012): 140–157.

Foucault, Michel. "Different Spaces" ("Des Espaces Autres," 1967), tr. Robert Hurley, in *Essential Works of Foucault, 1954–1984*, vol. 2: *Aesthetics, Method, and Epistemology*, ed. James D. Faubion (New York: The New Press, 1998): 175–185.

Foucault, Michel. "Of Other Spaces" ("Des Espaces Autres," 1967), tr. Jay Miskowiec, *Diacritics* 16.1 (1986): 22–27.

Foucault, Michel. *'Society Must Be Defended': Lectures at the Collège de France 1975–1976* tr. David Macey (New York: Picador, 2003).

Fukuyama, Francis. "The End of History?" *The National Interest* 16 (1989): 3–18.

Fukuyama, Francis. *The End of History and the Last Man* (New York: Avon, 1992).

Gallagher, Mary. *World Writing: Poetics, Ethics, Globalization* (Toronto: U of Toronto P, 2008).

Genette, Gérard. *Narrative Discourse: An Essay in Method*, tr. Jane E. Lewin, foreword by Jonathan Culler ("Discours du récit," in *Figures III*, 1972; Ithaca NY: Cornell UP, 1980).

Gerber, David A. "Haley's *Roots* and Our Own: An Inquiry into the Nature of a Popular Phenomenon," *Journal of Ethnic Studies* 5.3 (Fall 1977): 87–111.

Gilroy, Paul. *The Black Atlantic: Modernity and Double Consciousness* (Cambridge MA: Harvard UP, 1993).

Gintis, Herbert. *Individuality and Entanglement: The Moral and Material Bases of Social Life* (Princeton NJ: Princeton UP, 2016).

Girard, René. *Violence and the Sacred*, tr. Patrick Gregory (*La violence et le sacré*, 1972; Baltimore MD: Johns Hopkins UP, 1979).

Gleason, William. "'Go There': The Critical Pragmatism of Charles Johnson," in *Charles Johnson: The Novelist as Philosopher*, ed. Marc C. Conner & William R. Nash (Jackson: UP of Mississippi, 2007): 82–105.

Gleaves, Whitney, ed. *American Presidents: Farewell Messages to the Nation, 1796–2001* (Lanham MD: Lexington, 2003).

Glissant, Édouard. *Caribbean Discourse: Selected Essays*, sel., tr. & intro. J. Michael Dash (*Le discours antillais*, 1981; Charlottesville: UP of Virginia, 1989).

Glissant, Édouard. *La Cohée du Lamentin* (*Poétique V;* Paris: Gallimard, 2005).

Glissant, Édouard. "Creolization in the Making of the Americas," *Caribbean Quarterly* 54.1–2 (2008a): 81–89.

Glissant, Édouard. "Tous les jours de mai, ... Pour l'abolition de tous les esclavages," *Institut du Tout-Monde* (2008b): online (accessed 8 November 2016).

Glissant, Édouard. "The Deferred—The Word" (1986a), in Glissant, *Faulkner, Mississippi*, tr. Barbara Lewis & Thomas C. Spear (Chicago: U of Chicago P, 2000): 193–223.

Glissant, Édouard. "Le différé, la parole," in Glissant, *Faulkner, Mississippi* (1986b; Paris: Gallimard, 1998): 263–293.

Glissant, Édouard. *Introduction à une Poétique du Divers* (Paris: Gallimard, 1996).

Glissant, Édouard. "The Open Boat" ("La barque ouverte"), in *Poetics of Relation*, tr. Betsy Wing (Ann Arbor: U of Michigan P, 1997a): 5–9.

Glissant, Édouard. *Poetics of Relation*, tr. Betsy Wing (Ann Arbor: U of Michigan P, 1997b).

Glissant, Édouard. *Philosophie de la Relation: Poésie en étendue* (Paris: Gallimard, 2009).

Glissant, Édouard. *Poétique de la Relation* [*Poétique III*; Paris: Gallimard, 1990).

Glissant, Édouard. *Le quatrième siècle* (Paris: Seuil, 1964).

Glissant, Édouard. *Sartorius: le roman des Batoutos* (Paris: Gallimard, 1999).

Glissant, Édouard. *10 mai, mémoires de la traite négrière, de l'esclavage et de leurs abolitions* (Paris: Galaade éditions, 2010).

Glissant, Édouard. "10 mai: Mémoires de la traite négrière, de l'esclavage et de leurs abolitions" (Excerpt), *Les Mémoires des Esclavages et de Leurs Abolitions* (2013): online (accessed 9 November 2017).

Glissant, Édouard. *Traité du tout-monde* [*Poétique IV*; Paris: Gallimard, 1997).

Glissant, Édouard, & Patrick Chamoiseau. *Quand les murs tombent: L'identité nationale hors la loi?* (Paris: Galaade éditions, 2007).

Glissant, Édouard, & Patrick Chamoiseau. "The Unforeseeable Diversity of the World," in *Beyond Dichotomies: Histories, Identities, Cultures, and the Challenge of Globalization*, ed. Elisabeth Mudimbe-Boyi, tr. Haun Saussy (Albany: State U of New York P, 2002): 287–296.

Goodman, Amy. "The Undiscovered Malcolm X: Stunning New Info on the Assassination, His Plans to Unite the Civil Rights and Black Nationalist Movements & the 3 'Missing' Chapters from His Autobiography," *Democracy Now: Independent Global News* (21 February 2005): online (accessed 14 January 2017).

Grandin, Greg. *The Empire of Necessity: Slavery, Freedom, and Deception in the New World* (New York: Metropolitan, 2015).

Gratton, Peter, & Marie-Ève Morin, ed. *The Nancy Dictionary* (Edinburgh: Edinburgh UP, 2015).

Gronniosaw, James Albert Ukawsaw. *A Narrative of the Most Remarkable Particulars in the Life of James Albert Ukawsaw Gronniosaw, An African Prince, As Related By Himself* (1772; Gutenberg EBook, 14 February 2005).

Hainsworth, George. "West African Local Colour in *Tamango*," *French Studies* 21.1 (January 1967): 16–23.

Haley, Alex. *Roots: The Saga of an American Family* (1976; New York: Vanguard, 30th Anniversary Edition, 2007).

Haley, Alex. *Roots: The Saga of an American Family* (1976; New York: Dell, 1977).

Hallward, Peter. *Absolutely Postcolonial: Writing Between the Singular and the Specific* (Manchester: Manchester UP, 2001).

Hardack, Richard. "Black Skin, White Tissues: Local Color and Universal Solvents in the Novels of Charles Johnson," *Callaloo* 22.4 (Fall 1999): 1028–1053.

Hayden, Robert. "Middle Passage" (1962), in Hayden, *Collected Poems*, ed. Frederick Glaysher (New York: Liveright, 2013): 48–54.

Hayek, Friedrich. *Law, Legislation and Liberty*, vol. 3: *The Political Order of a Free People* (Chicago: U of Chicago P, 1981).

Hayes, Jarrod. *Queer Roots for the Diaspora: Ghosts in the Family Tree* (Ann Arbor: U of Michigan P, 2016).

Hegel, Georg Wilhelm Friedrich. *The Philosophy of History*. tr. J. Sibree (1837; Mineola NY: Dover Philosophical Classics, 2004).

Heidegger, Martin. *Being and Time*, tr. John Macquarrie & Edward Robinson (1927; Oxford: Blackwell, 2001).

Heynen, Hilde. "Engaging Modernism," in *Back from Utopia: The Challenge of the Modern Movement*, ed. Hilde Heynen & Hubert-Jan Henket (Rotterdam: 010 Publishers, 2002): 378–399.

Hijiya, James A. "*Roots*: Family and Ethnicity in the 1970s," *American Quarterly* 30.4 (Fall 1978): 548–556.

Hobbes, Thomas. *Leviathan*, ed. Edwin Curley (1651; Indianapolis IN: Hackett, 1994).

Hoffmann, Léon-François. "Victor Hugo, les noirs et l'esclavage," *Françofonia* 16/31 (1996): 47–90.

Howe, Russell Warren. "An Elusive Past," *The New Leader* (3 January 1977): 23–24.

Hutcheson, Francis. *An Essay On the Nature and Conduct of the Passions and Affections, with Illustrations on the Moral Sense*, ed. Aaron Garrett (1742; Indianapolis IN: Liberty Fund, 2002).

Hyatt, Vera Lawrence, & Rex Nettleford, ed. *Race and the Origin of the Americas: A New World View* (Washington DC: Smithsonian Institution Press, 1995).

International Organization for Migration (IOM). "IOM Learns of 'Slave Market' Conditions Endangering Migrants in North Africa," International Organization for Migration (IOM): The UN Migration Agency (4 November 2017): online (accessed 31 December 2017).

Jaucourt, Louis, chevalier de. "Slave trade," in *The Encyclopedia of Diderot & d'Alembert Collaborative Translation Project*, tr. Stephanie Noble (Ann Arbor: University of Michigan Library, 2007); tr. of "Traite des nègres," *Encyclopédie ou Dictionnaire raisonné des sciences, des arts et des métiers*, vol. 16 (Paris, 1765): online (accessed 21 March 2018).

Johnson, Charles. "Ralph Ellison: Novel Genius," *The New Crisis* (March–April 2002): 17–20.

Johnson, Charles. "The End of the Black American Narrative," in *Charles Johnson: Embracing the World*, ed. Nibir K. Ghosh & E. Ethelbert Miller (New Delhi: Authorpress, 2011): 59–72.

Johnson, Charles. *Middle Passage* (1990; New York: Scribner, 1998).

Kadish, Doris Y. "Mérimée's *Tamango*: Texts, Contexts, Intertexts," paper presented at the Nineteenth-Century French Studies Colloquium, University of Arizona (October 2003): online (accessed 20 July 2016).

Kadish, Doris Y. "The Black Terror: Women's Responses to Slave Revolts in Haiti," *French Review* 68.4 (March 1995): 668–680.

Kant, Immanuel. "An Idea for a Universal History with a Cosmopolitan Purpose," in *Kant's Political Writings*, ed. H.S. Reiss (Cambridge: Cambridge UP, 1970): 41–53.

Kaufmann, Michael W. *Institutional Individualism: Conversion, Exile, and Nostalgia in Puritan New England* (Middletown CT: Wesleyan UP, 1999).

Klein, Herbert S., Stanley L. Engerman, Robin Haines & Ralph Shlomowitz. "Transoceanic Mortality: The Slave Trade in Comparative Perspective," *William and Mary Quarterly* 58.1 (January 2001): 93–118.

Kleingeld, Pauline. "Kantian Patriotism," *Philosophy and Public Affairs* 29.4 (Autumn 2000): 313–341.

Knapp, Peggy A. "Barry Unsworth's *Sacred Hunger*: History and Utopia," *Clio* 38.3 (Summer 2009): 319–337.

Laborde, Cécile. "From Constitutional to Civic Patriotism," *British Journal of Political Science* 32.4 (October 2002): 591–612.

Lacoue-Labarthe, Philippe, & Jean-Luc Nancy. "The Retreat of the Political," in *Retreating the Political*, ed. Simon Sparks (Warwick Studies in European Philosophy; London: Routledge, 1997): 117–128.

Lautréamont, Comte de [Isidore Ducasse]. *Les Chants de Maldoror*, tr. Guy Wernham (1868; tr. 1943; New York: New Directions, 1965).

Lautréamont, Comte de [Isidore Ducasse]. *Maldoror and Poems*, tr. & intro. Paul Wright (1868; tr. 1978; London: Penguin Classics, 1988).

Lévi-Strauss, Claude. *Race and History* (Paris: UNESCO, 1952).

Leavy, Walter. "The Mystery and Real-Life Tragedy of Dorothy Dandridge," *Ebony* 49.2 (December 1993): 36–41.

Lingis, Alphonso. *The Community of Those Who Have Nothing in Common* (Bloomington: Indiana UP, 1994).

Little, Jonathan. *Charles Johnson's Spiritual Imagination* (Columbia: U of Missouri P, 1997).

Little, Jonathan. "An Interview with Charles Johnson (1993)," in *Passing the Three Gates: Interviews with Charles Johnson*, ed. Jim McWilliams (Seattle: U of Washington P, 2005): 97–122.

Lobis, Seth. "'Self-Reliance'—The Prehistory of Emerson's Famous Word," *In Character: A Journal of Everyday Virtues* (1 January 2007): online (accessed 30 July 2014).

Lock, Helen. "The Paradox of Slave Mutiny in Herman Melville, Charles Johnson, and Frederick Douglass," *College Literature* 30.4 (Fall 2003): 54–70.

Locke, John. *An Essay Concerning Human Understanding*, ed. Peter H. Nidditch (1689a; Oxford: Oxford UP, 1979).

Locke, John. *Two Treatises of Government*, ed. Peter Laslett (1689b; Cambridge: Cambridge UP, 1988).

Lowe, Lisa. *The Intimacies of Four Continents* (Durham NC: Duke UP, 2015).

Lucas, Paul R. "Colony or Commonwealth: Massachusetts Bay, 1661–1666," *William and Mary Quarterly* 24.1 (January 1967): 88–107.

Mackin, Glenn David. *The Politics of Social Welfare in America* (New York: Cambridge UP, 2013).

Macpherson, C.B. *The Political Theory of Possessive Individualism: Hobbes to Locke* (1962; Oxford: Oxford UP, 2011).

Mandeville, Bernard. *The Fable of the Bees: Or Private Vices, Publick Benefits*, intro. Philip Harth (1723; London: Penguin Classics, 1989).

Marable, Manning. *Malcolm X: A Life of Reinvention* (New York: Viking, 2011).

Marx, Karl. *The Eighteenth Brumaire of Louis* Bonaparte, tr. Daniel de Leon (*Der 18te Brumaire des Louis Napoleon, 1852;* Chicago: Charles H. Kerr, 1907).

Marx, Karl. *The Poverty of Philosophy: A Reply to M. Proudhon's Philosophy of Poverty*, tr. Institute of Marxism-Leninism (*Misère de la philosophie: Réponse à la philosophie de la misère de M. Proudhon,* 1847; Moscow: Progress, 1955).

Matthews, Daniel. "A Spirit of the Common: Reimagining 'The Common Law' with Jean-Luc Nancy," in *Space, Power and the Commons: The Struggle for Alternative Futures,* ed. Samuel Kirwan, Leila Dawney & Julian Brigstocke (New York: Routledge, 2016): 75–90.

Mbom, Clément. "Édouard Glissant: De l'opacité à la Relation," in *Poétiques d'Edouard Glissant: Actes du colloque international, Paris-Sorbonne, 11–13 mars 1998* (Paris: Presses de l'Université de Paris-Sorbonne, 1999): 245–254.

McFadden, Robert D. "Alex Haley Denies Allegations That Parts of 'Roots' Were Copied From Novel Written By Mississippi Teacher," *New York Times* (24 April 1977): 4.

Médina, José. "Toward a Foucaultian Epistemology of Resistance: Counter-Memory, Epistemic Friction, and Guerilla Pluralism, " *Foucault Studies* 12 (October 2011): 9–35.

Mérimée, Prosper. "Tamango" (1829a), in Mérimée, *Carmen and Other Stories*, tr. Nicholas Jotcham (Oxford: Oxford UP, 2008): 72–92.

Mérimée, Prosper. "Tamango" (1829b), in Mérimée, *Romans et nouvelles* (Paris: Garnier, 1967).

Miano, Léonora. *La saison de l'ombre: roman* (Paris: Bernard Grasset, 2013).

Mill, John Stuart. *On Liberty, Utilitarianism and Other Essays*, ed. Mark Philp & Frederick Rosen (Oxford: Oxford UP, 2015).

Miller, Christopher L. *The French Atlantic Triangle: Literature and Culture of the Slave Trade* (Durham NC: Duke UP, 2012).

Miller, Ethelbert, & Charles Johnson. "All You Need to Know About the Allmuseri," *The E-Channel* (17 April 2011): online (accessed 24 July 2014).

Mills, Gary B., & Elizabeth Shown Mills. "*Roots* and the New 'Faction': A Legitimate Tool for Clio?" *Virginia Magazine of History and Biography* 89.1 (January 1981): 3–26.

Monaghan, Peter. "Winner of National Book Award Won't Be a 'Voice of Black America' (1991)," in *Passing the Three Gates: Interviews with Charles Johnson*, ed. Jim McWilliams (Seattle: U of Washington P, 2005): 48–52.

Montesquieu, Charles de Secondat, Baron De. "De l'esclavage des nègres," in Montesquieu, *De l'esprit des lois* (1748a; Paris: Garnier, 1956), Book xv, Ch. 5.

Montesquieu, Charles de Secondat, Baron De. *The Spirit of the Laws*, ed. Anne M. Cohler, Basia Carolyn Miller & Harold Samuel Stone (1748b; Cambridge: Cambridge UP, 1989).

Morel, Lucas E. ed. *Ralph Ellison and the Raft of Hope: A Political Companion to Invisible Man* (Lexington: UP of Kentucky, 2004a).

Morel, Lucas E. "Ralph Ellison's American Democratic Individualism," in *Ralph Ellison and the Raft of Hope: A Political Companion to* Invisible Man, ed. Lucas E. Morel (Lexington: UP of Kentucky, 2004b): 58–90.

Morin, Marie-Ève. "Putting Community Under Erasure: Derrida and Nancy on the Plurality of Singularities," *Culture Machine* 8 (2006): online (accessed 26 October 2016).

Nancy, Jean-Luc. *Being Singular Plural*, tr. Robert D. Richardson & Anne E. O'Byrne (*Être singulier pluriel*, 1996; Stanford CA: Stanford UP, 2000).

Nancy, Jean-Luc. "La Comparution/The Compearance: From the Existence of 'Communism' to the Community of 'Existence'" ("La comparution: politique à venir," with Jean-Christophe Bailly, 1991a), tr. Tracy B. Strong, *Political Theory* 20.3 (August 1992): 371–398.

Nancy, Jean-Luc. "Of Being-in-Common," in Nancy, *Community at Loose Ends*, ed. Miami Theory Collective (Minneapolis: U of Minnesota P, 1991b): 1–12.

Nancy, Jean-Luc. "Conloquium" (1999), tr. Janell Watson, *Minnesota Review* 75 (2010): 101–108.

Nancy, Jean-Luc. "*Cosmos Basileus*," in Nancy, *The Creation of the World, or Globalization*, tr. Raffoul & Pettigrew, 109–112.

Nancy, Jean-Luc. *The Creation of the World, or Globalization*, tr. & intro. François Raffoul & David Pettigrew (*La Création du monde ou la mondialisation*, 2002; Albany: State U of New York P, 2007).

Nancy, Jean-Luc. "*Ex Nihilo Summum* (Of Sovereignty)," in Nancy, *The Creation of the World, or Globalization*, tr. Raffoul & Pettigrew, 96–107.

Nancy, Jean-Luc. *The Experience of Freedom*, tr. Bridget McDonald, foreword by Peter Fenves (*L'Expérience de la liberté*, 1988; Stanford CA: Stanford UP, 1993).

Nancy, Jean-Luc. *The Inoperative Community*, ed. Peter Connor, tr. Peter Connor et al., foreword by Christopher Fynsk (*La Communauté désoeuvrée*, 1983, rev. 1986; Minneapolis: U of Minnesota P, 1991).

Nancy, Jean-Luc. *Listening*, tr. Charlotte Mandell (*A l'écoute*, 2002; New York: Fordham UP, 2007).

Nancy, Jean-Luc. *The Sense of the World*, tr. & intro. Jeffrey S. Librett (*Le sens du monde*, 1993; Minneapolis: U of Minnesota P, 1997).

Nancy, Jean-Luc, & Aurélien Barrau. *What's These Worlds Coming To?* ed. Stefanos Geroulanos & Todd Meyers, tr. Travis Holloway & Flor Mechain. foreword by David Pettigrew (*Dans quels mondes vivons-nous?*, 2011; New York: Fordham UP, 2015).

Nash, William R. *Charles Johnson's Fiction* (Urbana–Champaign: U of Illinois P, 2002).

Neyrat, Frédéric. *Le communisme existentiel de Jean-Luc Nancy* (Paris: Éditions Lignes, 2013).

Nobile, Philip. "Alex Haley's Hoax: How the Celebrated Author Faked the Pulitzer Prize-Winning 'Roots'," *Village Voice* (February 1993a): 1.

Nobile, Philip. "Was *Roots* One of the Great Literary Hoaxes?" *Toronto Star* (8 March 1993b): A13.

Norrell, Robert J. *Alex Haley and the Books That Changed a Nation* (New York: St. Martin's, 2015).

Noudlemann, François. "Édouard Glissant's Legacy: Transmitting Without Universals," tr. Celia Britton, *Callaloo* 36.4 (Fall 2011): 869–874.

Obrist, Hans Ulrich, & Édouard Glissant. *Édouard Glissant & Hans Ulrich Obrist: 100 Notes – 100 Thoughts / 100 Notizen - 100 Gedanken* (DOCUMENTA (13): №038 Series; Ostfildern: Hatje Cantz, 2012).

OECD. "Reaping the Benefits of Globalisation: The Importance of Public Policies," *Remarks by Angel Gurría, Secretary General of the OECD, Foreign Relations Commission, Chamber of Deputies, Rome* (22 February 2007): online (accessed 2 January 2018).

Omi, Michael, & Howard Winant. *Racial Formation in the United States from the 1960s to the 1990s* (New York: Routledge, 2nd ed. 1994).

Ottaway, Mark. "Tangled Roots," *Sunday Times* (10 April 1977): 17, 21.

Page, Clarence. "Alex Haley's Facts Can Be Doubted, But Not His Truths," *Chicago Tribune* (10 March 1993): online (accessed 12 February 2017).

Paine, Thomas. "Common Sense" in *Paine: Political Writings*, ed. Bruce Kuklick (1776; Cambridge Texts in the History of Political Thought; Cambridge: Cambridge UP, 2nd ed. 2000): 1–47.

Parent, Yvette, "L'esclavage et *Bug-Jargal*: Victor Hugo entre histoire et mémoire dans la version de 1826," *Groupe Hugo* (Université Paris 7; 16 June 2007): online (accessed 11 November 2017).

Park, Mungo. *Travels in the Interior Districts of Africa*, 2 vols. (1795–97; Teddington: Echo Library, 2006).

Parry, Tyler D. "The Politics of Plagiarism: *Roots*, Margaret Walker, and Alex Haley," in *Reconsidering "Roots": Race, Politics, and Memory*, foreword by Henry Louis Gates, Jr. (Athens: U of Georgia P, 2017): 47–62.

Philip, M. NourbeSe. *Zong!* (Middletown CT: Wesleyan UP, 2008).

Phillips, Caryl. *The Atlantic Sound* (London: Vintage, 2001).

Piersen, William D. *Black Legacy: America's Hidden Heritage* (Amherst: U of Massachusetts P, 1993).

Posnock, Ross. *Color and Culture: Black Writers and the Making of the Modern Intellectual* (Cambridge MA: Harvard UP, 1998).

Price, Richard, ed. *Maroon Societies: Rebel Slave Communities in the Americas* (1979; Baltimore MD: Johns Hopkins UP, 1996).

Prabhu, Anjali. "Interrogating Hybridity: Subaltern Agency and Totality in Postcolonial Theory," *Diacritics* 35.2 (Summer 2005): 76–92.

Quadagno, Jill. "Race, Class, and Gender in the U.S. Welfare State: Nixon's Failed Family Assistance Plan," *American Sociological Review* 55.1 (February 1990): 11–28.

Radović, Stanka. "The Birthplace of Relation: Édouard Glissant's *Poétique de la Relation*," *Callaloo* 30.2 (Spring 2007): 475–481.

Rampersad, Arnold. "*Roots*, by Alex Haley," *New Republic* 175.23 (4 December 1976): 23–24, 26.

Rampersad, Arnold. *Ralph Ellison: A Biography* (New York: Alfred A. Knopf, 2007).

Rediker, Marcus. *The Amistad Rebellion: An Atlantic Odyssey of Slavery and Rebellion* (New York: Viking, 2012).

Rediker, Marcus. *The Slave-Ship: A Human History* (New York: Viking, 2007).

Rigby, Graeme. *The Black Cook's Historian* (London: Constable, 1993).

Robbins, Sarah. "Gendering the History of the Antislavery Narrative: Juxtaposing *Uncle Tom's Cabin* and *Benito Cereno*, *Beloved* and *Middle Passage*," *American Quarterly* 49.3 (September 1997): 531–573.

Roberts, Neil. *Freedom as Marronage* (Chicago: U of Chicago P, 2015).

Rockman, Seth, & Cathy Matson. *Scraping By: Wage Labor, Slavery, and Survival in Early Baltimore* (Baltimore MD: John Hopkins UP, 2008).

Rousseau, Jean-Jacques. *Discourse on the Origin of Inequality*, tr. Donald A. Cress, intro. James Miller (1754; *Discours sur l'origine et les fondements de l'inégalité parmi les hommes*, Pléiade ed. 1965; Indianapolis IN: Hackett, 1992).

Rousseau, Jean-Jacques. *Émile, or On Education*, tr. Allan Bloom (*Émile, ou De l'éducation*, 1762; New York: Basic Books, 1979).

Rowell, Charles H. "An Interview with Charles Johnson," *Callaloo* 20.3 (Summer 1997): 531–547.

Rucker, Walter C. "Haley, Alex," in *Encyclopedia of African American History*, ed. Leslie M. Alexander & Walter C. Rucker (Santa Barbara CA: ABC–CLIO, 2010): 791–792.

Rushdy, Ashraf H.A. "The Phenomenology of the Allmuseri: Charles Johnson and the Subject of the Narrative of Slavery," *African American Review* 26.3 (Summer 1992): 373–394.

Salamone, Frank A. "*Roots* (Haley, 1976)," in *Encyclopedia of Slave Resistance and Rebellion*, ed. Junius P. Rodriguez (Santa Barbara CA: Greenwood, 2006), vol. 2: 425–427.

Sarkozy, Nicolas. "Le discours de Dakar de Nicolas Sarkozy: L'intégralité du discours du président de la République, prononcé le 26 juillet 2007," *Le Monde* (9 November 2007): online (accessed 10 March 2018).

Sartre, Jean-Paul. "Black Orpheus" ("Orphée Noire," 1948), tr. John MacCombie, *Massachusetts Review* 6.1 (Autumn 1964–Winter 1965): 13–52.

Sawyers, Pascoe. "Black and White," *The Guardian* (13 September 1997): 6.

Scott, Daniel M. "Interrogating Identity: Appropriation and Transformation in *Middle Passage*," *African American Review* 29.4 (Winter 1995): 645–655.

Seaton, James. "Affirming the Principle," in *Ralph Ellison and the Raft of Hope: A Political Companion to* Invisible Man, ed. Lucas E. Morel (Lexington: UP of Kentucky, 2004): 22–36.

Segalen, Victor. *Essay on Exoticism: An Aesthetics of Diversity*, ed. & tr. Yael Rachel Schlick (*Essai sur l'exotisme: une esthétique du divers* (*notes*), 1904–18; Durham NC: Duke UP, 2002).

Selzer, Linda F. *Charles Johnson in Context* (Amherst: U of Massachusetts P, 2009).

Shumway, Rebecca. *The Fante and the Transatlantic Slave Trade* (Rochester NY: U of Rochester P, 2011).

Singh, Amritjit. "Afterword: Charles Johnson's Quest for a New African-American Narrative and His Literary Genealogy," in *Charles Johnson: Embracing the World*, ed. Nibir K. Ghosh & E. Ethelbert Miller (New Delhi: Authorpress, 2011): 269–292.

Sloterdijk, Peter. *You Must Change Your Life*, tr. Wieland Hoban (*Du mußt dein Leben ändern*, 2009; Cambridge: Polity, 2013).

Smallwood, Stephanie E. *Saltwater Slavery: A Middle Passage from Africa to American Diaspora* (Cambridge MA: Harvard UP, 2007).

Song, Sarah. "What Does It Mean to Be an American," *Daedalus* 138.2 (Spring 2009): 21–40.

Spielberg, Steven, dir. *Amistad* (Dreamworks/HBO, USA 1997; 155 min.).

Steckel, Richard H., & Richard A. Jensen. "New Evidence on the Causes of Slave and Crew Mortality in the Atlantic Slave Trade," *Journal of Economic History* 46.1 (March 1986): 57–77.

Stein, Howard F. "In Search of 'Roots': An Epic of Origins and Destiny," *Journal of Popular Culture* 11.1 (Summer 1977): 11–17.

Stephanson, Anders. *Manifest Destiny: American Expansionism and the Empire of Right* (New York: Hill & Wang, 1995).

Storhoff, Gary. *Understanding Charles Johnson* (Columbia: U of South Carolina P, 2004).

Stowe, Harriet Beecher. *Dred: A Tale of the Great Dismal Swamp*, intro. Robert S. Levine (1856; Chapel Hill: University of North Carolina Press, 2006).

Schwieger Hiepko, Andrea. "Creolization as a poetics of culture: Edouard Glissant's 'archipelic' thinking," in *A Pepper-Pot of Cultures: Aspects of Creolization in the Caribbean*, ed. Gordon Collier & Ulrich Fleischmann (Matatu 27–28; Amsterdam & New York: Editions Rodopi, 2003): 237–260.

Schwieger Hiepko, Andrea. "L'Europe et les Antilles: Une interview d'Édouard Glissant," *Mots Pluriels* (8 October 1998): online (accessed 5 August 2017).

Thaden, Barbara Z. "Charles Johnson's *Middle Passage* as Historiographic Metafiction," *College English* 59.7 (November 1997): 753–766.

Tise, Larry E. *Proslavery: A History of the Defense of Slavery in America, 1701–1840* (Athens: U of Georgia P, 1987).

Tocqueville, Alexis de. *Democracy in America*, tr. Arthur Goldhammer (*De la démocratie en Amérique*, 1835; New York: Library of America, 2004).

Tucker, Lauren R., & Hemant Shaw. "Race and the Transformation of Culture: The Making of the Television Miniseries *Roots*," *Critical Studies in Mass Communication* 9.4 (December 1992): 325–336.

United Nations. "Mediterranean Situation," *The United Nations High Commissioner for Refugees* (22 December 2017): online (accessed 31 December 2017).

United States Supreme Court. *"Loving v. Commonwealth of Virginia, 1967,"* in *Interracialism: Black–White Intermarriage in American History, Literature, and Law*, ed. Sollors, Werner (Oxford & New York: Oxford UP, 2000): 26–34.

Unsworth, Barry. *The Quality of Mercy* (New York: Random House, 2011).

Unsworth, Barry. *Sacred Hunger* (New York: W.W. Norton, 1993).

Valkeakari, Tuire. *Precarious Passages: The Diasporic Imagination in Contemporary Black Anglophone Fiction* (Gainesville: UP of Florida, 2017).

Veyne, Paul. *Comment on écrit l'histoire: essai d'épistémologie* (Paris: Seuil, 1971).

Walcott, Derek. "The Sea Is History" (1979), in *Selected Poems*, ed. Edward Baugh (New York: Farrar, Straus & Giroux, 2007): 137–139.

Wald, Gayle. *It's Been Beautiful: "Soul!" and Black Power Television*, photos by Chester Higgins (Durham NC: Duke UP, 2015).

Walker, David. *David Walker's Appeal, In Four Articles; Together with a Preamble, To The Coloured Citizens Of The World, But In Particular, And Very Expressly, To Those Of The United States Of America* (1829; Baltimore MD: Black Classic, 1997).

Weiler, A.H. "By Way of Report," *New York Times* (13 September 1959): X9.

White, Richard. *"It's Your Misfortune and None of My Own": A New History of the American West* (Norman: U of Oklahoma P, 1991).

Wiedorn, Michael. *Think Like an Archipelago: Paradox in the Work of Édouard Glissant* (Albany: State U of New York P, 2018).

Williams, Eric. *Capitalism and Slavery* (1944; Chapel Hill: U of North Carolina P, 1994).

Williams, Linda. *Playing the Race Card: Melodramas of Black and White from Uncle Tom to O.J. Simpson* (Princeton NJ: Princeton UP, 2002).

Winthrop, John. "A Modell of Christian Charity" (1630), *Collections of the Massachusetts Historical Society*, 3rd series 7 (1838): 31–48.

Wright, Donald R. "The Effect of Alex Haley's *Roots* on How Gambians Remember the Atlantic Slave Trade," *History in Africa* 38 (2011): 295–318.

Wright, Donald R. "Uprooting Kunta Kinte: On the Perils of Relying on Encyclopedic Informants," *History in Africa* 8 (1981): 205–217.

Young, Kevin. *Ardency: A Chronicle of the Amistad Rebels* (New York: Alfred A. Knopf, 2011).

Index